JOHN SURTEES

MOTORCYCLE MAESTRO

MV Agusta four-cylinder, c.1959/60. Drawn by Christopher Marshall.

JOHN SURTEES

MOTORCYCLE MAESTRO

MICK WALKER

First published in Great Britain in 2003 by
The Breedon Books Publishing Company Limited
Breedon House, 3 The Parker Centre,
Derby, DE21 4SZ.

Paperback edition published in Great Britain in 2012 by The Derby Books
Publishing Company Limited, 3 The Parker Centre, Derby, DE21 4SZ.

Dedication
To my dog Jessie, whom I found and adopted
while writing this book in Caithness, Scotland.

Picture Credits
Thanks to Castrol and Nick Nicholls for providing the pictures.

ISBN 978-1-78091-215-8

Printed and bound by Copytech (UK) Limited, Peterborough.

Contents

Thruxton, 6 August 1951: John with his 499cc Vincent Grey Flash during a very wet 1,000cc Festival of Britain race in which he finished second behind Norton works star Geoff Duke. The press labelled him in their reports as 'The man who made Geoff Duke hurry'.

John in winning form at Crystal Palace, Easter Monday, 19 April 1954, riding Bob Geeson's superb home-crafted dohc 249cc REG twin.

Preface

THE IDEA for writing *John Surtees: Motorcycle Maestro* came out of a conversation with Rupert Harding, of Breedon Books. It was important that John Surtees should cooperate, and after a meeting between Rupert, John and myself, agreement was reached. I wanted to write about John's life because, in my opinion, he had had such a varied and interesting career, as a rider, driver, mechanic, engineer, team owner, sidecar passenger and special-builder.

I soon discovered that John was someone with whom I could share old world values, besides our mutual love and enthusiasm for motorcycles and mechanical things. We had both grown up in a world far different from today, where happiness didn't have to mean money.

John grew up part of a close-knit family and his parents played a pivotal behind-the-scenes role in his rise to the top – not by bankrolling their son, but by their experience and enthusiasm for his chosen sport. Certainly John Senior (more commonly known as Jack to avoid confusion with John Junior) was a hard taskmaster, but his heart was in the right place and John is the first to relate how close he was to his dad and mum.

Being responsible for writing *John Surtees: Motorcycle Maestro* has been a real challenge – I feel the man has achieved so much in his life. The book is written in the same way as I see John himself, truthfully recording the facts without in any way making it all sound more glamorous than it really was.

John (more commonly known as Jack) Surtees Senior (centre, standing behind bike) and the 998cc HRD Vincent Rapide sidecar combination which he raced on both tarmac and grass c.1947. Surtees Senior was a major three-wheel star before and after World War Two. His experience and enthusiasm played a major part in his son John's motorcycle racing career.

A happy time. John and his great friend and MV teammate John Hartle after the pairing had finished one-two in the 1959 Isle of Man Junior TT on their four-cylinder models. Also in the picture is John Surtees's mother, Dorothy (behind her son), John Hartle's wife and child and, directly to the rear of Mrs Hartle, MV's team manager, Nello Pagani.

Certainly anyone aspiring to reach the top in any sport could learn a lot from John Surtees's life – the combination of talent, commitment, enthusiasm and professionalism is a winning formula. Second best is not good enough.

I would like to thank John Surtees for letting me take a close look at his life and career; without his help it would have been an impossible task.

Finally it is left to me to say to you, the reader, that I hope you have much enjoyment from reading *John Surtees: Motorcycle Maestro*, as I have had in compiling it.

Mick Walker
Wisbech, Cambridgeshire
March 2003

A previously unpublished photograph of John winning at Silverstone on the 350cc MV Agusta on 18 April 1959. He set a new lap record for the class during the race.

Chapter 1

Beginnings: motorcycles in the family

B ORN in the pretty village of Tatsfield on the Kent-Surrey border, a couple of miles south of Biggin Hill Airfield on 11 February 1934, John Surtees Junior (his father was also christened John), arrived into a world just recovering from the effects of the Great Depression. Shortly after his birth the family moved to be near a motorcycle shop that John Senior had opened in Tamworth Road, Croydon, Surrey, so John spent the greater part of his very early childhood in the Croydon area of south London.

John, aged two, on the tank of his father's B14 Excelsior-JAP at Layhams Farm Mountain Mile grass track, near West Wickham, Kent, c.1936.

Aged five, with his mother and younger brother Norman, Brands Hatch, 1939.

John's father and his passenger Frank Lilley at Crystal Palace in July 1938. John's upbringing revolved around motorcycle racing. The machine is a 596cc overhead camshaft Norton.

Two years prior to John Junior's birth, John Senior had begun grass track racing with a B14 Excelsior-JAP, then came four meetings with an early Velocette, before beginning a successful sidecar racing career (see separate boxed section within this chapter). His mother Dorothy was also an expert motorcyclist. So with this background it is perhaps hardly surprising that John Surtees was to take the path that he did.

When World War Two broke out in September 1939, the late Graham Walker, at that time the editor of *Motor Cycling*, was asked by the British Government to co-operate in the enlistment of well-known motorcyclists to act as instructors at the army training schools for DRs (Despatch Riders). John's father was one of those who answered Graham Walker's call and he was posted to the Royal Corps of Signals establishment at Catterick in North Yorkshire as an instructor and to organise the workshops.

In the 1940 Luftwaffe air raids a German bomb landed in the Surtees' family garden in Shirley, Surrey, blowing in the front of the house. So Surtees Senior decided he would feel a whole lot happier if his family could be removed from the Blitz area. He took his wife, John, younger son Norman (who had been born in 1938), and the latest arrival Dorothy, from Croydon to Yorkshire. They occupied a flat opposite the Catterick barracks, where John says 'we were all crammed in'.

Childhood memories die hard. And in John Surtees's case the move to the North of England, first to Catterick and later to near Huddersfield, saw him develop a love of the countryside which has remained to the present day.

Another early passion was drawing and painting, and a particular village church fascinated John in the period when the family was living on the edge of the moors near Huddersfield. Their home was actually two cottages knocked into one and the church was on the way to Huddersfield. To his young eyes it was as he says 'a most beautiful building'. He would sit down whenever he could and paint or draw it – literally dozens of times.

Although money was tight and the family had to put up with wartime measures such as food rationing, the Surtees household was still a pleasant place to be and provided John with many happy memories of the time he spent away from the London area.

Moving back south

Towards the end of the war, the Surtees family moved back south. The old family home in Croydon was now occupied by another family, but John's father, who was still in the army, was fortunate enough to be allocated a council house at Mardel Road, Bywood, near Elmers End between Croydon and Beckenham. Opposite their home was a small primary school called Monks Orchard which John attended until he was 12, before going on to Ashburton secondary school in Long Lane, Addiscombe.

By this time it became clear that John was a natural when it came to sport of any kind. He was captain of the soccer eleven, he was a good cross-country runner and well above average in the boxing ring. In fact, strength and fitness are, John believes, vital ingredients for achieving one's full potential. He also confided 'I have only attempted to smoke once; when aged 11 I had a single puff and that was enough!'

At the age of 13, John was given his first ride on a Wallace-Blackburne speedway bike. He rode around the outside of Brands Hatch on the cinders of the spectators' path. As his father was later to recall when interviewed by *Motor Cycling* in their 27 August 1959 issue: 'Took to it like a duck to water; he kept going round and round until the petrol ran out'.

Of course John had been brought up with motorcycles.

John Surtees excelled at most sports. He is seen here aged 14 (far left, top row), as part of the Ashburton School soccer team, Long Lane, Addiscombe, in 1948.

They were his father's business, and many of his first indelible memories were linked with the sporting side of motorcycling. His parents took part virtually every weekend. During the winter months his mother often passengered in the Surtees trials outfit, while in the summer the couple were always off to grass tracks and road race meetings where the crowds thronged the trackside and the engines roared their battle cry. So, as a journalist of the day said, young John 'absorbed motorcycling with his rusks'. He genuinely loved the battles on the track at Cadwell Park and the other circuits between his father and men such as Eric Oliver.

But probably his greatest love in those early days was tinkering with anything mechanical. During the 1959 *Motor Cycling* interview his father said of John: 'Of course, as a youngster his riding ability didn't portend a great future. But his interest in engines was intense. He'd spend hours in the garden shed tinkering. A typical request would be: "Dad, can I skip school and help you today?" He tried that as often as he could. Happily his schoolmaster was a keen rider and John was always taking bits and pieces to the classroom for the most popular lesson of the week'.

Cadwell Park

John well remembers his first visit to Cadwell Park in 1946. The meeting at the famous Lincolnshire track took place on Good Friday and Easter Monday. He recalls: 'we were all loaded up into the family car, an early 1930s Ford V8, the three children – my brother Norman, sister Dorothy and myself – occupied the dicky seat'. In those early post-war days there were no

Cadwell Park, Easter 1946. Jack Surtees (Norton) leads the field. The whole family had travelled north to Lincolnshire in a Ford V8 car with the bike towed behind.

Competitors getting
ready for a race at
Cadwell Park in
1947. Jack Surtees's
outfit is to the right
at the rear. John
Surtees, then aged
13, is standing
between his father
and passenger.

Brands Hatch as it
was in 1948, with
Jack Surtees's HRD
Vincent Rapide
outfit. Note the
Morris 1000
convertible on the
left of the photo-
graph and Jack
Surtees's shop van
on the right.

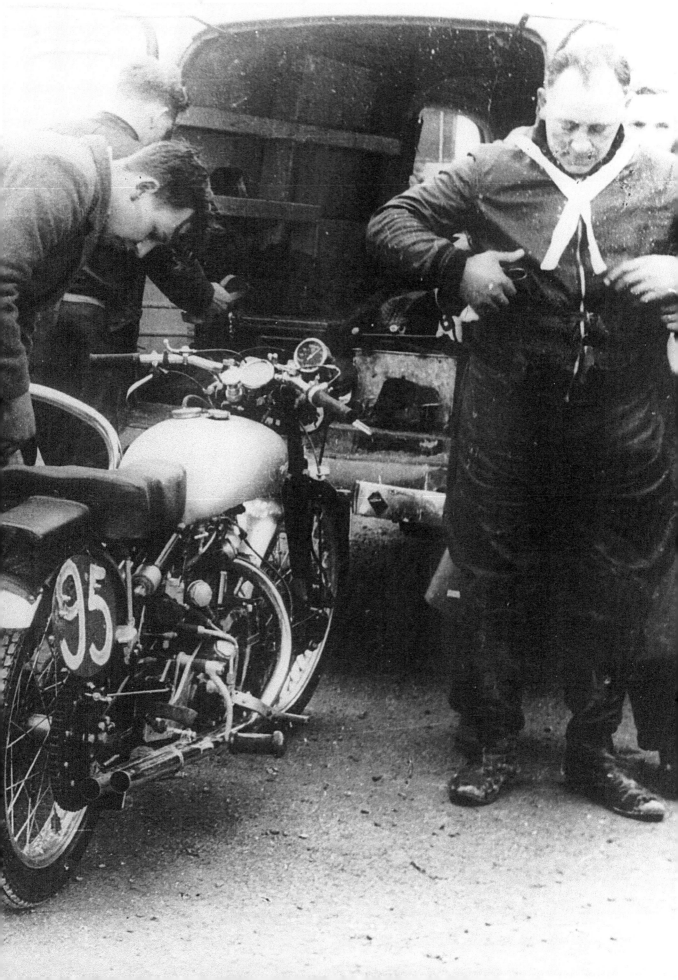

trailers or transporters, let alone motor homes! It was very much a case of towing the 596cc Norton – with a yoke attached to its front fork – and the sidecar, suitably weighed down with tool boxes, behind the children in the rear of the car.

Father and son with the Vincent, 1951.

The Surtees équipe – father, mother, the three children, bike, sidecar, tools and the like – arrived in rural Lincolnshire very late on the Thursday evening. John still vividly remembers: 'the antics we all had trying to set up the tent in which we were going to stay and finding what we thought would be a suitable location to pitch it.' Even though the family were nearly washed away in the middle of the night when torrential rain hit the area, it was such an exciting experience that the memories are still with him today.

The habit of travelling to race meetings and doing everything together was very much a regular affair for the Surtees family. As will become apparent throughout this book, this was one reason why John received such great support from both his father and mother during his racing career.

Competition debut

John's competition debut came when he was under age. He was just 14 when he passengered his dad in the chair of the Vincent outfit at Trent Park speed trials at Cockfosters, North London. Surtees Senior won the event, but was disqualified because of John's age. Then came the day, when approaching his 15th birthday, he was allowed to ride the Vincent one early morning at Warlingham Heights, near his Tatsfield birthplace. His father's words were: 'John, be careful, but have a ride!' It was a tremendous thrill for the budding young speedster.

John reached 15 years of age in early 1949 and with the birthday came thoughts of entering a race meeting. As he now recalls, 'Well, perhaps I shouldn't really have done so, because I didn't have a licence and I suppose I was under age, but some of the grass tracks were none too fussy.'

His first meeting was on the grass at Eaton Bray, just outside Luton. He rode a B14 Excelsior-JAP and he wore a pair of oversized leathers which belonged to his father. The B14 had come from John's father's shop and had been purchased for £25. Before the war both his father and Eric Oliver had raced similar models, so this machine played an important role in Surtees family history. Heavy falls of rain had turned the Eaton Bray track into a quagmire and John slid off 'more than once'. The machine was big and heavy for the teenage novice, but even so John did finish in his first race.

His racing debut had made him even more determined to do well, so the B14 was stripped and improvements were made with such materials as were at hand. But the fact remained that the bike was still a heavy piece of metal and certainly too powerful for a slight 15-year-old with underdeveloped muscles. As John once recalled, 'more often than not the machine was in charge of me, rather than the other way around.' He realised that for a really serious attempt at racing, it would be necessary to obtain a motorcycle that he could take charge of.

By now John had begun work at his father's motorcycle shop. So the whole business of acquiring a more suitable bike was talked over, but for some time it got no further than that – mainly, it has to be said, because of the financial considerations. However, eventually an understanding was reached that John should purchase and be responsible for maintenance of any machine that he chose, with his father advancing the purchase price and deducting it in instalments from the wages he was paying John. As a point of interest, John spent several months working: 'under his expert guidance' and was 'completely absorbed in the routine of the little workshop'.

Tiger 70

John's attention had been taken by a pair of pre-war Triumph Tiger 70 250cc singles which were performing well in competition events at the time. A bike like this would be suitable in terms of both competitiveness and size. One day when John was collecting some spares from Harold Daniell's shop (which was not far from the Surtees' own dealership in Forest Hill), his eyes focused on one of the 250cc Triumphs for sale in the showroom. He went over and inspected the bike. And as he says: 'The longer I looked, the more convinced I became that this was just the machine for me.' A price tag was hanging from the handlebars and, very gingerly, John put out a hand and turned it so he could read the figures written on the label – £32. At that time he didn't have that sort of money, and his first reaction was 'that it was out of the question'. When John returned home, he told his father about the Tiger 70, more as a subject of conversation than with any direct suggestion that perhaps it would be just the machine for him. His father didn't say much, but John must have shown that he had really fallen for the Triumph, because a little later on John's father suggested that he would take him over the next day to have another look at it, telling him: 'If you are sure that's what you want you'd better have it.'

Actually John need not have worried. Harold Daniell had an excellent reputation and later on was to prove of great help on the young Surtees's debut in the Isle of Man. In fact, in Joe Craig's opinion, Harold and Artie Bell, another great Norton works rider: 'were two men who were really worth listening to'.

John's father had not only known Harold Daniell for many years, but had also done a considerable amount of business with him as well, both before and after the war. Although he came to the shop with John the following morning, he left his son to decide whether he really wanted the Triumph or not and went off into a corner of the shop to chat to Harold. As John certainly did want the bike, the transaction was very soon completed. As John recalled many years later: 'The idea that I was now the owner of a Triumph Tiger 70 took some getting used to. Not until it was actually standing in our workshop could I really believe it.'

His father, in his usual businesslike manner, insisted that before anything else was done to John's new acquisition, the Triumph would have to be stripped down. As John says: 'I thought he might be intending to help me but he told me to get on with it myself. That, he reckoned, was the only way I could really get to know it – which of course is absolutely true.'

So the Triumph was stripped down, with John cleaning everything thoroughly as he went. Although he had a good range of hand tools, the only electrical one was a power drill: 'which came into play polishing the cylinder head'. In addition the carburettor was replaced by a racing type remote needle instrument from a pre-war International Norton. Thus equipped, John presented his handiwork to his father for final approval.

Next came the first try out for the Tiger 70. This took place at Pirbright, Surrey. The event was not a grass track nor a road race, but the one and only scramble (motocross) that John Surtees ever contested. John set off for the course with his father, transporting the Triumph in a van, and he discovered that racing over the rough was a tough sport – not just on the rider, but the bike too – as the front forks of the Tiger 70 broke in two!

To John this was a major disaster. However, eventually he discovered a pair of ex-AMC WD Teledraulic forks which were available 'free of charge'. Deciding that scrambling wasn't for him, John then took in a couple of grass track events before the 1949 season ended; one at Folkestone Heights and the other at Barham, near Canterbury. At that time Kent was a hot-bed of grass track racing, with events throughout the county virtually every weekend during the season. As for the Triumph, as John recalls: 'it had no

Triumph Tiger 70

John Surtees began his tarmac racing career with a tuned, pre-war Triumph Tiger 70. The Tiger 70 had been designed by Edward Turner, who was also the man behind such outstanding motorcycles as the Ariel Square Four, Triumph Speed and Ariel Red Hunter. Turner was a designer who understood the importance of power-to-weight ratio. He kept the weight down from the drawing board stage. If anything broke on test it was strengthened, otherwise it remained as it was and this ensured light machines with decent performance.

Jack Sangster bought Triumph in early 1936 and one of his first moves was to transfer Edward Turner from Sangster's Ariel company to his new acquisition. What Turner did was simple and effective. He took the existing 249cc (63 x 80mm) single together with the larger 343 and 493cc versions, and equipped them with tuned engines and additional bright work (such as chrome tank panels) and named them Tiger 70, 80 and 90 respectively.

From 1937 there were some major changes with new frames, forks and gearboxes. And from January 1937, the range of Tigers was extended to include competition versions. These were intended for trials use, so the fittings were altered to suit, as were the gearbox ratios and state of engine tune. The Turner touch worked wonders and before long enthusiastic sporting riders turned to the Tiger singles in droves, making it one of the most popular of the immediately pre-war British motorcycles.

In March 1937 Triumph gained the prestigious Maudes Trophy for their Standard Production Test carried out at Donington Park. Three Tigers, a 250cc, a 350cc and a 500cc, were chosen from the stocks of various agents. The machines were then taken to Donington, briefly run-in, and then put through their paces, which included a 3-hour high speed test. The 500cc covered 84 laps at an average speed of 54.4mph; the 350cc 89 laps at an average of 57.4mph and the 250cc 79 laps at 50.72mph.

Maximum speed tests were also carried out at Brooklands in Surrey. The 250cc Tiger 70 achieved a flying lap of 66.39mph; the 350cc Tiger 80 74.68mph and the 500cc Tiger 90 82.31mph.

Although production of the Tiger 70/80/90 singles did not survive the war, the military 350cc 3HW was based on the civilian Tiger 80 model. In the early post-war years many of the surviving Tiger 70s were used not only for road racing but also for grass track, scrambles and sprinting with varying success. The Triumph factory even prepared a number of works Tiger 70s for trials and road racing. Percy Tait rode one of these modified machines and nearly beat Moto Guzzi-mounted Maurice Cann at Silverstone; John Surtees now owns the actual machine.

really impressive turn of speed but it was a good little machine and I was very proud of it.'

The meeting at Folkestone brought with it a reminder that racing is not always a bed of roses and it taught John that everybody's definition of sport is not the same. There was a novice's class for first-year riders, which he entered. Prior to this meeting, the only other events John had taken part in had been the couple or so on the old heavyweight B14 Excelsior and the unsuccessful scrambling episode. So it came as a nasty shock, after finishing

Brands Hatch

Brands Hatch holds special memories for John Surtees, because it was here that he took part in his first road race in April 1950 and where he scored many of his early victories on two wheels. Even today there are many Brands stalwarts who remember those far off performances.

The beginning of the famous circuit, situated on the Kentish Downs to the south east of London, dates back to 1926, when a group of passing cyclists noticed what they saw as a natural bowl – at that time a mushroom field – beside the road. This belonged to Brands Hatch farm. After discussion with the farmer agreement was reached to allow the cyclists to compete there. Motorcycles arrived in 1928 and throughout the 1930s there were regular grass track events in the chalky bowl. In 1947, after the war, Brands Hatch Stadium Limited was created and during the closed season of 1949–50 the track was tarmaced; the first race meeting being staged there on Easter Sunday, 4 April 1950.

This original circuit was kidney-shaped and without the Druids Loop. It was just under one mile in length, the main corners being Clearways and Paddock. The races were run anti-clockwise. Although perfect for club events, it was too short for international races, so during the winter of 1953 major changes were instigated. First racing switched to a clockwise direction and the track was widened with the addition of the uphill Druids section. Pits and spectator banks were also constructed. In the middle of 1955 a permanent grandstand was purchased from the Northolt trotting ground in north London which was closing down. This was re-erected at Brands just in time for John Surtees's victory over Geoff Duke in early October that year. John Surtees's fastest lap over the new 1.24-mile circuit in that race was 74.40mph.

When, at the beginning of the 1960s, the circuit was increased in length to 2.65 miles, it attracted many of the world's top motoring events, including the car Formula 1 Grand Prix (1964) and much later World Super Bikes. Today the circuit length remains at 2.65 miles, even though in the last decade there have been plans to alter this by removing much of the wooded section on the back part of the circuit. At the present time these moves have stalled because of environmental concerns.

runner-up in the novices race at Folkestone, that some 'fellow sportsman' should lodge an official protest. Even now John can only think that this incident came about because of his name Surtees and that his father was known as such a successful rider. As John says: 'it brought me into open contact with the petty jealousy which sometimes lurks below the surface in sport.' Throughout his motorcycle racing career he is rather proud of the fact that he never once resorted to the official protest; and he always considered it wrong that the name of the person making the protest should be concealed. As he was once to recall: 'If a man has the courage of his convictions, he should not mind saying what he thinks straight out, in public.'

Sidecar ballast

Besides his solo antics in these formative years of his racing career, John

Surtees often acted as 'ballast' for his father's sidecar, when Jack Surtees's usual passengers, Frank Lilley, Jack Noble or Charlie Rous, were unable to make a meeting. As he related in his 1963 book *Speed*, John found sidecar racing 'extremely thrilling'. He went on to paint the picture:

> *At first I tended to be too enthusiastic and, in my eagerness, was inclined to leap about too briskly. I was not too keen on the right-handers, where you have to drape yourself over the back wheel and can't see very much of what is going on, but loved the left-handers. My father and his passengers were among the first to adopt the continental style of sidecar racing and, lying out forward of the sidecar wheel, with your shoulder just establishing contact with the ground as it rushes past, you get a wonderful sensation of speed. I was still a growing lad of course and at that time, I remember I used to find some difficulty in hanging on when the outfit was acceler-ating hard and nearly pulling my arms out of their sockets.*

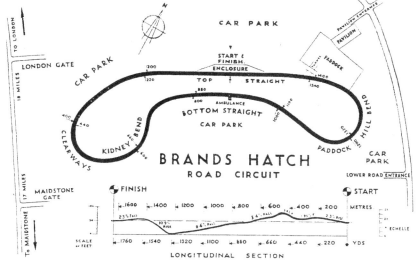

The original 1950s Brands Hatch circuit.
Lap length: 1 mile.

Road racing debut

John Surtees's road racing debut came in the very first race staged over the newly tarmaced Brands Hatch circuit, in a 250cc heat on Easter Sunday, 9 April 1950, not long after his 16th birthday. The new surface was an impor-tant development in the history of the circuit – since it had first opened in pre-war days, Brands had been a grass track venue only. The historic race was started by none other than the 1949 500cc World Champion, Les Graham, and in contrast to today's Brands, it ran backwards – anti-clock-wise. The circuit was also less than a mile in length. John's baptism on

A 16-year-old John (Triumph Tiger 70, No.23) on the start line for the very first race over the new tarmac Brands Hatch circuit, Easter Sunday, 9 April 1950.

tarmac went extremely well and he finished third in the heat. But in the final, unlike the heat in which conditions were dry, it was very damp. Coming into the final lap John found himself on the heels of another Tiger 70 ridden by Harry Pearce (who later became head of the McLaren F1 machine shop). With the scent of victory John's inexperience then got the better of him and as he says 'I thought I could go by him, I think I did, but the only problem was that I wasn't on my bike.'

During the spring of 1950 John rode the Triumph at other meetings, both on the road and grass. However, on the road it was very much a case of either the machine failing or the young Surtees falling on his ear. The main problem with the Tiger 70 was the bottom end, with the big-end proving the real weakness. Also the fastest models, ridden by the likes of Percy Tait, sported works-developed Conway and Lilley square aluminium cylinder heads and barrels, and, though John and his father didn't know it at the time, these modified engines were usually fitted with an Excelsior Manxman connecting rod. To make his bike more competitive, John acquired a Conway and Lillley top end, and he grafted on a sprung hub to provide a degree of rear suspension. The new hub came from a bike in his dad's showroom.

The revised Surtees Tiger 70 was entered for a Silverstone race meeting in late spring 1950. John felt elated, the Triumph was finally ready for action. But rounding Abbey Curve at the Northampton track the con-rod broke, locking the engine and throwing our would-be racer 'down the road'. Sadly that was the end of John Surtees's Triumph racing exercise. On one of his visits to the Vincent factory in Stevenage John managed to sell his blown up Tiger 70 engine to one of the lads there.

The next idea was to fit a JAP engine in the Triumph chassis, but instead, on another visit to the Vincent works, John's father found the answer to his son's prayers in the shape of a partially disman- tled Grey Flash bike that had been used for road test and development work. As the next chapter reveals, the Vincent era was really the start of John Surtees's climb up the motorcycle racing success ladder.

John's first-ever road race, with the Surtees Tiger 70 sporting AMC Teledraulic forks. Brands Hatch, April 1950.

John Surtees Senior

John Norman Surtees (later known as Jack Surtees), 'Dad' to John, was born on 28 March 1901, the youngest of two brothers, but didn't enjoy a particularly stable or happy childhood. This was because in the years prior to the outbreak of World War One, his father had become involved in attempting to form union representation in one of Sainsbury's stores, the result being domestic prob- lems, resulting in the two sons being taken in by the Salvation Army. But, not happy there, the two brothers ran away and joined the army. They both ended up in France early in the war and sadly the older of the two, Henry, was fatally injured when the ambulance he was driving was blown up.

John Surtees Senior had learned to drive while in the forces and emerged from the war unscathed, at least physically. But earning a living in 'civvy street' wasn't easy post-Armistice, so he remained in the army. He spent the next six years in Egypt and Palestine, driving the GOC (General Officer Commanding), the military man in charge of the combined civilian/military commission in various parts of the Middle East previously administered by the defeated Ottoman Empire.

After he left the army he found himself in an identical position to many former military personnel, jobless. However, this state of affairs was addressed when he became a bus driver. Yet as John Junior recalls: 'His competitive nature and, I suppose, a bit of the inherent Surtees family cussed- ness meant he didn't stop there. He didn't like the way things were done, so he upped and left.' By this time, John Senior had met Dorothy Cynthia Gray, whom he married at Croydon, Surrey in early 1933.

Shortly after the arrival of their first child (John, on 11 February 1934) John Senior opened a small motorcycle business in Tamworth Road, Croydon. Two years earlier he had had his first outing on a racing motorcycle, a B14 Excelsior-JAP, at Layhams Farm Mountain Mile grass track near West Wickham, Kent. And as John Junior describes: 'This had a one-in-three climb called Bob's

Jack Surtees (with helmet) and passenger Frank Lilley after winning the Sydenham Vase, Crystal Palace, summer 1938.

Knob, with a hump near the bottom, a downhill S-bend and an acute hairpin leading to the bumpy straight.' Surtees Senior led on the first lap, then applied a shade too much throttle, which resulted in his looping the Excelsior-JAP. After that, with a sidecar attached, and his wife in the chair, he gained useful experience prior to the birth of the couple's first child. As John Junior says: 'but then I came along and perhaps spoilt it all!'.

John Senior didn't stop racing, and in fact he was to become probably the most successful sidecar exponent on the mountain grass tracks (hillside tracks in south-east England) prior to the outbreak of World War Two in September 1939. At that time, during the late 1930s, there were very few permanent tarmaced circuits, though he did compete around the Campbell circuit at Brooklands, and at Alexandra Palace, Crystal Palace, Cadwell Park and Donington Park. By then the Excelsior-JAP had given way to a 596cc camshaft Norton.

All forms of motorcycle sport had to be forgotten when war came again. John Surtees Senior was now 38 years of age, above the normal recruitment age, but he was one of the first to volunteer and was accepted into the Royal Signals. This was thanks to a scheme devised by Graham Walker (former racer, editor of *Motor Cycling* and father of Murray) for recruiting some of the stars of road racing, grass track and trials into the Royal Signals in order to help with the training of DRs (Despatch Riders) as well as establishing the servicing workshop facilities needed.

Surtees Senior was posted to Catterick in North Yorkshire and given responsibility for both the setting up of the workshops and for ensuring new recruits received a thorough grounding in their training to become Despatch Riders. As he was to reveal to John Junior much later: 'it was necessary to try and train the lads to have a better than average chance before they were sent to the front'. Obviously the carnage of World War One and the loss of his brother in that conflict had influenced the way he felt about his task.

By the time John Surtees Senior was posted to Catterick, the family was living in a flat above another shop at Elmers End near Beckenham, Kent, to which the motorcycle business had been relocated. By this time John Junior had been joined by brother Norman and sister Dorothy. Since John Junior and Norman shared their father's two christian names, John Senior became increasingly referred to as Jack.

The London Blitz bombing campaign by the German Luftwaffe prompted Jack to arrange for the family to join him in Yorkshire. As John now admits, 'the real significance for me of that period is that it instilled in me the feeling of not wanting to make my home within a city or town.'

Later in the war, Jack arranged for the rest of the family to return south, while he remained at Catterick. This meant that to be reunited with his wife and children he had to travel from North Yorkshire to South London and it was on one of these journeys (there being no motorways in those days) that disaster struck one winter's night on a return visit to Catterick. The pressures of his hectic schedule caught up with him. He fell asleep and his motorcycle crashed down into a quarry. The result was a fractured femur and several other broken bones. This left Jack with one leg an inch or so shorter than the other and thereafter he walked with a limp. By now it was early 1945 and the war was almost at an end. He was invalided out of the army. The combination of six years of war and the injuries Jack had sustained in the crash meant that the Surtees family's finances were in a poor state. Jack had also been in and out of hospital for many months, but finally in early 1946 he was able to concentrate on the resumption of his business. John remembers: 'travelling around with him looking at various shops until he found one not very far from where Harold Daniell and Steve Lancefield were operating in Forest Hill, south London.' With their help and that of other friends, Jack Surtees was able, slowly and by dint

Jack Surtees leading on his 998cc Vincent Rapide V-twin and sidecar, Haddenham Airfield, Essex, May 1949. The large aircraft at the rear is a Handley Page Halifax bomber of the Royal Air Force.

FOREST HILL, S.E.23

JACK SURTEES MOTORS LTD.

We learn by racing successfully.
You can learn successfully by
visiting us. We can supply any
make. Personal attention to
all your requirements, backed
by experience.

2 SUNDERLAND ROAD, S.E.23

Forest Hill 1733

of sheer hard work, to earn enough money to support his family and eventually make a return to racing. In fact a return to racing had come as early as Easter Monday, 22 April 1946, with a journey north to Cadwell Park in Lincolnshire.

The remainder of the 1940s was spent running the business and racing either a 596cc Norton (not the one owned pre-war) or the 998cc Vincent V-twin. The latter marque was to play a major part in not only reshaping Jack's racing and business (he became a Vincent main agent at the end of 1946), but also son John's early racing career. As John recalls: 'Dad loved Vincents and at times he would display what I can only describe as an over-abundance of enthusiasm for the marque.'

There is also no doubt that John Surtees has a high regard and true affection for both his father and mother:

> Obviously there were the usual disagreements that arise between parents and their children, but on the whole I cannot imagine any parents doing a better job. I think it is important to emphasise just what a close relationship I enjoyed with my parents. My brother, sister and I grew up in a really close-knit family environment. Make no mistake, Dad worked very hard indeed. After those initial disappointments when he returned from Yorkshire, he gradually built up quite a reasonable business and a nice family home.

From the early 1950s, when his son's career was in its infancy, Jack slowly ran down his own racing to help his son. Not so much in a financial sense, but with his contacts, experience and considerable enthusiasm for the sport. Even when John switched from bikes to cars his father (and mother) were still deeply involved. When one journalist asked recently: 'What sort of a chap was Dad?' John replied: 'Oh, Dad was a wonderful character. He had a reasonable degree of temper, but a great heart. He would always be a sucker for someone's sob story. If he had a couple of shillings in his pocket and some kid came along he'd give them to him. He was a good dad and a good friend as well.'

Jack Surtees died in 1972, aged 71. He is buried, together with John's mother who died in 1998, at St Mary's Church, Tatsfield.

John as passenger on his father's 998 Vincent combination, Brands Hatch, 1950.

The Triumph Tiger 70 with John aboard grass-track racing at Stokenchurch, near High Wycombe, Buckinghamshire, May 1950.

Percy Tait's works
development Tiger 70
with aluminium head
and cylinder barrel.

Chapter 2

Apprenticeship: Vincent

JOHN SURTEES owed much to his father. It was Jack who was responsible for discovering the motorcycle which, today, is seen as setting John on the road to success, the Vincent. If the Tiger 70 had been the bike which began John's career, it was the Stevenage-built bike with which he was to serve his apprenticeship.

By late spring 1950, as recounted in the previous chapter, John had finally realised that his Triumph Tiger 70 wasn't going to make the grade as a racer. At first he thought that putting a JAP ohv single engine into the Triumph frame was the answer. But instead it was his father Jack who discovered a much more suitable machine. While visiting the Vincent factory in Stevenage (he was then one of the company's main agents) Jack happened to notice a half-dismantled Grey Flash, the racing version of the company's 499cc Comet roadster. Painted a non-standard black, it looked like little more than 'a heap of spares', but in fact it was a road test machine which had been returned from Stan Hailwood's Kings of Oxford dealership. Jack Surtees, with his knowledge of motorcycles, realised that here was a machine that would be a suitable mount for his son. He asked Vincent what they were going to do with it and was told it was in the process of being stripped down. Would they be prepared to sell it? Certainly if there was a buyer. How much then? The figure that was named (after Jack had explained it was for his son who would be joining Vincent when he reached 17) was acceptable and within a short space of time Jack had written out a cheque and was stowing the bike and its loose component parts into the back of the Surtees van.

Jack Surtees's first post-war motorcycle shop at 2 Sunderland Road, Forest Hill, south London. He became a Vincent dealer in 1946, finally passing on the agency to Deeprose Bros in 1954.

As John was to recall years later: 'I still remember vividly Dad coming home that evening and telling me to come and have a look at what he had found. The name "Vincent" was already a magic word for me and the fact that this one was largely in boxes with bits and pieces lying on the floor of the van could not dim that magic. I was so excited I could scarcely wait to start work on it.'

Getting the Grey Flash ready

Unlike the factory supported Grey Flash models which had been used in that year's TT, John's machine: 'was a standard specification bike which was going to be produced for the public', and this included an Amal TT10 $1^{5}/_{32}$ inch carburettor. John already had a fair amount of experience in stripping and rebuilding Vincents. He also remembered the mistakes he had made with the Triumph – an approach he says was: 'rather like a bull at a gate'. His new acquisition was treated in a much more considered fashion. He 'drilled and lightened with great caution. I polished everything I could, even the timing gears, and I buffed such components as the rockers, flywheels and crankcase.' But apart from cleaning the head thoroughly, 'I did not touch it.' John then

> ...set off to Brands Hatch for the first race with great optimism. In my boyish enthusiasm [he was only just 16 years of age] I was quite sure that the jinx [which surrounded his previous racer, the Tiger 70] would at last have retreated as the result of such care and attention. But that jinx was more conscientious – resolute, vengeful, or whatever jinxes are – than I had ever imagined. On the Vincent's first outing, the big-end locked.

Jack Surtees had a word with Philip Vincent and his chief designer Phil Irving about the problem and they suggested using one of their Type 4 plain aluminum big-ends. This consisted of a plain sleeve in RR77-type material, which was counter-sunk into the crank flywheels, on which the connecting-rod ran directly, held together by a pin through the centre. John remembers watching them put the crankpin in the fridge and the flywheels in the oven at the Vincent works, where they managed to assemble the whole thing successfully, despite people casting doubt on whether it would all hold together. 'Well, this was towards the end of the 1950 season, and when I unfortunately had to sell the bike at the end of 1952 in order to pay for my first Norton it had run two full seasons without a spot of bother'. Other modifications to the Grey Flash are contained in a boxed section within this chapter.

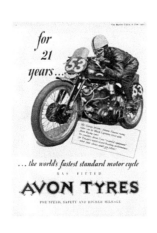

for 21 years...

...the world's fastest standard motor cycle

HAS FITTED

AVON TYRES

FOR SPEED, SAFETY AND HIGHER MILEAGE

First race victory

Now that the suitably tuned and modified Vincent was ready an entry was made for the Aberdare Park meeting, held on a Saturday in late August 1950. John remembers not only gaining his first victory that day at the Welsh circuit, but the hospitality he received: 'Marion Pryse and her husband David, the chief organisers, extended their activities far beyond the actual running of the races. Like most other riders we were found friendly accommodation for the night in the home of one of the local Aberaman Club members and after the racing, which takes place in a park right in the centre of the town, there was a prize-giving at the circuit, high tea and the sing-song inseparable from any club activity in Wales.'

Over the winter much time had been spent on the 499cc Vincent. Its first meeting of 1951 came on 26 March at the Thruxton circuit, where in the 480-1,000cc Non Experts event, John brought his machine home second behind the 998cc Vincent V-twin of F. Taylor. His next race came at the Boreham Airfield track, situated just north of the Essex town of Chelmsford, on 30 April. Again, lining up with the larger displacement bikes, John finished an excellent third with only the very experienced pairing of George Brown and John Hodgkin, both mounted on 998cc Vincent twins, in front.

On Sunday 3 June 1951, John had what he was later to call: 'my first taste of success, made particularly sweet because I had the opportunity of getting my own back on the rider who had proved himself better than me when I had given the Triumph Tiger 70 its first outing.' This came at the

George Brown riding one of the special Vincent Grey Flash models that the Stevenage factory built for the 1950 TT at Scarborough in September that year.

John, left with father and a friend, on his 17th birthday, 11 February 1951, testing the Grey Flash (it was actually painted silver) at Boreham.

Greenwich club's open-to-centre (meaning that members of ACU local centres could enter) road race meeting at Brands Hatch. John had entered three races: the 500, 1,000cc and handicap events. The rider John was particularly keen to beat was Harry Pearce, who had a 499cc ohv JAP-engined Triumph, as well as his 250cc Triumph Tiger 70.

Even though Pearce won his first race in style – the 6-lap 250cc – John remembers 'thinking that if the Vincent behaved, and if I kept on, I should be quite satisfied if I could give him a good run when we met in the handicap.' In his first race John soon discovered that 'the Vincent was going to behave perfectly.' From the start he was soon challenging for the lead and went on to win from E.A. Brown (EAB special) and Peter Ferbrache (Hartley Ariel). This performance was a good omen for what was to come later in the day.

Then came John's duel with Harry Pearce, for duel was what it really was. On the Brands start line the two riders selected first gear and pulled their engines back on to compression, as the starter raised his flag. John got away to a good start but so did Harry Pearce. Although the two riders were circulating together John admits 'finding myself surprised at the comparative ease with which I was managing to hold on to him. Not only that, the Vincent still had something in reserve and as I realised this, all of a sudden I went coldly calm and quietly calculating. Urging on the Vincent, I went into the lead.' Even though Pearce got by again, he did not retain the lead for long. John describes the following stages thus: 'the Vincent still had power in hand, so I opened up and challenged Harry again. The Triumph-JAP, apparently, was at almost full stretch, because although he kept very close behind me he could not pull out enough to pass me again.'

John finished the day ended by completing a hat-trick, with victory in the 25-lap invitation race in which the likes of Brown, Ferbrache and Pearce all took part. As John recalls, that early June Sunday afternoon in 1951, 'Brands Hatch looking its best under a clear blue sky and a brilliant warm sun will, I think, remain in my memory for as long as it continues to tick over. I was so excited at my good fortune and so proud of the Vincent, that the world of motorcycle racing was my idea of paradise.' Indeed the joy that day in the Surtees family was unbridled. Not, John says, 'simply because of the wins, but also because the Vincent was certainly repaying me for all the many hours of thought and work I had put into it and was fully justifying my father's purchase of it.'

In the author's opinion, Sunday 3 June 1951 was one of those vital stepping stones which were to mark John Surtees's rise to a world-class rider. The following episode shows what a big role his family played in shaping John's career:

Fortunately I had the example of my father's experience to help me keep things in perspective. If he gave me encouragement, he also made sure that I didn't get too big for my boots. Not long after this hat-trick day I was at Brands Hatch again and legged myself off through being over-confident and trying to overtake an experienced rider, Ernie Barrett, on the inside of a corner. First man on the scene was my father, who had run down from where he was standing near the finishing line. Having satisfied himself that I was none the worse for the tumble, he administered a hearty wallop, which certainly served to remind me that I was still a youngster with a lot to learn.

Keeping one's feet on the ground

John was then 17 years of age – very young to be racing at the time. The Brands episode should serve as a useful reminder to many a budding young racer of today and to their fathers, whose relationship is often compromised by getting carried away with the first sign of potential, resulting in that potential often going to waste through inappropriate guidance. Also it should be remembered that being a racing parent is not an easy task, because on the one hand you want your offspring to make the grade and become a star, but on the other hand, as any parent, you are fearful of a serious accident occurring. The late Charlie Rous, family friend, journalist and at one time Jack's regular sidecar passenger, confirmed: 'John wasn't a crasher because if he did he got a good telling off from his father – "Motorbikes are not made to fall off", Jack used to say, "and that is that".'

Rous also said: 'I often thought he [John] should have been a works rider a lot earlier, but his career was probably planned to some degree by his father; bringing up a fast rider slowly.' Another of Rous's recollections helps to explain why. 'When John had one of his first races, on the grass at Stokenchurch, near High Wycombe, John's father had said: "Go up to the line with him and make sure everything's ok." I did that and the race started. Jack climbed into the back of the lorry and sat there until the race ended. He couldn't bringing himself to watch. And he was a hard man, tough.'

During the 1951 season John competed several times at the Boreham airfield track in Essex. This circuit, which might once have become a serious rival to Silverstone, was where John made his Norton debut, albeit on an older 'Garden Gate' plunger-framed model, rather than the newly introduced Featherbed Manx bike. The one John rode at Boreham on 21 July 1951 was a borrowed 350cc. Finishing sixth in the 350cc final, he was racing against riders of the calibre of Robin Sherry, Ken Kavanagh and Cecil

Father Jack adjusting John's helmet, spring 1951.

Sandford. His other finishes that day (on the Vincent) were fifth in the 500cc and sixth in the 1,000cc event.

John's international debut came at the 1.895-mile Thruxton circuit on bank holiday Monday 9 August 1951 – and what a debut it was to be. Competing against a star-studded entry, John was to leave the Hampshire airfield venue unbeaten with the exception of double 1951 World Champion and Norton team leader Geoff Duke. In terribly wet conditions the 17-year-old put on an inspired display and in doing so clearly marked his potential as a future champion.

1951 was Festival of Britain Year and the sports governing body, the Auto-Cycle Union, had organised a six-race programme (plus heats), including a sidecar race in which John passengered for his father in the latter's 998cc Vincent outfit. The race programme consisted of:

Ultra Lightweight (125cc – 4 laps)
Lightweight (250cc – 10 laps)
Junior (350cc – 15 laps)
Festival of Britain Invitation (all classes – 12 laps)
Passenger Race (sidecars and three-wheelers up to 1,200cc – 8 laps)
1,000cc (15 laps)

Surtees v Duke

The Festival of Britain race was the first meeting between Geoff Duke and

John Surtees, and before the flag dropped no one could have realised just how the latter was to push the former. The entry list also included Johnny Lockett (Duke's Norton teammate), Albert Moule, Frank Fry and Auguste Goffin on 499cc Nortons; Roland Pike, Robin Sherry, Syd Lawton, Basil Keys and Ralph Rensen on 348cc AJS 7Rs; the remainder of the field comprised A.A. Fenn (249cc Moto Guzzi), Brian Purslow (499cc BSA), H. Hutt (348cc Velocette), Cyril Julian (348cc Douglas), John Hodgkin (998cc Vincent) and G.W. Andrews (498cc Matchless twin); plus Duke (499cc Norton) and John's 499cc Vincent. As *The Motor Cycle* said: 'There was a mixture of makes and a wide range of engine sizes, but on the face of things, there could be little challenge to Duke.' However, there was a shock in store.

Of course, it was Duke's race, but it was also a personal triumph for Surtees on his half-litre Vincent. Duke got away well, but at the end of lap 1 he was only about 30 yds ahead of Surtees, who was twice that distance in front of Sherry. Goffin was fourth, Purslow fifth, Hutt sixth and Hodgkin, on the big Vincent, seventh. Slowly Duke added to his lead but Surtees was holding on. At the end of lap 5 the gap was about 200 yds and by then Duke had lapped nearly half the field. These two riders had the entire limelight. Lockett was well back and by the end had been lapped by Surtees as well as Duke.

The final order was Duke, Surtees, Sherry and Purslow. A truly outstanding performance, but there was more to come.

The last event of the day was the 1,000cc race and weather-wise it brought no respite from the continuous downpour. As *The Motor Cycle* reported: 'John Surtees on his Grey Flash Vincent again distinguished himself.' And in fact, after getting a good start, it took Geoff Duke a full seven laps before he could finally overtake the flying youngster.

The race report went on to say: 'However, Surtees would not let Duke get away and hung grimly on his tail.' At the end of the meeting Geoff Duke praised 'the remarkable riding of young John Surtees – who made me ride so fast in the last race'.

By now John had started his apprenticeship at the Vincent works in Stevenage and he acknowledges the relationship he enjoyed with the company. 'I must say Philip Vincent was enormously understanding and indulgent of my own racing activities. I was allowed to turn up at nine o'clock rather than eight o'clock in the morning, everybody knowing full well that every spare moment of my time was spent either racing or

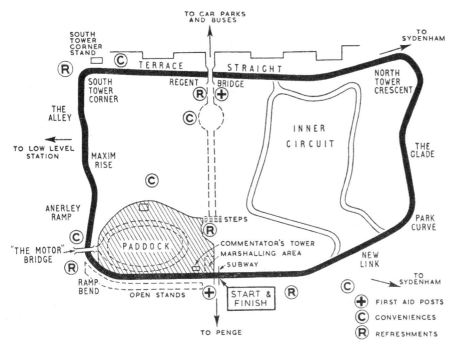

Crystal Palace.
Lap length: 1.39 miles.

preparing my bike, and there's no doubt that I have a great deal to thank them for.' Vincent also provided a TT machine dating from 1950, which was used as backup and for spares if they were needed.

John's recollections of his attitude to his racing career at this time are revealing: 'It would be rather romantic, in retrospect, to say I had much interest in what was going on in the outside world, that I studied the results of every motorcycle Grand Prix and major international race, because, to be honest, I don't think I did. I was completely involved with the family, my own racing and my apprenticeship with Vincents.'

After the excitement of his duels with Duke at Thruxton, John was back at Boreham on 1 September 1951. Again the conditions were wet and John passengered his father in the sidecar race. The main race of the day, the Chelmsford 100, began in the dry, but from the second lap the rain, which had been threatening for some time, arrived and steadily increased. George Brown, riding a Featherbed Manx Norton and Harry Bostock (Triumph twin) initially had a tremendous tussle at the front. However, soon these two were joined by P.E.J. Webb (JAP Special) and John Surtees on his Vincent single. Bostock, who was leading, fell on the 14th lap and John stormed into first place, a position he held to the flag. George Brown eventually passed Webb to take the runner-up spot. George Brown was a rider of considerable note and also chief tester at Vincent, so John's victory was a remarkable feat. Brown was later to win worldwide fame for his straight-line performances with his record breaking Nero and Super Nero Vincent V-twins. His brother

Cornering the Grey Flash in very wet conditions at Thruxton on 6 August 1951. With only months of racing experience John finished second to World Champion and Norton works star Geoff Duke in two races that day against a star-studded field.

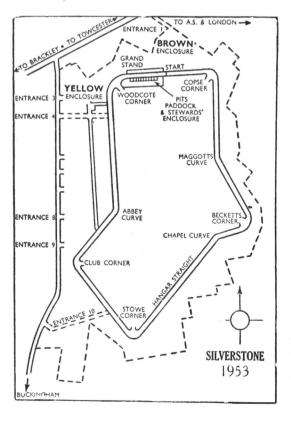

Cliff also worked at the Stevenage factory.

More victories were recorded at Brands Hatch on 16 September and 30 September with the Vincent. In between, on Saturday 29 September, John took part in an international meeting at Thruxton. This included the British Aerodromes Invitation Race, in which he came home an excellent third behind Les Graham (MV Agusta four) and David Bennett (works Norton). Once again he had shown his ability to compete at the highest level.

When the new 1952 season got under way John continued to do well on the Vincent. He started with first and second positions at Brands Hatch in 1,000cc-class races on Good Friday 12 April. Two days later, on Easter Sunday 14 April at Thruxton, John finished runner-up to David Bennett (Norton) in his heat of the Senior (500cc) class and third in the final, behind Bennett and Robin Sherry (also Norton mounted).

Then came an outing at Silverstone, in front of some 40,000 spectators, at the British Motor Cycle Racing Club (BMCRC) organised Motor Cycling Saturday International meeting held on 20 April. The entry included Duke, Doran, Brett, Bennett, Sherry and Storr, but John didn't have a particularly successful day. However, at Brands Hatch on Sunday 21 April, John gained two more victories on the trusty Grey Flash, in the 1,000cc scratch and invitation races.

Philip Vincent

Philip Conrad Vincent (PCV) was born in 1908 and grew up on a ranch in Argentina owned by his wealthy British parents. He was sent to study in England at Harrow School and it was there that his interest in motorcycles first began. He left Harrow at 18 to study Mechanical Sciences at Cambridge in 1927. Before leaving Harrow he had designed an ingenious cantilever system of rear suspension, with near-horizontal springs positioned beneath the saddle. This system, modified over the years and patented, would become a feature of all his future motorcycle designs. To appreciate the forward thinking of PCV one has to realise that the vast majority of motorcycles would remain unsprung for the following quarter of a century, and that it would be a full half century before cantilever systems were to start appearing on Japanese motorcycles. In his first year at Cambridge PCV constructed the first Vincent motorcycle, incorporating the spring frame.

Then, with his Cambridge course unfinished, the young Vincent persuaded his father to visit England and assist him financially in his bid to set up as a motorcycle manufacturer. Part of this involved the sum of £400 (around £40,000 in today's terms) to purchase the name and stock of the former HRD marque. HRD (Howard R. Davis) had been a rider of considerable note, having won the 1925 Isle of Man Senior TT on a machine of his own design. The Vincent-HRD company was established on the Old North Road in Stevenage, a Hertfordshire town some 20 miles north of London.

In 1932 PCV hired the Australian engineer Phil Irving as chief designer and together they famously designed the first brand-new model in a hectic 11-week period. The legendary motorcycles which followed are generally agreed to have been the fruits of both men's combined labour and design skills. As a sign of his commitment to his company during these early years Philip Vincent lived in a half-timbered old house adjoining the factory's main office block, with only an ageing aunt as company.

Under-funding was always a problem for Vincent and often his design genius, and that of Irving, was stunted by a lack of capital to develop ideas. However, Vincent-HRD was a firm which in many ways showed the rest of the British motorcycle industry how to go on. Their best-known machines were the 499cc single and later 998cc V-twin motorcycles, but there were other projects as well. For example, the superb 500cc opposed-piston two-stroke twin-cylinder marine power plant which so completely outperformed the Admiralty's existing engine that its tester concluded: 'It's far too good to be true'. There was also a light industrial engine, a superlative 3-wheeler with a

Philip Vincent (left) and engineer Phil Irving with an HRD machine, in the early 1930s.

Jack Surtees with John in the chair of the Vincent sidecar combination, 1951.

The famous 998cc (84 x 90mm) 47.5 degree angle V-twin Vincent engine, showing details of the transmission components.

Rapide V-twin motorcycle engine and the remarkably efficient water scooter – in effect a jet-ski four decades before the advent of the modern marine vehicle.

Unfortunately, following an accident on the airfield where the company tested its bikes in the immediate post-war period, Philip Vincent was never really himself again. This led to a financial crisis, which resulted in the appointment of E.C. Baillie, the official receiver, who took over control of the company in September 1949. 'To save costs' Phil Irving departed shortly afterwards, and was followed over the next few years by the majority of the key engineering staff. Eventually only PCV was left and the last Vincent motorcycle was built in late 1955.

In 1971 Philip Vincent suffered the first in a series of strokes and he died in April 1979. He was buried at Horndon-on-the-Hill, Essex, less than a quarter of a mile from High House, the old Vincent family home.

Vincent Black Lightning Series C racing model, *c*.1951. In John Surtees's opinion the Vincent company was considerably more advanced than the majority of mainstream British marques, but Philip Vincent's accident in 1949 and subsequent cost-cutting led to poorer quality.

The Featherbed Manx Norton threat

A rare engine problem caused John's retirement while battling for the lead in the main 500cc event at Boreham's national road races on Saturday 27 April. As at Silverstone, it was becoming increasingly difficult for John, as an ever larger number of the latest Featherbed 500cc Manx Norton's arrived on the scene. Consequently, he was forced into constantly attempting to improve the Vincent's performance by 'tiny increments'. Even so John had victories on the Grey Flash at Brands Hatch on 25 May and 13 July; he also crashed the Vincent there in the 1,000cc race on 29 June.

On Sunday 6 July John had journeyed up to Cadwell Park in the Lincolnshire Wolds. His best result was in the solo handicap, where he and G. Grant (498cc Triumph twin) dead-heated for fourth place, causing a bit of controversy – this was the first time a dead heat had been returned at Cadwell. John also competed at Ibsley, near Ringwood, Hampshire, on Saturday 12 July, finishing fourth in the 350cc final on the borrowed 'Garden Gate' Manx Norton.

Even though John had by now purchased the new Featherbed 500cc

John and Cyril Quantrill with the Norton-Vincent, a machine that John built in an attempt to beat Geoff Duke during his apprenticeship with the Vincent company. He began building it at the end of 1952, but his other racing commitments meant that it was never raced.

Manx Norton on which he had made his debut at Boreham, and had raced it shortly thereafter at the Ulster GP in mid-August (see Chapter 4), the faithful Vincent was still used to win at Brands Hatch on 24 August and finally at Aberdare Park on Saturday 30 August. At this latter venue John not only won the 500cc race, but also had the satisfaction of setting a new course lap record of 51 seconds for the ⅞-mile Welsh parkland circuit.

The Vincent is sold

John recalls he received around £150 for the Vincent (with his winnings he had already repaid his father the original £65 purchase price), whereas the Norton cost £280. Obviously, these are only the financial parts of the equation. In truth the two-year period spent with the Vincent had provided John with the basis upon which to build his racing career. In his time with the Stevenage push-rod single, he had learned much about racing – not just the actual riding, but tactics, starting techniques, tuning and preparation. But the time had come when, with ever increasing numbers of the Featherbed Manx Norton coming into service, the days of any pushrod model, whether it be Vincent, JAP or Triumph twin, was at an end. Certainly a rider couldn't expect to succeed on one, and John Surtees not only wanted success, he was hungry for it.

Vincent Grey Flash

The Grey Flash was developed from the series production Meteor and Comet roadsters, which had first been seen under the old HRD names of pre-war days.

Essentially the 499cc (84 x 90mm) engine was one cylinder from the famous 998cc ohv V-twin series. First mooted in mid-1949, the Grey Flash made its public debut at the London Earls Court Show in November that year. The idea had come from George and Cliff Brown (the latter being John Surtees's foreman in the Picador shop at Vincent) and it was ultimately to be built in three variants – as a stripped racing model for £275 plus purchase tax, as a roadster with lights, horn and other components for £290 plus purchase tax, or as a roadster supplied with racing equipment for easy conversion for an additional £10. The stock Grey Flash engine was tuned to Black Lightning specification and produced 35bhp at 6,200rpm; maximum speed, depending on model, ranged from 109 to 115mph.

As recorded elsewhere, John Surtees's Grey Flash (it was actually black before it was sprayed in Ford Silver Fox) was essentially a works hack, which had been used for test purposes. Thereafter it was modified, tuned and lightened in a successful attempt to create a competitive racing motorcycle. John's father Jack was a leading Vincent agent and John was for much of the time campaigning the Grey Flash as a Vincent employee. These two connections made a tremendous difference in the overall preparation of the bike.

Although the Surtees Grey Flash was built from a collection of component parts in mid-1950, it was pretty much a stock machine. Certainly it didn't benefit from the specification of the works 1950 big-port TT engines.

Initially it was assembled with the standard TT10 1⁵⁄₃₂-inch carburettor and original roller bearing big-end. But this latter component seized in its Brands Hatch debut and was replaced by a plain sleeve component in RR77-type material with an aluminium pin. At the same time John increased the delivery of the oil pump, fitted a fabric filter and then knocked up a special quill which he fitted to the main-shaft on the timing side end, hoping in this way to reduce oil losses from the shaft and so increase the pressure; and it worked perfectly, the big-end lasting for the rest of the time it was in Surtees's ownership.

In addition, the inlet port was bored out and an Amal RN remote needle carburettor (from a Norton) fitted. John then went to work on the piston, getting the compression ratio up to 9:1. There was also considerable experimentation in achieving the optimum length, shape and diameter of the exhaust pipe. Another area of modification and improvement was to the dampers. The stock Vincent assemblies were prone to lose their oil, something which had been found to happen on the standard roadster models in the Surtees dealership. This resulted in John and his father producing a different type of sealing for the shaft – a modification which was also made to John's racer.

The tank was replaced by one from his father's Black Lightning, which was in fact a standard component with the bottom cut off halfway up. This provided more space for the carburettor and held less fuel, which was perfect for the relatively short races which John's Grey Flash contested. The tank was further modified to provide a more comfortable 'tucked in' riding stance. A considerable amount of effort was expended on a weight-saving exercise; in this John sought his father's advice in an attempt to prevent the mistakes he felt he had made with his Triumph Tiger 70.

In the spring of 1951 a new cylinder head was fitted. It was of the type with which the factory was experimenting, mainly for use with alcohol fuels by John Hodgkin, who held the Cadwell Park lap record. Later it was employed for successful speed record attempts by the American Rollie Free and the New Zealander Russell Wright. It featured a 2-inch inlet valve and employed a 1³⁄₁₆-inch bore carburettor. John 'found this gave a definite improvement in the machine's performance'.

After these modifications had been carried out, it was very much a case of making small adjustments and changes in the final 12 months or so of the Vincent ownership, in an ever more difficult attempt to remain competitive with the latest pure-bred racing machinery which was coming on stream. Even so John Surtees's performances on the Vincent Grey Flash over two years played a vital role in his future development. It also helped teach him the importance of machine preparation. John recalled the period in his book *Speed*, published in 1963:

> There were meetings every weekend and I took part in as many events as possible, because I wanted all the riding I could get and realised that I needed all the racing experience available to me. Each race taught me something valuable and not least, I learnt how essential it is to give constant attention to one's machine. If you work seriously – and, obviously, you are not going to work at all unless it is seriously – every hour, or fraction of an hour, that you spend going over your machine will be time well spent. Later on, when I joined a works team, most, if not all, of the preparatory work was done for me, but I am convinced that even when this happens, if you know all about your motorcycle yourself, you will be a much better rider.

Chapter 3

Privateer

BESIDES his early achievements with the Vincent and various Nortons, John Surtees also scored a large number of victories aboard the likes of Bob Geeson's home-brewed dohc REG parallel twin (1954) and the German NSU Sportmax single (1955). In addition, he was also courted by BMW and rode one of the German twins with great skill at the feared Nürburgring in the 1955 German Grand Prix. In light of his rides on the works development Manx Nortons, followed by his career with MV Agusta, this period in John's career is best described under the 'privateer' banner.

As has already been made clear in the two earlier chapters, John Surtees had to make his way by dint of his own skill and determination, as there were no rich parents or well-off sponsors in the wings to bank-roll his racing career. Instead he had to be largely self-funded. However, John's performances by the end of the 1953 season had been enough to impress several parties – including the Norton factory. But a practice crash when the forks

Bob Geeson (seated on bike) built a series of superbly constructed home-crafted 250cc REG twins. Here John and his dad are with the bike as it was raced during late 1953 and most of 1954 by the future World Champion.

Bob Geeson

R.E. (Bob) Geeson not only enjoyed a successful racing career, but also design-ed and built the famous twin-cylinder REG, a double overhead camshaft 250cc racer, with which John Surtees scored a number of victories during his early career.

Geeson, who was living in Croydon, South London, began racing before World War Two, riding a 250cc Excelsior Manxman at venues such as Brooklands, Donington Park and the Manx Grand Prix. His racing career, like so many others, was rudely interrupted by Hitler in 1939.

In 1948, 12 years after the last win by a British bike in the Lightweight (250cc) Isle of Man TT, a a letter appeared in the BMCRC magazine, which sparked Bob Geeson into a decision which was to make a mark on motorcycle history.

A long-time member of 'Bemsee', as the BMCRC was more commonly known, Geeson viewed the letter, which suggested a consortium of qualified parties should build a motorcycle with which Great Britain could once again successfully contest the quarter-litre class, with considerable interest.

As Bob was both a qualified engineer and a rider he responded to the 'Bemsee' letter. This brought him into contact with Gordon Allen, a toolmaker, who was already well advanced with the construction of a prototype 250cc parallel twin. But up to his first encounter with Bob Geeson, Gordon Allen's efforts had been solely directed towards the bottom end of the engine, and he hadn't given much thought to the top end, let alone the chassis.

The meeting saw Allen and Geeson decide to pool their talents, the result being that within the very short space of three months, they had designed, constructed and tested a brand-new racing 250cc twin, named the Allen-REG. The frame and cycle parts were entirely Geeson's work – many in fact coming from the REG Rudge single which its creator had raced during the 1948 season.

The new twin, which is described on p.50, didn't enjoy a fairytale entry into the world. In fact the results gained – three starts and three retirements through big-end failure – could well have caused its premature end. However, as its technical development history reveals, the REG, with Geeson in sole charge from the end of 1949, flourished.

Geeson proved this when, riding his own creation, he came home 12th in the international Lightweight TT in June 1950, and the REG would have finished considerably higher up the ladder had not a broken oil pipe caused Geeson to lose 16 minutes on lap 3. This machine was actually a redesign, including a new bottom end. In 1951 an unfortunate mix-up in the Geeson pit resulted in the wrong type of lubricant being put into the oil tank. As a conse-quence he was forced to retire at Ballaugh with a badly damaged engine. His best position that year was seventh place in the Ulster Grand Prix. Ignition trouble put Geeson out of the TT in 1952, but in 1953 he realised a long standing ambition, finishing 10th and winning a Bronze Replica. His average speed for the four-lap race was 71.74mph. Further successes that year were also posted at Silverstone and the newly opened Crystal Palace circuit near Geeson's south London home.

He then decided to hang up his leathers and let someone else – John Surtees – do the riding. John made his debut on the REG at Blandford in August, taking the home-built machine to a magnificent third place in the 250cc final behind the Moto Guzzis of Fergus Anderson and Maurice Cann. As is described elsewhere in this chapter, the Geeson/Surtees collaboration was a highly successful exercise, since John dominated the British short circuit scene in 1954 with victories at Brands Hatch, Crystal Palace, Cadwell Park and Castle Combe.

At the end of 1954 Geeson sold his number one machine to Australian Jack Walters and laid plans for a second engine which was completed in April 1956. It was not until May 1957 that the REG again hit the headlines – which it did in notable fashion, making the fastest 250cc practice lap in the German Grand Prix at Hockenheim, with John Hartle aboard. Clocked at 125mph, Hartle finished eighth in the race, a wet affair in which he was slowed by magneto trouble. Then a few weeks later at the Dutch TT Hartle and the REG were robbed of a certain seventh place by a last-lap crash caused by oil on the circuit. Even more unfortunate was the fact that the accident caused the engine to, as *The Motor Cycle* described it, 'burst at astronomical rpm'.

Besides John Surtees and John Hartle, other notable riders who campaigned the REG were Derek Minter, who scored a number of victories, notably at Brands Hatch; Arthur Wheeler (1956), Jim Baughn (1956), Jack Brett (1957), Bob Anderson (1959), 'Ginger' Payne (1959–61), Norman Surtees (1960), Syd Mizen (1960–1), Ray Fay (1961) and finally Fred Hardy (1961–2).

With this array of riding talent and the number of wins and lap and race records, there is no doubt that Bob Geeson was a gifted engineer who could have taught the major British factories a thing or two about designing competitive racing motorcycles. Even today John Surtees has fond memories of his time with Bob Geeson and the remarkable REG twin, and as is recounted in Chapter 9 he has brought back to Britain the original engine and gearbox from Australia – and is in the process of rebuilding it into a complete motorcycle.

Bob Geeson, the creator of the famous home-brewed dohc REG twin, with John Surtees seated on the bike, 1954. This was to prove the most successful combination in British 250cc short circuit racing that year.

John Surtees as he was in 1954, then 20 years of age. Already he had become the number one rider in British short-circuit racing; before long he was to establish himself on the world stage.

John with the NSU Sportmax he raced so successfully during the 1955 season and upon which he won his first World Championship race at the Ulster Grand Prix on 13 August 1955.

broke on his EMC during the TT that year, forced him to pass up the chance of a works Norton ride which had been offered by the Bracebridge Street company's racing chief, Joe Craig. So, instead of being a fully-fledged Norton factory rider for 1954, John was still a privateer.

The REG debut

John's first outing on the Bob Geeson-built REG had occurred on 3 August 1953. This was followed by racing at Brands Hatch, where on 27 September he won both his heat and final. *The Motor Cycle* had this to say in their 1 October 1953 issue: 'In spite of intermittent rain during last Sunday's Brands Hatch Championship Meeting, it produced spirited racing and two new race records. An entry of high calibre contested seven events. The new figures were established by J. Surtees (REG) with a 10-lap speed of 62.35mph in the 250cc final, and by reigning World Sidecar Champion Eric Oliver (Norton SC) who achieved 59.9mph for the six laps of the Sidecar Handicap final.'

John's 1954 campaign got under way at Silverstone on Saturday 10 April, with the first national road race. *The Motor Cycle* commented: 'Young John Surtees kept the REG twin in third place until the last lap, when he suffered the misfortune of an engine seizure, thus letting in B.W.T. Rood (later one of the co-founders of Cosworth Engineering) on his twin ohc Velocette.'

As John revealed in his book *Speed*, 'Perhaps the greatest satisfaction that year came, however, from my excursion into the 250cc class'. The REG's builder, Bob Geeson constructed the REG at his home workshop in Coombe

Road, Croydon, not far from John's own home at Addington. The title REG came from Bob's own initials, and as John says: 'It turned out to be the best by far of all 250cc machines that year in England, even including the crack Italians.'

The Silverstone seizure had been caused by lubrication problems. John was entered to ride at Brands Hatch the following Friday and at Crystal Palace on the Monday, and, as John recalls 'Bob worked like a galley slave but was not sure that he had cured the trouble until Thursday. I shall always remember those two 1954 Easter meetings. I don't think I could have gone wrong if I had tried. The REG went like a bird and we won our Brands Hatch race at an average speed of 62.40mph. It was a wonderful experience, but more was to come at the Palace on Monday. It was an absolutely brilliant day and a crowd of over 20,000 streamed into the Crystal Palace grounds to watch more than 200 competitors.' John goes on to say: 'from the stage management point of view, quite the best I had experienced up to then. The machine went even better than it had gone on Good Friday. E.W. Tinkler, on a Pike-Rudge, made a fantastically quick getaway, but the REG went after him and before the first lap was completed we had passed him. After that the REG drew farther and farther ahead. We broke the lap record with a speed of 69.31mph and set up a new 250cc race record at an average speed of 65.98mph.' John had also won his heat on the REG so he scored two victories at the Palace that day. Another REG victory was chalked up at the Gravesend Eagle Club's meeting at Brands Hatch on Sunday 25 April.

On Saturday 8 May, John rode his Nortons to a trio of victories at Aberdare Park, but the REG didn't make the journey to Wales, instead Bob Geeson rode it himself at Snetterton to finish third behind Maurice Cann (Moto Guzzi) and Bennie Rood (Velocette).

At Brands Hatch on 9 May no fewer than 329 entries had been received. As *The Motor Cycle* was able to report: 'In winning every heat and every final in which he rode, Surtees set up new race records for 250, 350 and 1,000cc classes, and also raised the outright lap record to 70.86mph.'

Although John didn't ride the REG in either the TT or Ulster GP which followed a week later, he was back in the saddle of Bob Geeson's machine on 4 July 1954 at the Louth Club's road race meeting over the 1.25-mile Cadwell Park circuit. It was another impressive performance. *The Motor Cycle* reported: 'John Surtees (REG and Nortons) won every event in which he was entered. It was his first appearance at Cadwell this year and only the second occasion on which he had competed there.'

The winning steak on the REG continued at Crystal Palace on Saturday 17 July, with a repeat performance the following day at Brands Hatch.

The original Gordon Allen/Bob Geeson prototype dohc parallel twin in 1949.

REG twin development

The story of the REG twin began back in 1948 with the publication of a letter in the Bemsee club magazine, suggesting a way of putting Britain back on top of the 250cc class. In Croydon, South London, Bob Geeson, a long-time Bemsee member and pre-war competitor at Brooklands, Donington and the Manx Grand Prix, read the letter with considerable interest. This brought him into contact with Gordon Allen, who had already started work on a prototype 250cc parallel twin. Allen and Geeson decided to join forces, the result being the Allen-REG, a 249cc (54 x 54mm) all-alloy construction, gear driven, double overhead cam engine, with roller bearing big-ends and a three-bearing crankshaft. Allen had been responsible for the bottom end of the engine, with Geeson designing the cylinder head and valve gear, plus the chassis. Completed in an amazingly short three-month period, the results in 1949 were not impressive – three starts and three DNFs – all due to seized big-ends.

During the closed season of 1949–50 Bob Geeson took over sole responsibility for the project, now renamed simply REG. The main differences of the subsequent engine redesign, completed in January 1950, were to the bottom end; Allen's built-up crank being discarded in favour of a one-piece Nitralloy assembly machined from solid and supported on lipped roller bearings at each end and a plain centre bearing; the seizure-prone roller big-ends making way for Hiduminium connecting rods running directly on the crankpins. The valve gear and its drive train had also displayed weaknesses during 1949 and had been modified.

Other technical details of the REG's specification included camshaft drive via six spur gears, each supported on either side by ball races, thus reducing friction to a minimum. The oil pump was driven from the timing and lubricant for the dry sump system fed under pressure to both camboxes. Oil was pumped through the hollow crankshaft to a point midway between the big-end journals, from which an oilway led to each big-end. Both bearings were thus assured of an equal supply of lubricant.

Con-rods were RR56 forgings and ran directly on the crankshaft; the small ends being unbushed. An outside flywheel was a feature of the power unit, with the crankcase and timing cover casting being magnesium; ignition was by magneto.

Several modifications were carried out for 1952. The central main bearing was removed. Another change was that the piston-type tappets were discarded in favour of square section tappets and the valve stems shortened. Interviewed in 1958 Bob Geeson revealed that: 'whilst a cylindrical tappet was easier to make, it was heavier than its square-section counterpart'. And with a square-section tappet 'the only limitation on the amount of metal that can be removed is the wall thickness required to provide adequate strength'. In fact the modifications reduced the weight of the reciprocating parts of the valve gear by a quarter.

In 1953 Geeson altered the valve spring arrangement and as a result the engine would operate safely in excess of 9,000rpm. But, unfortunately, a cracked piston in that year's Ulster Grand Prix resulted in a major engine blow-up. Modifications to the webs around the gudgeon-pin bosses cured the problem in future pistons and, with John Surtees riding in place of its creator, the REG's first ever victory came on 27 September 1953 at Brands Hatch in Kent.

The next year, 1954, with Surtees in the saddle, saw the REG unbeaten except for two occasions, when mechanical trouble was encountered. The actual record was 15 firsts (plus another victory by Bob Geeson himself), plus no fewer than seven occasions when the Surtees/REG combination set new race and lap records! At the end of that year the machine was sold to the Australian Jack Walters.

The following year, 1955, was devoted entirely to manufacturing sets of components for two more complete bikes, one of which Geeson assembled as

Fred Hardy working on the final version of Bob Geeson's remarkable REG at his home in the summer of 1961.

John Surtees with Bob Geeson's REG dohc twin at Crystal Palace in April 1954.

soon as it was ready, which was in the following summer, when it made its debut with Jim Baughn in the saddle. The only technical improvements over the original design were confined to the porting and the use of shorter connecting rods.

But it wasn't until three years later that circumstances permitted the simultaneous operation of both REGs. Experimentally, during 1958, a switch was made to the coil ignition, then after a season back with the magnetos, Geeson adopted twin plug ignition. But this dual ignition experiment did not prove a success and, in combination with certain other factors, led to a spate of stripped timing gears.

In its final incarnation – with Fred Hardy aboard in 1961 and 1962 – the REG employed a frame which featured a massive top tube and much smaller twin front downtubes, Girling rear shock absorbers, Norton Roadholder front forks, and an AJS 7R front hub; there was also a separate four-speed close ratio gearbox, dry multi-plate clutch and simplex primary chain.

Finally on 24 July came John's last victory on the REG at Castle Combe – another '1' was chalked up on the victory scoreboard.

However, at Snetterton on 1 August the REG was extensively damaged in a practice accident. Although John finished runner-up behind Arthur Wheeler (Moto Guzzi) in the shorter morning 250cc event at Silverstone's Hutchinson 100 meeting on 7 August, he was forced to retire (with water in the works) during the main 250cc Championship event at the pits, after 7 laps, in horrendously wet conditions.

At this point John switched from the REG to Ian Telfer's 250cc Manx Norton. He was not to make a winning debut on this machine, since it was slowed by gearbox gremlins. John finished in the runner-up spot, behind race winner Maurice Cann's Moto Guzzi at Ibsley Airfield, near Ringwood, Hampshire on 21 August. Victories were to come on the sleeved-down Norton at Aberdare Park (28 August) and Brands Hatch (12 September).

1954 had been a brilliant year for John Surtees – he had won 50 of the 60 races he had taken part in. Much of this success had been achieved riding Norton 350cc and 500cc Manx models; however, the 250cc class had also been a productive venture, with many successes on Bob Geeson's rapid REG twin and afterwards on Ian Telfer's 250cc Norton. These achievements were officially recognized when John was presented with the Pinhard Prize; this memorial award being made annually to the most meritorious contribution to motorcycling by an ACU licence holder under the age of 21. As John was later to recall: 'It was the first recognition granted to me by the pundits of the sport and I was very happy to receive it.'

John's mother made an important contribution to his success. He received enormous support from her. He recalls:

> *...right from the start she had taken all the paperwork off me. She would send away for the entry forms and fill them in. I would sign them when I came home and she would mail them off. She also attended every meeting in which I raced, at home and abroad, right up to my last season on motorcycles. And nearly always, in the latter years when my father was too busy looking after the business to get away, she would also drive the bikes and me to and from meetings.*

Family friend Charlie Rous confirmed this: 'She was just as much interested in bikes as Jack [her husband]. Dorothy was an expert sidecar driver – not in racing but on the road – a superb motorcyclist and car driver. John [Junior] was born a natural. Without question he inherited his father's ability and his mother's.'

The NSU debut

The 7 April 1955 issue of *The Motor Cycle* carried a story revealing that although the German NSU factory had quit racing, it was nonetheless going to supply a number of its former works riders with the new Sportmax

Isle of Man TT

First used in 1911 (though in slightly different form), the famous Mountain Course measured 37.73 miles in length and comprised roads which were the normal traffic arteries of the Isle of Man. To avoid too much interference with everyday trade on the Island, therefore, the pre-race practice periods largely took place in the early hours of the morning. Closure of the roads for both practising and racing required a separate Act of the Man Parliament every year.

The start, grandstand, scoreboard and pits were situated in Glencrutchery Road high above the town of Douglas. Soon after leaving the start riders rocketed down the steep but bumpy Bray Hill, then followed the slight rise of Brown's Hill, followed by the drop to Quarter Bridge, a slow right-hander necessitating hard braking, engagement of bottom gear and usually the use of the clutch.

Braddan Bridge was the next landmark, a spectacular S-bend over the railway and river, then on to the village of Union Mills three miles from the start, winding and undulating, the course dropped down to the Highlander and through the bends at Greeba to Ballacraine (7.25 miles); a sharp right-hander.

The course was now very much out in the country, with the road twisting and turning through the leafy tunnel of the Neb Valley past Laurel Bank and Glen Helen, then up the 1-in-10 rise of Creg Willey's Hill on to the heights of Cronk-y-Voddee. The descent of Baaregarroo before the 13th milestone section was generally held as being the fastest section of the course. It was followed by a tricky section ending with Westwood's Corner, a relatively fast left-hander.

Soon riders reached Kirkmichael (14.5 miles) with its second gear right-hander followed by a trip through the narrow village street, after which there was a winding but fast run to Ballaugh – with the famous hump-back bridge where both wheels left the ground. Left, right, left – the trio of Quarry Bends were taken in the region of 100mph or more; the bends leading out on to the start of the famous mile-long Sulby Straight, with at its end an extremely sharp right-hand corner at Sulby Bridge (20 miles). Then came hard acceleration up to and around the long, sweeping left-hander at Ginger Hall. Through wooded Kerromoar and the foot of Glen Auldyn, the circuit wound its way on to the town of Ramsey, where riders flicked right and left through Parliament Square in the very middle of the town. Then came the beginning of the long mountain climb, the road rising up May Hill to the testing Ramsey Hairpin (24.5 miles) and up again to Waterworks Corner and the Gooseneck.

Still climbing, riders passed Guthrie's Memorial and reached East Mountain Gate (28.25 miles) where the long gruelling ascent at last began to flatten out. A further mile on led to a quartet of gentle bends at the Verandah section, followed by the bumpy crossing of the mountain railway tracks on the bend at the Bungalow. The highest point on the course was at Brandywell, a left-hand sweep beyond the Bungalow, and from there the road began to fall gently, through the aptly named Windy Corner, a medium fast right-hander and the long 33rd milestone bend.

Kate's Cottage (300 yards past Keppel Gate) marked the beginning of the flat out, exhilarating sweep down to Crag-ny-Baa (34.5 miles). Still dropping, the course swept towards the left-hander at Brandish Corner and down yet more to the fast right-handed curve at Hillberry.

With less than two miles to the finish there followed the short climb of Cronk-ny-Mona and the sharp right-hand turn at Signpost Corner. Bedstead Corner and The Nook followed in swift succession and within a quarter-of-a-mile it was a case of hard on to the brakes for Governor's Bridge, an acute hairpin, which was the slowest corner on the course. The short detour through the hollow was a link to earlier days when it formed part of the main road. Once out of the hollow, riders accelerated into Glencrutchery Road less than half-a-mile from the grandstand and pit area.

In essence the course remains the same today, when at the beginning of the 21st century, the TT has long since lost its World Championship status. However, it still remains one of the most famous names in motorcycle racing history and attracts huge crowds every June; although the 2001 event was not held, due to the foot-and-mouth outbreak on the British mainland.

production racing model and a few were also to be sold for use by leading privateers. As described elsewhere within this chapter, the machine was an overhead camshaft single, producing around 30bhp. Non-German riders were to include: 'Reg Armstrong, J. Surtees and P. Monneret'.

This story did not make it clear how the arrangement with John Surtees would work. In fact the deal was organised through his then-employers, Vincent of Stevenage. The Vincent company had been appointed British agents for the entire range of NSU motorcycles, and before agreeing to ride the NSU John discussed the matter with Bob Geeson. So, together with his works Norton contract, John began 1955 with five machines: two works-development Manx Nortons, his own pair of privately financed Manx models, and the Sportmax.

John's debut on the German bike came at Brands Hatch on Good Friday 8 April 1955. There was a considerable air of excitement. *The Motor Cycle* report captured the occasion in the following manner: 'There were no fewer than 188 entries, of which 24 were sidecars, and it was estimated that nearly 30,000 spectators were present. As expected, John Surtees, riding 348 and 499cc Nortons and a 248cc NSU Sportmax production racer, had effortless runaway wins in every race in which he rode.' The NSU had been brought from Germany only the previous week and, at its first outing, the Brands Hatch 250cc race record speed was raised by 1.71mph. It was the same story at Snetterton on Easter Sunday 10 April, where it was reported: 'John Surtees had a field day'. This run of success continued the following day at Crystal Palace. So in its first weekend the NSU had proved a winner every time it had been wheeled to the starting line. This record indicated not only

its rider's skill, but also the machine's speed and reliability. Then on 23 April came the annual *Motor Cycling* Silverstone Saturday, where all the top riders of the day appeared. The two solo stars were undoubtedly Geoff Duke (Gilera) and John Surtees (NSU and Norton). About John's Sportmax ride *The Motor Cycle* had this to say: 'Riding his NSU at the top of his brilliant form, the young Londoner led the race from the fall of the starter's flag and notched a lap record of a speed of 85.34mph.' Actually, John won two 250cc races that day; one a five-lap affair, the other main event held over 10 laps of the Northamptonshire circuit. And a day later, on 24 April, it was back south to Brands Hatch and another NSU victory.

Next outing with the German 250cc machine was on 7 May at the Cheshire Oulton Park venue. *The Motor Cycle* report said it all: 'As on so many previous occasions this year, the outstanding rider was J. Surtees (NSU and Norton). Making lightning-quick starts and riding with superb dash and judgement, the 21-year-old Londoner won all the races in which he competed.'

Then a week later came a busy weekend when John rode at Aberdare Park on the Saturday and Brands Hatch the following day. In Wales he won every heat and every final on his NSU and 348 and 499cc Nortons. *The Motor Cycle* had this to say about his smaller mount: 'So reliable is the NSU, incidentally, that after 10 events the cylinder head has not been lifted.' The winning trend continued the next day. John arrived at the Kent circuit for the Rochester and Chatham Club's meeting and by the time he left Brands he had won two heats and three finals, and established record laps in two classes at a record 10-lap time for the 350cc.

Then, as described in Chapter 4, John journeyed to the Isle of Man to race his Nortons, not taking the NSU: 'because I was in the Island as a team man'. Straight after the TT he was back in the thick of short circuit action, at his local Crystal Palace venue on Saturday 18 June. *The Motor Cycle* headline read: 'Sunshine at the Palace. Masterful performances by J. Surtees at BMCRC Meeting'. Riding the NSU in the 250cc final, so great was the superiority of man and machine that, after only four laps of the 1.39-mile circuit, John had built up a lead of 17 seconds over his nearest rival Dave Chadwick riding the Reg Dearden Special. He also set a new class lap record for the south London circuit of 69.89mph.

The Continental Grand Prix outing was at the German Nürburgring circuit (see p.61). This track and the Isle of Man Mountain Course were without doubt the most demanding tests of man and machine in motorcycle racing. And it was at the Nürburgring on 26 June 1955 that John Surtees was first able to demonstrate his skills to a wider audience. Since he displayed his talent on three different makes of machine, the Nürburgring outing is of particular interest in the progression of the young Englishman's career. The event marked his first visit to the fearsome circuit, and it was also his one and, as it turned out, only competitive ride on a BMW.

The BMW saga

BMW's Chief Engineer Alex von Falkenhausen saw the Englishman as 'the man who can win races for us'. And John's performance on the horizontal twin-cylinder machine was impressive to say the least, and is best summed up by the man himself: 'Riding the twin had certainly been different, but I was doing the same sort of times as regular rider Walter Zeller, despite the fact that I was not using a full works-specification bike like his, and was in third place. I think this is what convinced von Falkenhausen – and certainly convinced me – that I could have won the championship in 1956, and perhaps beyond, if BMW had given full support to a Grand Prix programme.'

But on the day the BMW suffered 'continued oiling-up of the spark plugs and float chamber problems'. These eventually conspired to cause John's retirement from the race. As history records, the names of John Surtees and BMW did not converge again – instead he was to sign for the Italian MV Agusta company later that year. However, as John points out: 'I think it was

The ride which got John Surtees noticed by MV Agusta team manager Nello Pagani was on this BMW Rennsport during the German Grand Prix on 26 June 1955 at the Nürburgring, even though he eventually retired because of plug and carburettor problems.

my performance on this bike (the BMW) which alerted Count Agusta to my potential and indirectly led to the invitation to race for MV the following year. In fact, if BMW hadn't dithered around, I might well have ended up riding for them in 1956 rather than the Italians.'

In reality, much as von Falkenhausen and John would have liked to have joined forces at the end of 1955, the behind-the-scenes state of the German motorcycle industry would have made it difficult for BMW to mount a really effective challenge. This was because after record growth during the first half of the 1950s, sales were about to go into free-fall. Almost overnight the German economic miracle, which had made the bike industry's customers so much more prosperous, enabled them to switch en masse from two to four wheels. Many famous marques such as Adler, DKW, Express and Horex ceased production altogether, while BMW only survived by the skin of its corporate teeth, thanks to a massive injection of cash from the Quandt family.

At the Nürburgring, John had mixed fortunes in his other races – a fall on the first lap with the NSU (caused by having to use foreign tyres with less grip) and, as recounted in the following chapter, a superb top three finish on his 350cc Norton. In many ways the 1955 German GP – the first time it had been run at the Nürburgring since 1931 – marked a turning point in John Surtees's career. He became an international star, not simply a British one.

After the glamour and excitement of the Nürburgring experience, it was back to the 'coal face' of British short circuit events. As there was no 250cc class at Scarborough in the first weekend of July, it was not until the following Saturday, 9 July, that the NSU was brought out to play again. The setting was Castle Combe, a 1.84-mile former airfield, but unlike the vast majority of these, the Wiltshire course was more undulating and provided with a reasonable variety of corners. Discounting the heats, John recorded three starts and three victories, in the 250cc, 350cc and 500cc events. As *Motor Cycling* reported, Surtees 'proved his mastery yet again by three convincing and unhurried victories. As a result of his supremacy, most of the interest lay in the private battles being fought to his rear.'

A week later, at Thruxton, John was back in action on the NSU. The setting was the ACU's sixth international road-race meeting. John not only won the 250cc race by a considerable margin, but also set a new class record of 81.09mph for the Hampshire airfield track. Overnight the Surtees équipe travelled up to Snetterton for the Norfolk circuit's first national meeting of the year. Yet again, as *The Motor Cycle* report proclaimed, 'A grand entry, the star of the solo category proved to be the incredible J. Surtees'. This was an all too-familiar comment by the press during John's final year before he joined MV Agusta. Again, not only did he score a comfortable victory on the NSU, but he set a new class lap record of 80.19mph.

His next outing was across the Irish Sea to compete in the Ulster Grand Prix, on works-supported Nortons and the NSU. The meeting was staged in: 'blazing sunshine under almost cloudless skies and with vast crowds'. The Dundrod circuit, which had replaced the old Clady course as the venue for the Ulster Grand Prix, measured seven miles, 720 yards to a lap, and was essentially a rider's course. Its many bends were varied in nature from very slow to very fast. The circuit also had some severe gradients – for example,

NSU Sportmax

The prototype of what was to emerge as the Sportmax was first seen at the end of 1953 during the Spanish Grand Prix. Thereafter, development continued both on the track and in the test shop. There were several race tests during the 1954 season at events such as Hockenheim, the Swiss Grand Prix and Italian Grand Prix; riders included Georg Braun and Kurt Knopf.

All these early development machines were essentially similar to the production version, but used a smaller diameter front brake and had a few other more minor differences. Dipl. Ing. Karl Kleinbach was responsible for the Sportmax's development, but there has always been some confusion as to just how many genuine Sportmax models were actually built. NSU publicity officer Arthur Westrup stated 17, while other well-informed sources go as high as 34. In addition, a number of other examples were built later from spare parts, when the race shop was sold to the Herz family in the late 1950s. Finally, there was a large number of converted Max, Special Max and Super Max roadsters; some of these being crude to say the least – they not only used the series production cycle parts, but also poorly-made replica Sportmax tanks and seats.

The genuine Sportmax or Type 251RS (250 one-cylinder Rennsport), had a displacement of 247cc (69 x 66mm) and a compression ratio of 9.8:1, giving 28bhp at 9,000rpm (maximum safe engine revolutions of 9,500rpm). The piston was a forged 3-ring Mahle and there was an Amal GP 1$\frac{3}{16}$-inch carburettor with remote float chamber. The distinctive 22-litre (4.84 imp gall) fuel tank was in hand-beaten aluminium. Both wheels were 18 inch diameter, with 2.75 front and 3.00 rear section tyres. With a dry weight of 112kg (246lb), maximum speed was 124mph and there was a wide variety of gearbox and rear wheel sprockets available for changing the gearing. Compared to the 1954 prototype machines, the production version built from early 1955 featured an increase in front brake size from 180 to 210mm drum diameter.

The Sportmax proved even more successful than NSU could ever have dreamed. During the 1955 Grand Prix racing season not only did Hermann Peter (Happy) Müller win the 250cc World Championship title, but a Sportmax also provided John Surtees with his first Grand Prix victory in Ulster during August 1955.

Other riders who went on to success with the Sportmax included Sammy Miller, Tommy Robb, Mike Hailwood (with the ex-Surtees machine), Hans Baltisburger, Georg Braun, Pierre Monneret, Horst Kassner, Jack Murgatroyd and Eric Hinton.

With a somewhat slower BMW, an R51/2, back home in England during the mid-1950s.

the 500ft climb from Cochranstown to Hole-in-the-Wall being a particular test of machine stamina.

A famous victory

The 250cc race, held on 13 August 1955, created yet another milestone in John Surtees's career – his first World Championship victory. Speculation was rife over the prospects for the race. In the 250cc World Championship standings Bill Lomas (MV Agusta) had a lead of one point from H.P. Müller (NSU). MV had a big team for the event, not only Lomas, but star names such as Umberto Masetti, Luigi Taveri and Remo Venturi. Cecil Sandford was mounted on an ex-works Moto Guzzi, while there were several NSU Sportmax models besides John's own machine, including those of Müller and Sammy Miller.

On the drop of the flag John Surtees streaked into the lead, with Müller and Miller in close attendance. And as *The Motor Cycle* said: 'Surtees was in scintillating form and his second lap speed of 88.70mph was a class record.' The race was run over 13 laps, a distance of 96.32 miles. At its conclusion John was 24 seconds ahead of the runner-up, Sammy Miller, and an amazing 77 seconds up on the first of the MV Agusta's, ridden by Masetti. Lomas was fourth and Müller sixth. In fact

The Nürburgring

Here we are only concerned with the long Nürburgring circuit, not the pale shadow of the original on which today's events are staged.

Laid out in 1927, the original Nürburgring was not only the pride of German racing, but also the most tortuous and demanding of circuits which one can imagine. In many ways it was an even more difficult course than the legendary 37.73-mile Isle of Man TT circuit.

The magnificence of the Nürburgring's setting and the concentration of its hazards were truly awe-inspiring. Having an average width of 27 feet, the tarmac surfaced road wound and dipped, in a confusing sequence of blind bends and undulations, over the beautifully wooded slopes of the Eifel mountains. In its 14.165-mile lap, the road fell and climbed nearly 1,000 feet.

The task of riders in attempting to memorize the circuit's 174 bends was made difficult by the similarity in appearance of the majority of its curves. There were precious few identification marks to distinguish one bend from another. Nor was that the only difficulty, for even after the circuit had been memorised, actual racing experience was indispensable if a rider was to perfect his technique in blending the exit from one curve into the entry of its successor and thus achieve a smooth, fluent style.

None of the bends were very slow; few of them really fast. Nevertheless, the Nürburgring ranked with the Isle of Man Mountain Circuit as the ultimate test of real riding ability for, with the exception of a 1.5-mile straight, there was no respite for the memory and concentration.

Of the 'old' Nürburgring John Surtees had this to say: 'I stayed in the Sport Hotel, with pictures of men such as Rosemeyer, Varzi and Stuck. Then there were the garages. When I closed my eyes I could almost hear the sounds of BMW, the supercharged NSU, or the Auto Union and Mercedes GP cars of the 1930s. It was a time warp when you went there in the 1950s.'

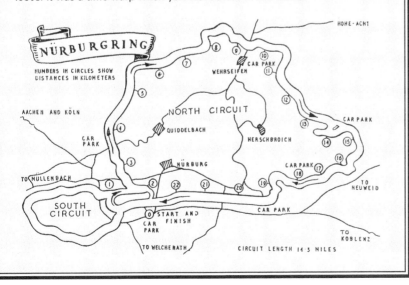

so conclusive was John's lead that he was able to ease the pace towards the end of the race.

At Ibsley Airfield near Ringwood, exactly seven days after his Ulster GP success, John had the satisfaction of breaking the lap record for each class that he rode in: 250, 350 and 500cc. In the former he totally dominated – after three laps of the 2.1-mile circuit he was no less than 20 seconds ahead of the second-placed rider Geoff Monty (GMV).

The following day at Brands Hatch, he gained another trio of victories to add to the Ibsley successes. But even these performances were eclipsed at Aberdare Park with four victories (250cc, 350cc, 500cc and 1,000cc). *The Motor Cycle* reported: 'Riding at the top of his form, J. Surtees not only repeated his successes of the May meeting at Aberdare by winning every race in which he rode, but he repeatedly lowered the lap record.'

After the excellent showing with the NSU in the Ulster GP John received a call from the NSU factory asking if he could contest the Italian round of the championship at Monza, in support of their rider Hermann Müller. John was keen to accept because riding there could strengthen his hand in obtaining a works contract. It was to be John's first visit to Italy, but certainly not the last. In the race, poor grade fuel caused his early retirement, due to a piston seizure. However, it was far from a wasted journey because, as Chapter 5 reveals, he was taken to the MV Agusta works in nearby Gallarate by fellow Englishman Bill Webster, and there was introduced to Count Domenico Agusta.

Then once again, after experiencing the excitement of travelling to pastures new, it was back home to England for the last of the short circuit events, including those at Snetterton (10 September), Cadwell Park (11 September), Brands Hatch (18 September) and Brough (25 September), which all produced victories for the NSU.

As is recorded in Chapter 5, the star-studded BMCRC Hutchinson 100 meeting of 1 October 1955 was the day John Surtees finally beat Geoff Duke in a straight race.

It also witnessed Norton's great team boss Joe Craig's final bow in a job he had held for so many years. But even though John won both the 350 and 500cc Championship races, what would have been an incredible trio of victories was not to be. The engine of his NSU Sportmax struck valve gear troubles when, as *The Motor Cycle* said 'he had the 250cc Championship virtually won by more than two miles'. His only consolation was a new 250cc lap record at 89.1mph. Since his final meeting of the 1955 season was the following day at Brands Hatch, he had no time to repair the German machine's engine. So his Silverstone exit thus proved to be the last time that

John would race the NSU in anger before signing for MV Agusta a few weeks later.

John's superb results on Norton and earlier Vincent machinery, and his performances as a privateer on Bob Geeson's REG, Ian Telfer's 250cc Norton and finally the NSU Sportmax, proved to be vital stepping stones to signing for MV and subsequently scoring the first of his seven World Championship titles for the Italian marque.

BMW Rennsport

In June 1939 the German BMW marque made Isle of Man history by becoming the first foreign company to win the Senior TT (if one discounts Irishman Stanley Woods's 1935 Moto Guzzi victory) with a foreign rider.

The 500cc BMW was a classic example of having a basically sound design and slowly developing it. The first example, the R32, made its bow at the Paris Salon in October 1923. When the flat twin was put into production and raced shortly afterwards, this machine featured a side-valve engine. Then a change was made from side to overhead valves and this set-up was progressively developed until 1935, when a supercharged double overhead camshaft unit was introduced. This made its Isle of Man debut in 1937, the year in which Ernst Henne regained the world's speed record on a streamlined version. Henne had first gained the world's fastest for BMW back in 1929.

A feature of the works model used by Walter Zeller in the mid-1950s was that of fuel injection, whereas the production Rennsport model ridden by John Surtees in the 1955 German Grand Prix at the Nürburgring employed conventional carburettors. The fuel injection, which debuted in 1953, was fitted to Zeller's Senior TT mount that year. Zeller lay ninth after the first lap but then came off, damaging his machine too seriously to continue.

There were in fact three stages in the development of the fuel injection: in the first the injector nozzle was mounted between the throttle slide and inlet port, spraying fuel into the induction tract at an angle. Next came the layout used by Zeller in the 1953 TT, in which the injector was mounted in the induction bellmouth, upstream of the throttles and injecting axially. Finally, from 1954, the nozzle was transferred to the cylinder head opposite the spark plug. It was found that this latter type, by removing a form of obstruction from the inlet system, improved the cylinder charging appreciably and thus resulted in increased power output.

If John Surtees had ridden a factory BMW in 1956 it would undoubtably have featured fuel injection and in this guise it would have put out 58bhp at 9,000rpm. The output of the production version, with carbs, was 52bhp. Zeller's works model had five speeds, the production Rennsport usually four ratios.

Even today John feels: 'I could have won the 500cc World Championship for BMW in 1956', and he recalls that in all his dealings with Alex von Falkenhausen he found him a 'real gentleman'. John also considers that the reason Geoff Duke did not get on with the BMW when he rode a works model in 1958 was 'because Geoff was not able to adapt to the wider range of riding styles which the BMW required'. John found the BMW twin 'needed to be ridden softly sometimes and physically on other occasions'.

Finally, it is worth mentioning the great success the BMW flat twin engine enjoyed in sidecar racing, winning 19 of the 21 World Championships between 1954 and 1974.

Chapter 4

Norton

EVEN today Norton is a famous name in motorcycling; half a century ago it was the greatest name in racing. Having begun in style by being a winner of the very first TT in 1907, the Birmingham marque had then gone on to win countless races, with such legendary riders as Alec Bennett, Stanley Woods, Jimmy Guthrie, Harold Daniell, Freddie Frith and of course Geoff Duke.

John Surtees's initial experiences with the double knocker Norton had come via a borrowed plunger-framed 'Garden Gate' 350cc model. as recorded in the previous chapter, not only was this machine heavy and prone to frame breakages, but compared to John's Vincent, suffered serious ground clearance problems. However, the arrival of the McCandless Featherbed chassis for the works bikes in 1950 meant that the 'Garden Gate' model was made obsolete and the first production Featherbed-framed Manx over-the-counter racers were available from 1951 onwards. However, at this time these could only be obtained by international licence holders intending to ride in events such as the GPs and the TT. Even so, by early 1952, with more and more riders equipped with the latest Manxes, bikes such as John's Grey Flash Vincent were at a severe disadvantage.

By mid-1952 the Surtees équipe realised that they simply had to have a Featherbed Manx to make further progress. So an approach was made to Norton to purchase a bike. Gilbert Smith, Norton's managing director, although he knew of John's performances with the Vincent, still took the view that he would only sell a new Manx to riders who were going to enter a World Championship event.

So it was decided that John should enter the Ulster Grand Prix; this enabled Norton to sell John (via Harold Daniell's dealership) a new 499cc model 30M Manx. The bike

John Surtees's first Norton race experience came with a 'Garden Gate' plunger-framed 350cc Manx model similar to the one shown here in 1951. Compared to his regular machine at the time, the Vincent Grey Flash, the Norton had insufficient ground clearance, causing the frame to ground far too easily.

arrived in July and, as a way of giving it an outing before setting off for Northern Ireland, an entry was made for the national road races at Boreham, near Chelmsford, on Saturday 27 July 1952. In a meeting dominated by full works supported riders, such as Ken Kavanagh (Norton), Robin Sherry (AJS Porcupine) and Les Graham (MV Agusta), John circulated with the leading privateers including George Brown, P.E.S. Webb and Allen Dudley-Ward. The Boreham outing made John realise how different the Featherbed Manx Norton was from his Vincent Grey Flash. Whereas the latter had been 'rather high, had a narrow tank and comparatively stiff suspension', the Norton was 'lower, wider and almost softly sprung'. He 'was glad to have the opportunity to adjust myself before crossing to Northern Ireland.'

The Ulster Grand Prix

The main object of competing at Boreham was to ensure the bike was ready for John's first world championship race, the Ulster Grand Prix. And what

By mid-1952 John had acquired his first Featherbed Manx Norton, on the premise that he would be contesting an event counting towards the World Championship. He made his classic debut in the 500cc Ulster GP held over the legendary Clady circuit on 16 August 1952. (This photograph was taken at a British short-circuit event that same year.)

Getting his newly acquired 30M Manx well over shortly after its acquisition. The brand new bike was authorised via Norton managing director Gilbert Smith and purchased (at full price!) from Harold Daniell.

a challenging debut it was to be, because the 500cc race was not only being run over the famous 16.5-mile Clady circuit for the last time, but the race distance was also an incredible 15 laps, totalling 247.5 miles.

Interestingly, on his arrival in Belfast John met Artie Bell for the first time, garaging his Manx Norton at the address in Woodburn Road where the former Norton works rider was in partnership with Rex McCandless, elder of two brothers, whose first claim to fame was that they had pioneered the type of swinging arm rear suspension which was subsequently to be found on many of the world's motorcycles.

Rex, who had been largely responsible for the design of the Featherbed frame, had by then retired from racing, but his younger brother Cromie was still riding and had that year finished sixth in the Senior and seventh in the Junior TTs, riding Francis Beart's Nortons.

Meeting men such as these only added to John's growing list of contacts and experiences. He was also taken around the circuit by car, to be shown its main features. However, this trip didn't prepare him for the shock which awaited him upon going out for practice on the Norton. John takes up the story: 'Everything went smoothly on the first few miles away from the start at Nutt's Corner and from there to Muckamore. Then came the Clady Straight and, as I headed into it, I opened the Norton up. The great feature

As part of the official Norton factory squad at the 1953 Isle of Man TT. Left to right: Ken Kavanagh, Ray Amm (on the Silver Fish streamlined kneeler), Jack Brett and John Surtees. Unfortunately, due to a practice accident when the forks of his EMC broke, John was unable to take part in any of the races, which set his entry into the ranks of the works-supported riders back several months.

of that straight was its series of undulations and the first one I hit, sitting in the saddle instead of poised on the footrests ready for what was coming, had me flying through the air for what appeared to be miles – to land with a crunch which effectively dampened my ardour for the next few miles.'

Also during practice John thought he had a carburation problem. However, back at Artie Bell's workshop, it was discovered that the ignition timing was eight degrees out; when remedied, the engine ran superbly.

The 1952 500cc Ulster GP was an incredible race with many retirements in a star-studded entry; there being works teams from Norton, AJS, Gilera and MV Agusta. For the first few laps Les Graham (MV), together with Norton factory riders Reg Armstrong and Ken Kavanagh, lapped in formation at over 103mph; Graham finally posting a lap of 105.94mph.

At the end, Cromie McCandless won on a Gilera four, averaging 99.79 for the near 250-mile race distance. After lying 12th on the first lap, John Surtees finished sixth (in the process scoring his first World Championship points), just prevented from going on for a 15th lap by being lapped by Rex McCandless' younger brother Cromie at Clady Corner, only a short distance from the finish. John recalls being 'very pleased with the result'.

After Ulster it was back to the short circuits, first a fifth behind Kavanagh, Graham and company at Boreham on Saturday 23 August, followed by a visit to Castle Combe in Wiltshire on Saturday 6 September, where John was to score his first ever Norton victory and set a new lap record of 81.98mph, when winning the 500cc from Sid Barnett (Norton) and Allen Dudley-Ward (DW Special).

Then came his first visit to Olivers Mount, Scarborough, for the International Trophy Meeting. With many of the top stars in attendance, John finished fourth at the demanding Yorkshire seaside venue, from Bill

John's mother Dorothy, a great supporter throughout his entire motorcycle racing career. She is seen here repairing the soles of his racing boots – worn away through hard cornering.

Doran (works AJS Porcupine) and the Norton pair of Phil Carter and Sid Barnett. Behind John were riders such as John Storr, George Brown, Denis Parkinson and the Australian Keith Campbell.

Up to now the vast majority of John Surtees' riding had been on 500cc bikes, in the shape of Vincent and Norton machinery. However, at the International Meeting at Thruxton on Saturday 4 October 1952, the name 'J. Surtees' appeared on the programme entered on a AJS 7R. There were no less than three heats. In the first Michael O'Rourke (7R) won from Bill Doran on a triple camshaft factory AJS. The second heat went to the diminutive Stan Dibben (riding a Norton, but more well known as a sidecar passenger). The fastest heat was the third, which brought John Surtees to the line. As *The Motor Cycle* report stated: 'Riding a works single knocker AJS, he made an ultra-rapid start and streaked away from the rest of the field to establish a commanding lead.' Then in the final he was again first off the mark and went on to a convincing victory, even though he eased off towards the end. He recorded a race record average speed of 78.52mph and in the process finished in front of O'Rourke and Doran. The AJS victory had another effect in that it brought an offer of a ride on one of the 500cc Porcupine twins. John says that this in turn brought a swift response from Gilbert Smith of Norton, who said 'We have you in line for the works team so forget AJS.' So he did.

Even though he was to stick with his private Norton at the time, there is no doubt that the Thruxton ride gave John a first-hand feeling for the 7R, and probably played a part in his choosing the power unit over the smaller Manx model when he built his lightweight special later in the decade.

The run of successes continued during 1953, thanks in no small part to the acquisition during the closed season of a second-hand 348cc long-stroke 40M Manx (formerly used by Ray Amm and Syd Lawton). This was added to the existing 500cc 30M model that had been purchased midway through the previous year. In fact John's maiden victory of 1953 came aboard the smaller Norton at Brands Hatch during the first meeting of the season on

Good Friday, 3 April. A crash at Clearways put him out of the 500cc race at the same meeting.

A record crowd estimated to have been 'roughly 73,000' turned up to witness some top-class racing at Silverstone on Saturday 18 April 1953. As *The Motor Cycle* was able to report: 'The 20-lap 350cc BMCRC championship race brought Geoff Duke to the starting line for the first time since last July (when he had been injured in a crash in Germany). Unfortunately, like the remainder of the Norton factory riders, he was mounted, not on a works machine, but on a standard Manx model'. This race was to witness 'a fantastic duel between J.A. Storr and J. Surtees (Nortons) who contested the lead for the entire 20 laps and frequently passed the timing box dead level.' The race ended with Storr just in front of Surtees, then Bob McIntyre (AJS). *The Motor Cycle* recorded that 'far behind the three flying leaders a secondary group involved Ray Amm (Norton), H.A. Pearce (Velocette), Ken Kavanagh and Geoff Duke (Nortons) and D.K. Farrant and Bill Doran, both AJS mounted. After many changes of position they finished in that order'. The 20-lap 500cc Coronation Championship race brought a repeat of the Storr-Surtees battle. Victory again went to Storr, this time by, as the race report said 'no more than a wheel'. And with the large number of 'names' in the entry list, the two 'S's' could be well pleased with their performances.

After Silverstone the Surtees bandwagon was really rolling and at venues such as Brands Hatch, Snetterton and Aberdare Park. John gained a series of wins and set record laps. No one was able to beat Norton-mounted John Surtees in either the 350 or 500cc classes.

Included among these results was the very first motorcycle race meeting held at Snetterton. The meeting, organised by the Snetterton Combine (Suffolk and Norfolk Motorcycle Clubs), was opened by Geoff Duke, who gave local fans a chance to see him when he completed a couple of demonstration laps. As for John Surtees, he won his heats and finals in the 350 and 500cc classes. *The Motor Cycle* said: 'He rode superbly to finish with the highest race speed of the day at 78.62mph, and the fastest lap at 82.23mph.'

TT disappointment

It has to be said that the 1953 Isle of Man TT was a major disappointment to John Surtees and one which still rankles with him today probably as much as any event during his long and varied motor sport career.

John's problems began when he agreed to ride Dr Joe Erhlich's 125 EMC-Puch. Erhlich, an Austrian who had settled in Great Britain just prior to World War Two, had in the late 1940s formed EMC (Erhlich Motor Company), producing both roadsters and racing motorcycles. Then at the

Featherbed Manx Norton

The Rex McCandless-designed Featherbed-framed Norton made its debut for 1950 on the works double overhead camshaft single only, as ridden by the likes of Geoff Duke and Artie Bell, with the first over-the-counter production examples arriving the following year. In both cases their arrival signalled the end for the plunger-framed models (which had first appeared in works guise during the 1936 TT and in production form from 1946).

The Featherbed (thus named thanks to rider Harold Daniell saying it felt like a 'feather bed' during a test session) created a sensation when it made its winning debut at Blandford in April 1950. Duke was in the saddle that day, as he was when, wearing his innovative one-piece skin-tight leathers, he won the Senior TT a couple of months later. Although Duke didn't win the 1950 World Championship (due to a succession of tyre problems), the same rider/machine combination took the 350/500cc World Championship double in 1951, retaining the 350cc crown for Norton in 1952.

For 1951 the production Manx models were given the Featherbed chassis for the first time, together with several other improvements pioneered on the 1950 works' machines. It is also worth pointing out that the production models were constructed in a different area of the Bracebridge Street, Birmingham, factory and were the responsibility of Edgar Franks (later design chief at the Ambassador works) rather than Joe Craig.

The pukka works specials were raced until the end of 1954. Then, with Joe Craig in charge, works development versions of the standard production version were entered in selected meetings by team riders during 1955 (John Hartle, Jack Brett and John Surtees). The over-the-counter customer Manx 40M (350cc) and 30M (500cc) continued with yearly updates until production finally came to an end in 1962. During the 1950s 'customer' meant someone who was approved by the company. This approval meant that the rider had to use his new machine in an international event, such as the TT, Ulster Grand Prix or a Continental European Grand Prix.

Also during the same period Norton engines were widely used in Formula 3 (500cc) racing cars. But Norton would not supply a separate engine and transmission, instead customers had to purchase a complete bike and dispose of the cycle components themselves. It was this procedure that gave rise to the now-famous Triton specials. These used redundant Norton Featherbed frames to house 500cc or 650cc twin cylinder Triumph engines – for road or racing use.

The Norton plunger frame as used on the Garden Gate series was totally eclipsed by the Featherbed during this period, as John Surtees found to his cost when racing a plunger-framed dohc Manx in late 1951 and early 1952. The Garden Gate frame not only limited the rider's ability to corner the machine due to poor ground clearance, but it was also prone to breakage of the frame tubes. John says: 'In contrast the McCandless Featherbed design was extremely forgiving and was thus able to be constantly driven to the limit and beyond.'

beginning of the 1950s, Erhlich began building and selling the EMC-Puch 125cc split-single two-stroke racer. More notable for their noise than their speed, John had agreed to ride an EMC, primarily because he was a newcomer to the Isle of Man Mountain Course, and felt (correctly) that he needed to gain as much experience as quickly as possible. So the name John

Surtees was entered for three races – Ultra-Lightweight (125), Junior (350) and Senior (500).

The practice week began exceptionally well and, as *The Motor Cycle* report revealed, 'last Thursday, young John Surtees was out on S. Lawton's Junior factory Norton (Lawton was in hospital after a Creg-ny-Baa crash). Surtees lapped confidently at 86.64mph, maintaining the stylish form he had displayed throughout the practice and in events on the mainland. After exchanging the Junior Norton for a 125cc EMC-Puch he spilled soon after passing through Ballaugh.'

The accident happened as he went over Ballaugh Bridge on the first lap with the EMC-Puch. The front forks broke, causing John to veer off from his chosen path. He recalls 'skating down the road, hitting a curb and breaking my scaphoid [a small bone deep within the wrist]'. This mishap not only ended John's first visit to the Isle of Man, but also, as he says, 'my chance to ride a works Norton, a unique opportunity for someone riding in the Island for the first time.'

Norton team boss Joe Craig was annoyed. There had originally been four or five works Norton entries: Ray Amm, Ken Kavanagh, Rex McCandless and Syd Lawton. When Lawton suffered the practice crash already mentioned (which ended his racing career), John could have taken his place. As John says, it was 'perhaps hardly surprising that Joe thought I had been extremely foolish in compromising my chances of an outing with the works Norton team by riding the EMC-Puch.'

In fact, John and his father did ask the other Joe (Erhlich) to release John from the arrangement, but Joe wouldn't agree, probably because of his commitment to sponsors. Being the honourable man that he is, John Surtees wouldn't welch on his agreement; hence the accident.

The author feels that this single event put back John Surtees's career by many months. And in fact when he finally did get into Joe Craig's team, the pukka works bikes had been moth-balled and instead he only received works development Manx models (for 1955). He also lost the chance to test the very secret F-Type Norton, which had been planned for 1955.

It took some six weeks for the wrist injury to improve sufficiently for John to resume riding and then it was back to the short circuit scene. John's first outing came at Ibsley Airfield, near Ringwood, on 11 July, and he was back in the winning groove immediately, recording victories in both his heat and the final of the 350cc event; he also set a new class lap record. On this occasion he did not ride his 500cc Norton.

Next came a busy weekend's racing, first at Castle Combe on 18 July, followed by Brands Hatch the next day. At the former venue *The Motor*

Cycle race report summed things up nicely: 'John Surtees was the star at the Wessex Centre's Castle Combe race meeting held last Saturday. He won both his heats and the 350 and 500cc finals in such a polished and unhurried manner that it was difficult to realise he was lapping at over 70mph.'

The fourth Blandford International Meeting on bank holiday Monday, 3 August, saw the lap record broken in all four classes. As recorded in Chapter 3, John Surtees had his first outing on Bob Geeson's REG twin in the 250cc race, finishing third. In the 500cc race he went one better, coming home runner-up to Derek Farrant (Matchless) after winning his heat. But after recording third on his 350cc Norton, John retired in the final with engine trouble.

During practice for the Crystal Palace meeting on Saturday 22 August 1953, John crashed, injuring an elbow, which stopped him taking part in the actual racing that day. But he was back in the saddle a week later at Aberdare Park, South Wales, on Saturday 29 August. There had in fact been much speculation as to whether John's elbow injury would prevent him riding. However, this was not the case. He won both his heat and final with some ease, the latter from no less than Bob McIntyre (Matchless G45).

McIntyre and John were again locked in combat at Snetterton on Saturday 5 September, with the honours being evenly shared, both setting a new lap record in the 500cc race at 84.10mph, during their titanic duel in the first heat. But in the final McIntyre's Matchless twin would only fire on one cylinder, leaving the field open for John to score an easy victory.

At the Scarborough International Road Races in mid-September Surtees rode his private Nortons, finishing third in the final behind World Champion Fergus Anderson (Moto Guzzi) and Derek Farrant (AJS). The 500cc race was the big one, with a battle royal between Geoff Duke and Dickie Dale (Gilera fours), Ken Kavanagh, Jack Brett and John Surtees. In the end power won with Duke beating Dale. But the Norton trio all struck trouble. First John crashed, then Kavanagh struck mechanical problems and Brett retired too with clutch trouble at Mere Hairpin. John would have to wait for some time longer before he was able to have another crack at Geoff Duke.

At Silverstone on 26 September 1953, the stars were out in force again, but this did not include Duke, even though Dale was there on his Gilera. John Surtees managed a victory in the first 500cc race of the day, beating Rod Coleman and Derek Farrant (AJS Porcupines). But in the main championship races he came sixth in the 350cc and fifth in the 500cc; both races being won by Ken Kavanagh (Nortons).

1954 was a new season, with new expectations. In retrospect, it was to mark John Surtees's arrival as star material. He not only contested far more

Ray Amm

Ray (William Raymond) Amm was the last of Joe Craig's many stars to claim TT and GP glory for the Bracebridge Street works. Born in Salisbury, Southern Rhodesia (now Zimbabwe) in 1927, he first raced in grass track events in his homeland and later in South African road events, such as the Port Elizabeth 200. Ray was by profession a draughtsman, although just before coming to Europe in 1951 he had entered into a partnership with his brother in the motor-cycle business. In December 1949 he married Jill, who accompanied him throughout his travels and who was a familiar figure in the race paddocks of the world in her own right.

First arriving in Great Britain for the TT races in 1951, Ray was known for his especially aggressive style and as *The Motor Cycle* once said 'was probably one of the most courageous riders ever to appear in racing circles'.

At first Amm was a private entrant, riding production Manx models, until he joined the official Norton works squad after the 1952 TT. He remained with Norton until their retirement from full-blown factory support at the end of 1954.

As well as many international victories, Ray Amm is best remembered for achieving the TT double in 1953 and his controversial victory in the 1954 Senior race. He also set a new lap record for the 37.73-mile Mountain Circuit in 1953 of 97.41 mph.

When his beloved Norton factory quit Ray finally signed for a foreign marque, in this case MV Agusta (who had, with other companies, been trying to gain his signature for some considerable time).

His first big race for his new team came at the international Shell Gold Cup at Imola, Italy in April 1955. He was riding a dustbin-faired four-cylinder model when he crashed in the 350cc event. Ray Amm suffered a fractured skull and died some 20 minutes after reaching hospital. The accident was probably the result of Amm fitting old tyres from his own Norton to the bike because he was unhappy with the handling of the MV after practice earlier that day. He did not seem to realise that the handling characteristics of his new mount would be less forgiving that the British single-cylinder machines that he had previously ridden.

The Rhodesian rider Ray Amm replaced Geoff Duke as team leader of the Norton factory when the former joined Gilera at the beginning of 1953.

Ray Amm, pictured during the 1953 Isle of Man Senior TT on his works Norton. He rode valiantly to keep British hopes alive until he joined MV Agusta at the beginning of 1955.

With his passing went one of Norton's hardest riders – in later years some would say he tried too hard at times. Certainly Amm was a hard rider rather than a tactical one, in contrast to Geoff Duke and John Surtees. But the fact remains that he was the man who succeeded the legendary Geoff Duke and did the task well – no mean feat.

On 11 April 1955, during his first race for MV on the 350cc four, Amm crashed fatally at Imola. His death was almost as big a blow for the Italian factory as that of Les Graham two years earlier, and it was not until the signing of John Surtees that the team was to finally make a recovery.

races than he had before, but also achieved an ever increasing amount of success, sometimes scoring many victories in a single weekend as the Surtees équipe travelled the length and breadth of Great Britain, taking in as many meetings as possible. This increased effort was financed by the monies John was now generating from his track performances. Yet even though he rode in both the TT and the Ulster, his priority in 1954 was the domestic short circuits.

For 1954, John had two brand-new, short-stroke Manx Nortons, having sold his previous year's models to George Catlin. There is no doubt, as John would be the first to acknowledge, that for the first time he had machinery to back up his own riding talent – the two new Manxes plus Bob Geeson's REG 250cc. Besides his new bikes John also had a new set of one-piece, made-to-measure leathers, replacing the bulky two-piece ones he had used in previous years.

The season opener could not have been a more testing occasion. In his first race John came up against the man who had narrowly beaten him a year before, John Storr. Like John Surtees, Storr had a pair of brand-new Nortons (provided by Ernie Earles). The two Johns met in the non-championship 1,000cc race. But unlike their previous Silverstone encounter Surtees enjoyed a comfortable win, showing how he had improved over the previous 12 months.

In the main 500cc championship event, John found himself up against the world's top riders, including Geoff Duke (Gilera) and Ray Amm (Norton). And as *The Motor Cycle* said: 'D.K. Farrant (AJS) rode a magnificent race to annex third place, while J.R. Clark (Matchless), R.D. Keeler (Norton), R. McIntyre (AJS) and J. Surtees (Norton) put up performances which were overshadowed only by those of Duke and Amm. In the 350cc championship race Amm won from McIntyre (on works Norton and AJS models respectively) with John Surtees third, Cecil Sandford (Velocette) fourth and the South African star Rudi Alison (Norton) fifth.

Following Silverstone came almost two months of unbroken race wins, at Brands Hatch (16 April), Crystal Palace (19 April), Brands Hatch (25 April), Aberdare Park (8 May), Brands Hatch (9 May) and Oulton Park (15 May). Of particular note was the weekend 8/9 May, when John recorded no fewer than seven wins in two days!

A return to the Isle of Man

In June 1954, John made a return to the Isle of Man TT. This time he rode his own Nortons in the Junior and Senior events, finishing 11th and 15th respectively. Actually, during practice John had, almost always, been on the leader-board. His average speed for the Junior race was 85.41mph. The Senior (500cc) race which followed a couple of days later, was as: *The Motor Cycle* headline said 'Catastrophic'. The weather was so awful that the start was postponed twice. When the race finally got going at midday on 18 June, it was staged in heavy rain, with swirling mist up on the mountain section. The event was eventually stopped on the fourth lap, with Ray Amm's Norton winning from Geoff Duke's Gilera by over a minute. John commented 'bearing in mind just how treacherous the conditions were over the Snaefell Mountain, I counted myself reasonably satisfied to have finished my first Senior TT in 15th place. I didn't yet know the circuit in good conditions and in the mist and rain I was lost.' For what it's worth John's average speed was 80.09mph, compared to race winner's Amm's 88.12mph. Probably the biggest thing to come out of the 1954 TT for John Surtees was that he had gained useful experience and had completed both races he had contested, without making a serious error. This experience also saw him making use of a masseur for the first time – something which he was to repeat in other years. John says 'In a long race like the Isle of Man you need to have flexible strength. And to achieve this you need to remain supple.' Also during his first TT he had experienced 'muscle cramps'.

'Brilliant Surtees' was the headline which described John's performance to the readers of *The Motor Cycle* who read of

With one of his Manx Nortons during the 1954 season in which he competed at virtually every mainland UK circuit, plus the Isle of Man TT and Ulster Grand Prix events.

John in winning form at Aberdare Park on his 499cc Norton on 28 August 1954. During this meeting he won eight races (four heats and four finals) and set a new outright lap record for the Welsh circuit.

his ride in the 1954 350cc Ulster GP: 'It was not until the eighth lap of the 350cc race that Amm forced his Norton into the lead, where he remained to the end. Surtees, riding his Manx Norton brilliantly, led the factory models for the first four laps; for the next half-dozen circuits he lay third behind Amm and Laing (both on works Nortons).' But a fuel stop at that stage, during which he overshot his pit, relegated John to sixth place behind Jack Brett (Norton) and the AJS works pair Derek Farrant and Bob McIntyre. There he remained, as the leading privateer, until engine failure ended his superb ride two laps from the finish of the 25-lap 185.39-mile race. John also finished the 500cc race in fifth position, averaging 81.74mph in wet conditions which saw the distance cut to 15 laps, 111.24 miles.

Sunshine and showers greeted riders and spectators alike at Cadwell Park on Sunday 4 July with John (REG and Norton) winning every event in which he was entered, including the main 20-lap Folbigg Trophy race for machines up to 1,000cc.

Then came the weekend of 17/18 July when on the Saturday at Crystal Palace, John had won five races: 250cc (heat/final), 350cc (heat/final) and his 1,000cc heat. He was prevented from making a clean sweep when water entered the carburettor of his 500cc Manx, forcing his retirement when leading the final in a day of incessant rain at the South London circuit. But he made amends the following day at Brands Hatch, winning every race he contested (250cc, 350cc and 1,000cc classes).

Geoff Duke was the rider that the young John Surtees always aspired to emulate. Geoff is seen here with the laurels of victory during his spell with Norton, which lasted from the late 1940s until the beginning of 1953 when he joined Gilera.

Geoff Duke

Geoff Duke was the man a youthful John Surtees aspired to match – and beat – during his early career. This was a feat he was finally to achieve, not once but twice in one weekend during October 1955; first at Silverstone and a day later at Brands Hatch.

Geoff had been born in St Helens, Lancashire, in 1923, the son of a baker. He first caught the motorcycle bug while still a small boy, watching sand racing on the beaches of Southport and Wallasey and riding pillion behind his brother Eric, some nine years his senior. Later Geoff, with a school friend, clubbed together to buy his first motorcycle when he was only 13. They could not ride it on the public highway but learned to ride on farmland.

After beginning work as a mechanic at a telephone exchange at the age of 16, he purchased a Dot two-stroke. Then at 18 Geoff Duke volunteered to be an Army despatch rider, but found he would only be accepted as an instrument mechanic. However, this did get him into the Royal Signals, so Geoff joined and subsequently made such a nuisance of himself that he was transferred to DR (Despatch Rider) duties. This led to the chance of riding for the army's display team and meeting a certain Hugh Viney (the legendary AMC trials rider and four-times winner of the Scottish Six Days Trial).

When Duke was demobbed in 1947 he used his gratuity to purchase a BSA single and got a job at the same factory preparing trials bikes and riding them. His trials results were noticed by Norton teamster Artie Bell, who after seeing him ride in Yorkshire, introduced Geoff to the Norton management. This resulted in the offer of a job, which was enthusiastically accepted. After riding a 500T ohv single in trials for his new employers, Geoff transferred to road racing.

During the 1948 Manx Grand Prix (his first ever race) he was leading when forced to retire with a split oil tank. The following June he returned for the Senior Clubman's TT and won at a record speed of 82.97mph. Three months later he won the Senior Manx and was runner-up in the Junior race. Geoff was then promoted to the full Norton works squad, managed by Joe Craig, for the 1950 season.

A series of tyre problems meant that Norton did not have a very good 1950, even though they debuted the new Featherbed chassis. But from then on, until he quit the Birmingham factory in the spring of 1953, Geoff and Norton could do no wrong; winning the 350/500cc world titles (the first time this had been achieved) in 1951, followed by the 350cc championship in 1952.

But by now the four-cylinder Italian models were at last outpacing the Norton singles, so Geoff signed for Gilera, winning the 500cc title for the next three years, 1953, 1954 and 1955.

Politics and accidents did much to restrict his efforts in 1956 and 1957 and then Gilera quit. Geoff followed two years later after racing a mixture of Norton, BMW and Benelli machinery. But the fact remains that Geoff Duke was the big star of the early 1950s and one of the smoothest top line racers of all time. But unlike John Surtees, Geoff's attempts to make the switch from two to four wheels, with Aston Martin in 1952, proved something of a failure. Like John, Geoff did this while continuing his motorcycle racing career (which at that time meant Norton); but ultimately he decided to stick with two wheels.

Duke with one of the factory Nortons in 1952. On both the British singles and the Italian four-cylinder models his style was always smooth; more suited to longer Grand Prix events than British short circuits.

The Motor Cycle chose another superlative – 'Again Invincible' – to describe John's performances at the national Castle Combe road races which followed on Saturday 24 July at the Wiltshire circuit. Again he won all his heats and the finals too. Then, in yet another of those 'double header' weekends which were becoming common in the Surtees calendar, John made successful visits on 1/2 August to Snetterton, followed by Thruxton. At the Norfolk venue John was able to take part even though, as *The Motor Cycle* reported, 'His 250cc mount, the well-known REG, was so extensively damaged in a practice spill that he was a non-starter in the 250cc class.' However, this did not prevent: 'The 350cc and 500cc races were both extremely fast and but rendered dull by Surtees' brilliance. Unperturbed by his unfortunate practice spill, and in spite of a grazed hip, he rode with particular verve and created race and lap records in both classes.'

And at the fifth ACU international road race meeting at Thruxton the next day John's Snetterton accident didn't seem to affect his performance in the least. After winning his heat and finishing runner-up to the Moto Guzzi works rider and World Champion Fergus Anderson in the 350cc event, John reversed roles in the 500cc final – beating Anderson and his bigger Guzzi single. Not only this, but he also set a new lap record of 86.17mph.

Nearly but not quite, is the best way of summarizing what happened at Silverstone's big international Hutchinson 100 meeting on Saturday 7 August 1954. Here John Surtees came very close to recording his first victory over the combination of Geoff Duke and the Gilera four. Appalling weather conditions were a feature of the 22nd Hutchinson 100, organised by Bemsee. Before the lunch break, the preliminary 250, 350 and 500cc races were run in fair conditions. But thereafter, when the BMCRC championships were contested, torrential rain fell almost continuously and flooded large areas of the Northamptonshire track. Before winning the 350cc championship race, John had been forced to retire in the 250cc event when the REG's engine began to misfire. Then, because of the extreme weather conditions, the stewards reduced the length of the last race – the 500cc championship – from 20 laps to 10. Ironically, the race was run in bright sunshine, though the track was still awash with water. John Surtees, Geoff Duke and Bob Keeler soon detached themselves from the rest of the field. *The Motor Cycle* takes up the story: 'Still in invincible form, Surtees gained about five seconds a lap on the Gilera champion; but at the halfway stage, stripped bevel gears (the bottom set) cheated him of almost certain victory.' John was later to recall: 'this robbed me of the win I really ached for'. The offending bevel gears still reside in a cabinet at his Surrey home today.

Many of the race meetings of 1954 were held in dreadful weather conditions, but the Ibsley Airfield Road Races held on Saturday 21 August were an exception – the day was warm, dry, and bright. In both the 350 and 500cc events John won both his heats and finals – setting new class lap records of 75.70 and 77.46mph respectively. He also rode a Norton, owned by Ian Telfer, to a debut runner-up slot in the 250cc race, behind the experienced Maurice Cann (Moto Guzzi).

More victories in the 350 and 1000cc races came at Brands Hatch the next day, 22 August, and at Aberdare Park on Saturday 28 August 1954 John recorded an amazing eight wins in a single day. He took four heat and four final victories at the Welsh venue and also set a new outright course lap record of 49 seconds. Another successful day came at Brands Hatch on 12 September, remaining unbeaten in the 250, 350 and 1,000cc events (Brands didn't run a 500cc class at this time).

Another crack at Duke

Huge crowds lined the tortuous Oliver's Mount, Scarborough circuit over Friday and Saturday 17 and 18 September to watch the International Gold Cup meeting; with fine weather race and lap records were broken in every class, partly helped by improvements made to the 2-mile, 728-yard Yorkshire course. The first 350cc heat was dominated by Bob McIntyre (AJS), with John winning the second in equally convincing fashion, and Phil Carter (Norton) taking the third, after Jack Brett (works Norton) had retired. In the final, John built up a commanding lead but thereafter allowed the works AJS pairing of McIntyre and Derek Farrant to close. However, signalled by his father that McIntyre's advances were becoming pressing, John drew away again to win easily, bettering the existing class lap record on his final circuit.

In the main race of the meeting, the 500cc Scarborough Senior event, John was up against a formidable array of talent: Geoff Duke and Reg Armstrong (Gileras), Dickie Dale (MV Agusta), Pierre Monneret, Bob McIntyre and Derek Farrant (AJS Porcupines). For this race John had been loaned a 1953 factory Norton. He responded by taking up the challenge but he did not enjoy the best of starts and had to fight his way through the pack. On the sixth lap he passed second-place man Bob McIntyre and thereafter set out after Geoff Duke. The Gilera World Champion responded by setting a new lap record at 66.94mph, but even he had to admit that the young Norton rider had given him some stiff competition.

The following day, Sunday 19 September, saw John in action at Cadwell Park, where he won both Junior and Senior races, including setting a new 6-lap race record for the 350cc class. His opposition at the Lincolnshire track included future MV teammate John Hartle plus Peter Davey, Percy Tait and Fred Wallis.

The first ever motorcycle meeting over the Aintree circuit near Liverpool was staged on Saturday 25 September 1954 under mainly dry, but windy conditions. Sponsored by *The Daily Telegraph* newspaper, the meeting attracted many top names including Geoff Duke, Reg Armstrong, Jack Brett, Dickie Dale, Bob McIntyre, Rod Coleman, Ray Amm, Derek Farrant and John Surtees. Third position in the 350cc race (behind McIntyre and Coleman) and runner-up in the 500cc (splitting the Gileras of Duke and Armstrong) was in truth, at this stage in Surtees's career, a magnificent achievement. The season was rounded off with 350 and 500cc victories at Cadwell Park (10 October) and 350 and 1,000cc wins at Brands Hatch (17 October).

As John was to recall later: 'The 1954 season was an extremely satisfactory one... despite the fact that Geoff Duke continued to hold me at arm's

Brands Hatch, 1955. Riders include Michael O'Rourke, Frank Perris, Alan Trow and Ginger Payne. John is seated on his 499cc Norton at the centre rear of the picture.

length, I notched up 50 wins in 60 races.' In addition, as related in the previous chapter, John was awarded the prestigious Pinhard Prize. But perhaps most important of all, considering that John was still apprenticed at Vincent and earning no more than about £4 a week, was the fact that he was beginning to earn good money from his racing.

I always paid for my machines, and bits and pieces I needed for them, out of my pocket. I had known how hard it can be for the budding racer to find all the cash he needs. The results of the 1953 season had eased the situation to some extent, but the wins of 1954 put a completely different aspect on things. I no longer had to pinch and scrape and, I am sure in my own mind, the freedom from too severe financial restrictions made a great difference to me psychologically. It could even have been the chief factor in my becoming increasingly successful.

Signing for Norton

For the 1955 season John Surtees joined John Hartle and Jack Brett as an official member of the Norton race team managed by Joe Craig. But unlike previous years, the machinery would not be works specials, but instead works development Manx over-the-counter models. Another company decision was that 'no streamlining would be allowed'. It was also stated that 'in 1955 Norton factory participation would be restricted primarily to events in the British Isles.' The full list of meetings it intended to support was as follows:

11 April	Oulton Park
23 April	Silverstone
1 May*	Mettet, Belgium
19-21 May	North West 200 N. Ireland
6-10 June*	TT Isle of Man
31 June–2 July*	Scarborough
23–24 July*	Swedish GP Hedemora
11–13 August*	Ulster GP, Dundrod
21 August*	Brands Hatch
3–4 September	Skarpnacksloppet, Sweden
16–17 September*	Scarborough
24 September*	Aintree
1 October*	Silverstone

* Those marked with an asterisk are the ones John Surtees competed in.

Dundrod.
Lap length: 7.49 miles.

John with his mother Dorothy at their Callender Road, Catford, home in October 1955, with some of the trophies he had won during 1955. This photograph was taken shortly after John had beaten Geoff Duke (Gilera) at Silverstone and Brands Hatch.

On 11 February 1955, John Surtees reached the age of 21. He also now agrees that 1955 was the year: 'I reached the peak of my performance'.

His first outing of the new season, riding his own private Nortons, came in front of some 14,000 spectators at Brough Airfield, near Hull. After winning his heat and the final of the 350cc event, John fell while leading Bob McIntyre (Potts Norton) in the main event, the Brough '25'. However, he climbed back on to the bike, still in third position, and although he got up to second, he couldn't make up lost time quickly enough and McIntyre took the victory.

A few days later at Brands Hatch on Good Friday, 8 April, not only did John have his very first outing on the NSU Sportmax (see Chapter 3), but also won the 350 and 1,000cc races in his private Nortons, and he set new lap records in each class. Two days later, on Easter Sunday 10 April, it was another Surtees field day at Snetterton. In what was fast becoming the norm his performance was described by *The Motor Cycle* as: 'a spectacle of consistent and impeccable riding'; which 'rather overshadowed the efforts of his opponents, for in all the races he streaked into the lead from the start'. He also set a new outright lap record for the Norfolk track.

Then, in order to fit three meetings at three circuits into a single weekend, John went on to Crystal Palace for Easter Monday, 11 April. And for this final day of the Easter holiday programme there was brilliant weather and a record crowd. John obliged by either equalling or breaking the existing lap record in every class he contested (250, 350 and 1,000cc). Then, during the handicap solo event for the 12 fastest riders (which besides John included the likes of Michael O'Rourke, Ernie Washer, Frank Perris, Percy Tait and the South African star Eddie Grant), *The Motor Cycle* said: 'Surtees scared spectators all round the circuit by the most brilliant exhibition of speed motorcycling they had ever seen. He was in unnerving form. Grant, by reputation a lurid rider, was subdued in comparison. The young Londoner won handsomely and, in doing so, equalled the 75.82mph lap record held by Reg Parnell with a Grand Prix Ferrari car.'

At the same time as John Surtees was breaking records and winning races at Crystal Palace, hundreds of miles away at Imola in Italy, the former Norton works star Ray Amm was having his first race with the Italian MV Agusta team. Sadly, Amm crashed on the 350cc four-cylinder model, and suffered a fractured skull, from which he subsequently died 20 minutes after being admitted to hospital. The significance of this event was that MV were to hire John a few months later. He thus became the next of MV's foreign riders and their team leader – a role Amm had been signed for.

Motor Cycling sponsored, BMCRC organised, the Silverstone Saturday meeting on 23 April 1955 was where John thought at first that he might finally achieve his ambition to beat Geoff Duke and his Gilera. John had already won the 250 and 350cc finals, and in the 500cc race he took the lead and held it for the first five laps. Then Duke screamed his Gilera up to maximum power and down the straight; no matter how hard Surtees pushed his Norton as he says in his own words: 'I could make no impression on him'. Bob McIntyre was third.

The annual Circuit de Mettet international meeting in Belgium every spring was for many years a testing ground used by many of the top continental riders as a dress rehearsal for the Grand Prix season. But in 1955 many were taking part in the Spanish Grand Prix that same weekend at Montjuich Park, Barcelona, ensuring that the ultra-fast Belgian course lacked some of the glamour seen in earlier years. However, it did mark John's debut on the other side of the Channel and there were still a number of riders of international repute, including Moto Guzzi World Champion Fergus Anderson. As the race report from *The Motor Cycle* dated 5 May 1955 stated: 'In both races Surtees provided a furious challenge to Anderson.' It went on to mention the Norton squad: 'Brett was there chiefly

John winning at Olivers Mount, Scarborough, on his 350cc Norton (works-supported model) on 16 September 1955. He also broke the class lap record.

John fighting tooth and nail at Scarborough on 17 September 1955 in the 500cc final with his great adversary, Gilera-mounted Geoff Duke (41). Although John was to be vanquished that day he came back two weeks later to score famous victories over the World Champion at Silverstone on Saturday 1 October, and the following day at Brands Hatch.

as a wise old watchdog, assisting Joe Craig and helping Surtees and Hartle with advice.' Although both the 350cc and 500cc events at Mettet saw an Anderson victory with Surtees second, Hartle third and Brett fourth, this only tells half the story; in the 500cc race, Anderson beat John by a mere three seconds after the 106 mile race, with Hartle another 48 seconds behind Surtees. The Mettet meeting also provides an excellent insight into John Surtees's riding style at the time, one journalist describing it in the following terms: 'His neat torso was never more than a fraction above the tank. His exit from one corner blended to perfection with his entry into the next.'

Back home in England, the next port of call for John was Oulton Park in Cheshire. The track had recently been extended to a lap of 2.76 miles and now represented one of the UK mainland's biggest tests of riding skill. Riding his own Nortons and the Vincent-supplied NSU (see Chapter 3), John won every race he contested. On his smaller Manx Norton he won his heat, followed by the final – from Cecil Sandford (Moto Guzzi) and Bill Lomas (AJS). He also set a new class record at 80.94mph. It was very much a repeat performance in the 1,000cc championship race on his 499cc Manx;

Joe Craig

Joe Craig was for over a quarter of a century a pivotal figure in British motorcycle racing; not as a rider (although he did compete with considerable success early in his career) but as a team manager and development engineer at the Norton factory during its greatest years, from the beginning of the 1930s until the mid-1950s.

Craig was born in the town of Ballymena near Belfast, Northern Ireland, on 11 January 1898. He served his apprenticeship in a local garage dealing almost exclusively with cars. Shortly after taking up employment he purchased his first motorcycle, a side-valve Norton Model 16 and was soon taking part in local hill climbs. His interest in two wheels developed, helped by reading copies of *The Motor Cycle* and thus gleaning information about racing events such as the Isle of Man TT. Then came the Ulster Grand Prix in the summer of 1922. Joe Craig was a spectator rather than a competitor at this event, but this fired his enthusiasm so much that he borrowed an ohv Model 18 Norton on which to take part in the event 12 months later; he won the 600cc class that year and again in 1924. In that latter year he made his Isle of Man debut in no less an event than the Senior TT, again riding the Model 18, but a leaking fuel tank meant he dropped down from sixth to twelfth at the finish. Results like these meant that he had been noticed by the Norton team and he became an official works rider from 1925 with the Birmingham marque.

Although he achieved considerable success he retired in 1929 to concentrate on helping run the team and developing the machinery; at first with Arthur Carroll and later solely in charge after Carroll died in a road accident in 1935.

Without doubt road racing was Joe Craig's life. He displayed a dedicated purpose that very few others could hope to emulate. His true mastery came in talent spotting and the patient development of the single-cylinder overhead camshaft Norton engine. Although not a designer like Carroll or his predecessor Walter Moore, Joe Craig somehow found more and more power from the Norton power unit long after many had thought its peak development

Joe Craig, who except for a brief period with AMC during the war years, was Norton race supremo from the early 1930s until the mid-1950s. The Ulsterman is seen here with one of his beloved cammy singles in 1951.

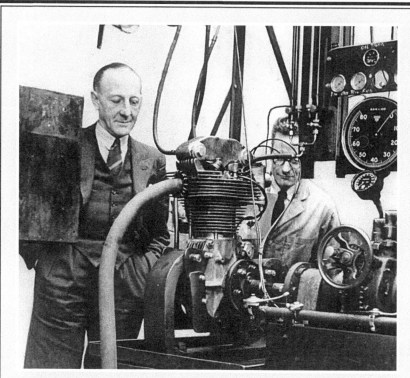

Joe Craig (left) with a Norton engine on the test bench at the Birmingham works. John Surtees commented after his death in 1957 'I was always grateful for the benefit of his wisdom and for the interest which he continued to take in me. Truly, racing lost a great man when he died.'

period was over. Such successes earned Craig the title of 'Professor' and a reputation which was equally as respected in continental European countries such as Germany, Italy and Scandinavia, as it was throughout the length and breadth of the British Empire.

He has been criticised for being too conservative, but one has to realise that he was paid on results, not innovation. Also Norton was in reality a tiny factory, its entire output hardly taking up one week of, for example, the giant BSA Group's yearly production.

Certainly those in the know, such as John Surtees, regarded Joe Craig highly. He was not one to suffer fools gladly and so riders of lesser talent probably didn't always have the ear of the great man to the same extent.

Joe Craig finally retired at the end of 1955. But even so, as John points out, Joe continued to keep in touch, taking an active interest in racing including visiting venues such as the Isle of Man TT during 1956. Sadly in March 1957 he died in a car accident while on holiday near Landeck, Austria. It was truly the end of an era.

a heat win followed by victory in the final, this time over Bob McIntyre and Phil Carter (both Norton mounted).

He also upped the lap record to 83.53mph. But that race was won after John locked his front brake up on the first lap and did a bit of grass tracking before resuming the race with much catch-up work to do. The following weekend, 14/15 May, at Aberdare Park followed by Brands Hatch, it was just the same. John took seven victories (excluding heats) and set a brace of new lap records for good measure.

Next came the 1955 Isle of Man TT. This had always been a major date in the calendar for the Norton factory. John freely admits 'I should have enjoyed riding in the Lightweight (250cc) race on my NSU', but he realised that he was over in the Isle of Man 'as a team man'. John was later to recall:

The racing team was really a separate unit within the Norton organisation. We had our own transporter; Joe [Craig] had his own secretarial staff; the development section worked exclusively for us; the tool room worked in cooperation with the racing department and provided any tools that we needed. Attached to us were four mechanics. It goes without saying that, besides being first-class mechanics, they were great racing enthusiasts. I got to know Arthur and Charlie Edwards best, because they were the two who usually travelled to the circuits with us, and have maintained a relationship right through to the present day.

The Norton policy of no streamlining made it difficult for the riders to match the full might of the Gilera and Moto Guzzi teams. John continues this: 'our Nortons stood little chance of winning but Joe Craig was hoping to get us home in good formation for a team prize.' However, even this hope died when Jack Brett fell at the Gooseneck during the Junior TT. John and Bob McIntyre (his Potts Norton featuring full streamlining) were neck-and-neck for the lead at the end of lap one. But slowly the speed, and the fact that they didn't have to refuel, as the Nortons did, played into the hands of the Guzzi riders, who went on to finish first (Bill Lomas) and third (Cecil Sandford). Splitting the Italian bikes was the flying Bob McIntyre on his streamlined Potts Norton. Even so John Surtees's fourth place, with an average speed of 90.63mph (Lomas's winning speed was 92.33mph) was certainly no disgrace. John was also a member of the winning Club Team, BMCRC (with McIntyre and Sandford).

The competition facing the Norton teamsters in the Senior (500cc) TT was fierce. Once again the race distance was seven laps, a distance of 264.11 miles. The 1955 Senior was also the race everyone expected to provide the first 100mph TT lap. In fact for a period of 41 minutes everybody thought it had been achieved, as an announcement saying Geoff Duke had done it was made before the corrected time of 99.97mph was made public. All this overshadowed the fact that Gilera dominated the race, with Duke and the Italian factory's other rider Reg Armstrong holding first and second from start to finish. And what of John Surtees? Tenth at the end of lap one, he had moved up to seventh by the next lap, a position he held off-and-on until

The engineer. Right from his earliest days, John Surtees has loved the preparation of machinery just as much as the actual racing. He is seen here in 1959 working on one of his Norton engines.

the last quarter of the final circuit when he ran out of fuel; so was left to push in for 29th position. His bike's performance and fuel consumption had not been helped by an over-rich mixture: 'Joe Craig had played too safe', he said. Teammate John Hartle also ran out of fuel, but Jack Brett had kept going to finish fourth. So the Surtees dream of TT success had to wait for another year.

The German GP was a private venture for John, so he rode his own unfaired Norton. Ranged against him was a truly impressive array of machinery and riding talent and the event gave him his first experience of the demanding circuit, which measures 14.165 miles to a lap, through undulating countryside with a myriad of bends. The 350cc race was held over seven laps, a distance of 99.16 miles. There was a wide range of machinery including Norton, AJS, DKW, Moto Guzzi, MV Agusta, NSU, Parilla and Horex.

In fact even though Bill Lomas (Moto Guzzi) and August Hobl (DKW) finished in front of him, John rode and performed like a true champion that day. The extent of this achievement is indicated by the fact that the next non-factory entry Keith Campbell (Norton) finished ninth. John's time was a mere 3.3 seconds behind runner-up Hobl and only 16 seconds off Lomas at the finish. The first eight finishers were:

1   Bill Lomas (Moto Guzzi)
2   August Hobl (DKW)
3   John Surtees (Norton)
4   Cecil Sandford (Moto Guzzi)
5   Ken Kavanagh (Moto Guzzi)
6   Karl Hoffmann (DKW)
7   Siegfried Wünsche (DKW)
8   Carlo Bandirola (MV Agusta)

This result, combined with his showing on the BMW in the 500cc race, played a vital role in John's subsequent MV Agusta contract.

By comparison, the British short circuits that John returned to must have seemed a bit tame. Even so, he was immediately back in the groove with victories at Scarborough (1 and 2 July) and Castle Combe (9 July). Then it was off abroad again with the Norton team to the non-championship Swedish GP at the tricky 4.34-mile Hedemora circuit over the weekend 22/23 July, where John gained two second places behind Geoff Duke and his Gilera in the 500cc race and teammate John Hartle in the 350cc event. It had also been Hartle who, on the Friday afternoon following practice, had saved John Surtees's life when the latter had jumped into the lake near the village in which the Norton team was staying. Not only was the water freezing cold, it was also so fresh that it had absolutely no buoyancy, and John was not able to swim at the time. Luckily John Hartle was a strong swimmer and came to the rescue. From then on the two were to remain firm friends – as John says, 'there was always a special bond between us'. John Hartle and John Surtees were not only Norton teammates, but later teammates at MV too.

Among the many British short circuit events of the day, Thruxton on Saturday 1 August 1955 was the big one – the ACU's sixth international road race meeting. After finishing runner-up to Bill Lomas (works Guzzi) in the 350cc and scoring a runaway victory on his NSU in the 250cc, John's win in the 500cc race (on the works Norton) was, as *The Motor Cycle* said: 'more of a surprise since the entry included 350cc World Champion, W.A. Lomas and his teammate R.H. Dale on Moto Guzzis.' Snetterton the following day saw John win all five races he contested, including heats.

As recorded in the preceding chapter, John Surtees gained his first World Championship victory on Saturday 1 August 1955 in the 250cc Ulster GP on his NSU Sportmax. Two days earlier he had been in a titanic four-way battle involving teammate John Hartle and the Moto Guzzi pairing of Bill Lomas and Cecil Sandford. The final result was: Lomas, Hartle, Surtees and Sandford. In the 500cc race the two Norton Johns were neck-and-neck, but then refuelling came into the reckoning in this 25-lap, 185.23-mile race. Shortly after his refuelling stop John Surtees's Norton stripped a bevel gear and he was out of the race.

Then came a quick succession of meetings at Ibsley (20 August), Brands Hatch (21 August) and Aberdare Park (27 August) in which John won every race he contested, followed by a trip to the Italian GP at Monza to race his NSU (see Chapter 3). This was followed by more short circuit events: Snetterton (10 September), Cadwell Park (11 September), Scarborough (16/17 September), Brands Hatch (18 September), Aintree (24 September) and Brough (25 September). Again he won everything with the exception of the 500cc races at Scarborough and Aintree, in which he was beaten on both occasions by Geoff Duke (Gilera). However, at Aintree John did manage to get the better of the Duke/Gilera combination in the Open Handicap (in which John rode his 350cc Norton). But this was still not the victory John was looking for over his adversary.

Two days of history

Then came two days of history. In the final weekend of the 1955 racing

John Surtees en route to victory in the 350cc race on his Manx Norton at Silverstone, 21 September 1957. The fairing was home-made and based on the MV dustbin type. Not only did he win at record speed, but he also set a new lap record of 92.87mph. Ultimately, however, Count Agusta decided not to allow John to race his own machines in non-championship events, which led him to switch from two to four wheels.

season, John finally beat Gilera-mounted Geoff Duke – not once but twice!

The first triumph came at the Silverstone International Hutchinson 100 on Saturday 1 October. Held in 'ideal conditions of bright sunshine and pleasant breezes', as one contemporary race report described it, John's performances that October Saturday set the seal on a season of brilliant successes. He won the 350cc championship race as well as the 500cc and established 250cc, 350cc and 500cc lap records (the latter shared with Duke at 96.28mph). Only engine failure prevented him taking the 250cc championship race as well – he had a lead of no less than two miles over the next competitor. As John was to later recall: 'I had waited a long time for this moment and it was a wonderful feeling to have succeeded.' It also meant a lot to Joe Craig; when John returned to the pits after the race, Joe had 'tears in his eyes'. All this made it a day John 'will always remember'.

The following day a record crowd of over 60,000 lined the 1.24-mile Brands Hatch circuit to see John Surtees repeat his Silverstone performance by winning both the 350cc and 500cc (actually listed as 1,000cc). In the main 15-lap event *The Motor Cycle* described the start thus: 'At the first twitch of the flag the Norton was moving; in a few yards it was flat out in bottom gear and Surtees astride, well in the lead and determined not to see the Gilera's rear tyre.' In fact John was never to see Geoff Duke as our hero went on to take a hugely popular victory, creeping away from second place man Alan Trow (riding John's old Norton), who in turn did the same to the Gilera World Champion. Riding his private Norton, John also set a new lap record for the Kent circuit at 74.40mph.

Even then John Surtees did not get carried away. He puts it this way: 'It was one thing to beat him [Duke] on the short circuits. To be in front of him at the TT or classic Continental Grand Prix circuits was quite another.' But that would be the challenge of the next part of his career and one he was to respond to in the most positive of fashions. However, before that could come about he had to sort out a full works ride. Who would it be with?

In his final year as a regular on the British short circuits, John Surtees took part in 76 races, winning 68 of them; some record.

Technique

'Brilliant'; 'incredible'; 'star performance'; 'breathtaking' – the list of plaudits used to describe John Surtees's two-wheel performance is virtually endless. But how did he do it? Here are some of the answers.

John says 'While at school I was keen on all sport, in particular athletics [100-yard sprint was his favourite], long jump, football [soccer, not rugby!] and walking'. He also thinks that his mother's cooking helped his fitness regime 'No rubbish food, just good wholesome fare'.

John was 'fit and strong', and he says he was able to maintain a weight of 11–11½ stone throughout his racing career on two and four wheels. As is revealed in the main text, John only smoked 'one puff when I was eleven' and except for 'an acquired liking for wine following my visits to Italy' he does not partake of alcoholic beverages.

John discovered very early on in his Isle of Man career that 'one does not need overdeveloped muscles, but flexible muscles.' This led him to a masseur in Douglas, and his fitness in this respect definitely paid off in the longest, most difficult races of his career.

Right from his earliest days on two wheels, John Surtees was known for his superb starts. In those days push-starts were the rule, not clutch starts as is the case today. John says 'being fit and strong I would thrust off 1-2-3 steps, bang, and normally the bike would fire up instantly. I would then concentrate on getting away – staying side-saddle longer than most people.' Fellow competitor Bernard Codd recalls:

> I'd watched John Surtees for several years, and if you watched him when the flag dropped, Surtees would be pushing first. He used to watch for a flicker of the starter's arm, I'm sure he did, instead of the flag, because he was always pushing first! One day I decided not to watch the flag. Instead I watched him out of the corner of my eye. When he started pushing I started pushing. In the first 50 yards that I had gone, he had gone 150! It was like trying to race an Austin Seven against a Jag!

What about the circuits? Did John have his favourites? He parries by saying: 'Circuits are like people. A living environment. You have to adjust – same for everyone. But I did get a lot of satisfaction from getting it right.' John also reveals that it was absolutely vital to learn circuits quickly. 'This made races that much easier. If I got into the groove quickly – almost from the off – I was able to dictate what happened, rather than having to worry about making up time.'

Being able to ride in all conditions was another vital factor. Some riders become demoralized as soon as they see a wet circuit. Not John. He says 'I always got on well in the rain – the smoothness was all-important.

Machine preparation was also extremely important to John. The knowledge that his engine would fire up instantly – and that it would finish the race – gave him confidence, which added to his natural riding ability proved a sure-fire winning combination.

John's biggest asset, however, was his 'love of racing'. I really don't think financial returns were ever very high on his list of priorities. Instead he loved what he was doing and certainly in his early days benefitted greatly from the moral support, enthusiasm and expertise that both his parents provided.

John Surtees didn't buy success as many modern motor sport superstars have done. Instead he achieved success by his own efforts out on the track and in the workshop, with a clear mind and a single purpose – winning races. This was how he achieved his incredible success.

Chapter 5

MV Agusta

LONG before the end of the 1955 season, John Surtees was caught up in considering his options for the following year. As he now recalls, 'My first thoughts were to stay with Norton. I had been happy with the little team under Joe Craig, with Charlie and Arthur Edwards looking after the mechanical side. Yes, we'd had our problems; we had worked at a disadvantage without streamlining or the backing of a thorough 100% works effort, but I had still enjoyed it enormously'.

John believed, and still does, that 'there was an outside chance I could win the championship in 1956 on a Norton'. He considered that he had 'the edge on Duke purely in terms of riding'. And at that time, new circuits were coming on to the world championship calendar which would place a greater emphasis on handling and road-holding than before, and this would work to the Norton's advantage. In addition, if Norton developed efficient streamlining to match that of their rivals (notably Moto Guzzi and Gilera) and with luck encountered a few wet races through the season, things would be more even than they had been in 1955 when Norton had raced the unfaired, production-type Manx models. But this would require Norton to commit themselves to a pukka works effort, preferably with the horizontal (F-type) model developed at the end of 1954. This design, which had already given more power under testing than the vertical engine, was also more suited to streamlining. Unfortunately this approach was vetoed by Norton's managing director, Gilbert Smith. However, he did agree to put the remainder of John's racing plans before his Board of Directors. The plans were rejected. The board felt that 'Surtees would do well', but realised that he would probably 'earn more than a director of the company'. This attitude indicates what was wrong with the British motorcycle industry at that time.

Actually, there was the offer of sponsorship from a national newspaper which was keen on the British rider, British motorcycle tilt at the world championship theme. To this end Joe Craig and John Surtees made an approach to Edward Turner, head of the Triumph factory at Meriden near Coventry, on the subject of his factory backing a racing programme. Triumph, at that time, was the largest manufacturer in Great Britain, many times the size of Norton. Here John met an example of what he describes as 'the overwhelming sense of conservatism and self-satisfaction which pervaded the British motorcycle industry at the time'. John continues, 'He [Turner] was totally negative. He shrugged the whole project aside saying it was no problem, Triumph could do three or four-cylinder engines, or whatever, but there was no point in going racing. Triumph could sell all the bikes they made, and more'. When Norton decided to decline John's racing plans he finally realised that he would have to go 'foreign'. At the end of November 1955 Joe Craig came to the same conclusion and announced his retirement.

BMW was one company for John to consider. He had ridden one of the Munich-built horizontally-opposed twins at the German GP in June 1955 and had not only put on a good performance before retiring, but found contrary to what certain 'experts' had said, that the bike's handling was not a problem. In fact John says: 'I was surprised by it. It was different and no doubt not so forgiving as the Norton, but certainly raceable'. BMW's engineering chief Alex von Falkenhausen firmly believed that John Surtees could win the world championship on one of their machines, and so did John. But because of BMW's less than satisfactory financial state at the time, the firm's directors, like Norton, failed to authorise a programme which would have allowed a full crack at the title.

There was also interest from both Moto Guzzi and Gilera for John Surtees's services. But as John says, 'these approaches expressed the view that, while they would very much like to do something with me, they had doubts about disturbing the Italian family atmosphere which existed in these teams. It was rather nice to see the way in which these companies acted in those times, the way in which they supported their riders and the manner in which they regarded their whole operation as a family'.

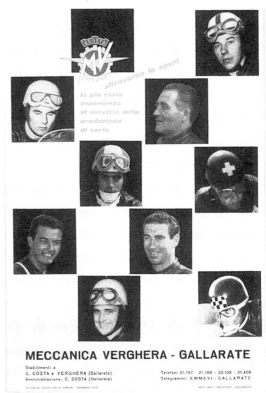

A visit to Gallarate

While John was at Monza in September 1955 with his NSU, he had a visit from Bill Webster. He had been a personal friend of the late Les Graham and had also been partly responsible for Ray Amm joining MV Agusta. Webster explained that MV team manager Nello Pagani had been very impressed by the way John had stayed in front of all the MVs

The first MV tests at Monza, autumn 1955. Left to right: John Surtees, the interpreter Signor Callatroni, Count Domenico Agusta and John's father.

while riding the BMW at the Nürburgring. After one of the Monza practice sessions Bill Webster took John and his father to the factory at Gallarate to meet Count Domenico Agusta. There they were shown the machines and the entire racing department and, even before he had a test ride, mention was made of the possibility of joining the team for the following year. However, as John says, 'Apart from the fact I would never have dreamed of accepting those terms until I had enjoyed the opportunity of trying the handling and performance of the big four-cylinder machines, I had to discuss the matter with the man who had given me my first contract as a works rider, Norton managing director, Gilbert Smith. So I could give no answer to the offer until I had been to Birmingham to see him. Mr Smith, when I saw him, could only confirm what I already knew, that Norton would be unable to "support all the 1956 championship races".' So John 'decided to ride for MV Agusta, if their machines suited me'.

By now the rumour machine was in full swing and as John says, 'all sorts of people had been warning me about the MVs'. The factory had certainly not been blessed by good fortune in the bigger classes since making its debut during the early 1950s. Just when it appeared that Les Graham was in a position to win the Senior TT for MV, he had been killed in a horrendous accident at the bottom of Bray Hill in June 1953; then in April 1955 Ray Amm, Graham's replacement, had been killed at Imola in his very first race for his new team; even their Italian rider Carlo Bandirola seemed to have more than his share of crashes. In truth, had John Surtees, or his father, been of the superstitious or worrying type, all the 'good advice' might have persuaded cancellation of the arrangements made to visit Italy in October 1955. But common sense prevailed with John of the mind: 'at least I would try the machines and make my own conclusions'.

It had been agreed at the initial meeting that John, together with his father, should fly out to Italy. He would then test the machines before they discussed terms. After arriving at Malpensa airport, Milan, they were taken to the Monza Autodrome for testing. However, the circuit was covered in leaves and it was raining hard, making it dangerous. So instead they journeyed to Modena, a track with which John was to become more familiar during his days with the Ferrari car firm. Here there were no leaves, but still plenty of rain.

The Agusta family

The founder of the Agusta empire, Giovanni, was born in the northern Italian town of Parma in 1879. He became one of the European aviation pioneers when he flew an aircraft of his own design in 1907, just four years after the Wright brothers had made their historic first flight at Kittyhawk, USA, on 17 December 1903.

Next Agusta designed a parachute in 1911, serving in the event of engine failure not only to save the pilot but also the aeroplane. This device weighed 15kg and could be said to be the forerunner of a similar principle used for the recovery of present-day space rocket capsules. That same year Italy became the first nation in history to employ an aircraft for the purposes of warfare when on 1 November the world's first bombing raid was carried out during the Italian conquest of Libya. Following this action Giovanni Agusta went to Libya as a government volunteer and was to serve his country in a similar capacity throughout World War One.

By 1919 Agusta was acknowledged as one of his country's premier aviation experts and the following year, 1920, heralded the beginning of the Agusta company, originally for the construction, overhaul and repair of both military and civilian aircraft, with facilities in Tripoli and Benghazi. Three years later, in 1923, the Agusta concern relocated to Italy, establishing its base at Cascina Costa, Gallarate, just outside the urban sprawl of Milan.

The company continued to expand but on 27 November 1927, Giovanni Agusta died at the premature age of 48 and the business passed to his wife, Giuseppina Agusta. She and Giovanni had four sons, Vincenzo, Mario, Corrado and Domenico, the eldest, who soon proved to have a natural flair for the rigours of commercial life. This was very quickly put to the test, as his father's untimely death had coincided with the most fearful industrial depression of the 20th century. Not only did the young Domenico, then 21 years old, weather this storm but he was to remain the head of the Agusta empire until his own death in 1971.

The Agusta family pose for the camera during the mid-1950s. Left to right: Corrado (the youngest and still alive), Domenico, Countess Giuseppina Agusta, Vincenzo and Mario.

During the 1930s, with the rise of Fascism in Italy under its leader Benito Mussolini, Agusta, like many other Italian industrial companies, decided to take military contracts rather than go out of business. When Italy finally joined the war on 10 June 1940, the Gallarate concern was swept into the war effort and grew rapidly – massive production requiring a much larger workforce. When the Allies landed in southern Italy during the autumn of 1943, Domenico Agusta could clearly see the writing on the wall and began to plan for peacetime production. Initially this would not include aviation – certainly not of the military variety – so the Count, as he now was, guessed that lightweight motorcycles would be needed in the aftermath of war for a transport-starved country. He turned his production facilities and workforce to this new venture, and production began with the 98cc Vespa (wasp) in late 1945. However, the name soon had to be changed because it had already been registered by Piaggio (another former aviation company) for its newly introduced range of scooters.

From the first powered two-wheeler was to come a whole family of motorcycles and scooters. In the beginning these were usually powered by two-stroke engines, but from 1950 attention switched to four-stroke power. By now MV (Meccanica Verghera) had added racing bikes to its offerings. As a way of increasing publicity for the new marque MV started to design and construct works specials rather than just over-the-counter customer racers.

The centrepiece of the MV racing effort was, from 1950, the 500cc four-cylinder Grand Prix project, joined from early 1953 by a smaller 350cc version. The descendants of these early fours were the machines which would take John Surtees to no less than seven World Championships between 1956 and 1960.

From the early 1950s Agusta had rejoined the aviation business, principally via a licence agreement with the American Bell helicopter firm. By the early 1970s helicopters had become the major feature of Agusta's commercial activities. But during the 1950s and 1960s motorcycles provided a significant part of Agusta's annual production.

There were three factors which finally conspired to cause Agusta's eventual withdrawal from the motorcycle industry. The first was the fatal heart attack suffered by Count Domenico Agusta in Milan on 2 February 1971. The second was that during the early 1970s the Italian government came to regard Agusta primarily as a defence contractor and to protect 'national interests' took a majority 51 percent shareholding in 1973, by which time the Agusta group was headed by Corrado, the youngest of the four brothers. These two factors alone might not have proved a fatal blow to the motorcycle division, except for the third and most significant – the plan to develop two brand new Agusta helicopters. These, the A109 and A129 Mangusta, were to bring the company's name to the forefront of world helicopter design, but at a price. Paradoxically, it was the very success of the A109 and A129 projects which contributed to the final demise of the MV Agusta motorcycle; the last of which was manufactured during 1978, the Grand Prix race effort having come to an end two years earlier in 1976.

Actually the rain began after the bikes had been unloaded from the van and, rather to John's surprise, the mechanics immediately began loading the machines back into their transporter. So he asked why. Via the interpreter Signor Callatroni, the chief mechanic Arturo Magni (still a staunch friend of John's today) replied: 'no one ever practises in the rain the first time on a machine'. To which John's response was 'as you sometimes had to race in the rain, why not practise as well'. He ended up doing many laps of the Modena course, his first impression being of a super-smooth power unit with a lovely sound and an over-soft suspension. On the subject of suspension, MV had at first used blade girders, then Earles type and finally in 1955 telescopics. John chose the latter, as they were the closest to what he had been used to with the Norton (the NSU having featured the leading link type). However the MV teles were of the leading axle type, similar to that found on Royal Enfield machines at the time, while the Norton Roadholders were of the central axle variety, which MV were to introduce later.

Basically, although the large tank felt 'a little cumbersome', once the riding position had been tailored 'it wasn't very much different from the Nortons'. The test session proved useful in analysing the bike. John says: 'My initial impression was that the bike felt a little too soft, demonstrating too much dive under braking and too much reaction to the application of power, although this only began to become apparent as the track surface started to dry.' Nevertheless, everyone ended up pretty happy as John had been within one second of the lap record. As he says, 'It had been a real experience'. All this was reported back to headquarters, with the reply being 'Come to Monza tomorrow. We are getting the track swept'.

The Count and Countess

John then went back to Monza for more testing. Although the circuit was relatively free of leaves, it was still greasy through the Lesmo

The 1956 MV Agusta team with Count Agusta centre. John Surtees is on the far left.

curves. Even so John got within four seconds of the fastest lap ever at Monza. Then he went back to the Agusta headquarters at Gallarate, through the arched gates at Cascina Costa, past the aircraft hangars and on to the office complex where Count Agusta was housed.

The Count was quick to come to the point of the meeting: 'We want you to be our rider and tester. Yes, you can have some machines for the early-

Count Domenico Agusta (centre) shaking hands with John Surtees after agreeing the terms of the original MV contract. On the left is Bill Webster who helped introduce John to the Italian company.

season events in England. We would like the contract to be for more than one year. This is the amount we will pay you, there will be a bonus for first, second and third places. We are on Mobil fuel and oil, but in response to your request, you can use whatever tyres you think best. Nello Pagani is the day-to-day manager and coordinator and the head of the racing department; the chief mechanic for the fours is Arturo Magni. What do you think?' John responded by saying 'Yes, we will go on from here, although there are one or two other aspects which I would like clarified as regards machines and development.'

John recalls that some time later, while Count Agusta chatted to Pagani and Callatroni, the door of the office opened and 'a lady came in completely clothed in black and wearing a black veil... I stood up and she came across, looked me over and went back to the table where she addressed Domenico. There was a brief exchange of words and she went out. I later asked Callatroni what this was all about. Callatroni replied "Ah, that was the Countess [Domenico's mother]. She was just here to check whether she liked the look of you and whether you were suitable to be allowed into the Agusta family." This is how it was – I now became a member of MV Agusta.'

John's father had also attended the test sessions and meetings, as John says, to 'keep an eye on proceedings'. He thought the arrangement was a good move and that, combined with Bill Webster's enthusiasm, 'sealed the whole thing'.

After the meeting, John had his own meeting with Arturo Magni (formerly with Gilera, who had followed Ing. Piero Remor when the latter left to join MV in early 1950). As he was to discover, Arturo was the man who could effect the technical changes needed on the bikes rather than Nello Pagani. Arturo and John got on from the start, with the latter explaining there were certain things he would like to try. John 'took all the various dimensions relative to suspension units' and asked Arturo for a couple of changes to be made to the riding position, saying he would return to Italy for more testing when they were ready. He duly returned to do another short test at Monza, but again the weather conditions were far from satisfactory. So it was mutually agreed that the main testing would take place in Britain at the beginning of the 1956 season, when the team would also decide whether to use Avon or Dunlop rubber.

At the end of October 1955, the British motorcycling press were able to publically announce that John had joined MV. The Italian press had previously published details of the test sessions. When interviewed by the editor of *La Moto*, Count Domenico Agusta had been reported as saying: 'Surtees rode like a veteran and we could detect no difference between his handling of the machine and that of our best riders. He rode, changed gear and used the throttle as if he had known the machine for ages – long enough to appreciate perfectly the qualities and weaknesses of a four.'

At around the same time there were changes at home in England. The family was about to move from Old Addington to Callendar Road, near Catford, not far from Jack Surtees's old business in Forest Hill. John also left the Vincent company. He was still carrying on his apprenticeship; recently he had been employed in the company's experimental department. At that stage this had entailed quite a lot of outside work at ML Aviation at White Waltham, with Vincent's Picador engine, rather than the motorcycle side. The motorcycle business was unfortunately by this time on its last legs. This decline was mainly a consequence of Philip Vincent's unfortunate accident (see Chapter 2). He had been quite severely injured and had lost his grip on the company. As a result the main engineering staff left and quality control slipped badly. John feels that this was all very sad, 'because that company undoubtedly had more potential than any other British marque when it came to meeting the demands which would be made of machines in the 1960s.'

By this time John's father was no longer involved with Vincents, his dealership having passed in 1954 to Deeprose Brothers of Catford. Even so Surtees Senior had to look for another firm in which John could finish the final year of his engineering apprenticeship.

The apprenticeship question was solved by one of John's father's old

The four-cylinder Gilera

Gilera first hit the headlines in April 1937 when Piero Taruffi broke the one-hour speed record, previously held by Norton rider Jimmy Guthrie at 114mph. Taruffi raised this to 121.33mph over a 28-mile course comprising a section of the Bergamo–Brescia *autostrada*. The machine the Italian was riding was a fully enclosed, water-cooled four-cylinder model developed from the earlier Rondine design, itself conceived from the even older GRB (Gianini, Remor, Bonmartini) air-cooled four of the mid-1920s. As for Gilera itself, the company had been founded by Giuseppe Gilera in Arcore, near Milan during 1911 and its owner had been shrewd enough to realise the Rondine's potential.

The basic design was steadily improved through an intensive racing and records programme until 1939. Gilera was on course to achieve supremacy in the Blue Riband 500cc category. Twice during that year, rider Dorino Serafini achieved magnificent victories – beating BMW on its home ground in the German Grand Prix and winning the Ulster Grand Prix at record speed.

When racing resumed again after World War Two the use of supercharging had been banned, so Gilera returned with new air-cooled fours designed by Ing. Piero Remor. Then in late 1949, Remor quit to join rivals MV Agusta. However, Remor's exit left his former assistants at Gilera, Franco Passoni and Sandro Columbo to carry out a redesign, which meant that in effect Gilera stayed ahead of MV, thanks to a lighter, more powerful engine during much of the 1950s.

Gilera's first world title came in 1950 (the second year of the FIM official championship series), when Umberto Masetti took the crown. From then on success followed success, particularly after Geoff Duke joined the Arcore factory in the spring of 1953. Duke brought with him the ideas of a new chassis which greatly improved the handling.

In eight seasons from 1950, Gilera riders Masetti, Duke and finally Libero Liberati won the 500cc championship no less than six times, winning 31 races in the process. It was on a Gilera too that Bob McIntyre scored a Junior and Senior TT double in 1957 and became the first man to lap the 37.73-mile Mountain Course at over 100mph. In addition, there were also the performances of the sidecar star Ercole Frigero,

Gilera's famous badge celebrating 500cc World Championship titles in 1950, 1952, 1953 and 1954 – they also won in 1955 and 1957.

Ing. Piero Remor (left) and Arcisco Artesiani with the Gilera four in summer 1949. Both men left to join MV Agusta at the end of that year.

who was consistently brilliant, but is today often overlooked. For several years he was second only to the legendary Eric Oliver (Norton) in the World Sidecar Championship.

When Gilera retired from the sport it did so on a crest of a wave, with a series of record-breaking achievements at Monza in November 1957, crowned by Bob McIntyre's incredible 141.37 miles in a single hour on a 350cc four (the Monza surface for the speed bowl being in such poor repair that riding the 500cc would have been dangerous).

Although Gilera made a number of comebacks during the next decade, notably with Scuderia Duke in 1963 and the diminutive Argentinian Benedicto Caldarella a year later, the Arcore company was unable to recapture its former glory.

In John Surtees's opinion Piero Taruffi's involvement was an important feature of Gilera's success, both before and after the war. It was Taruffi who championed the use of a lighter power unit. This John believes was the critical difference between Gilera and MV Agusta during the early and mid-1950s. This also allowed the use of a smaller overall motorcycle than MV built at the same time.

John is also pleased to see that Gilera has returned to Grand Prix racing at the beginning of the 21st century, sharing technology with the Spanish Derbi concern, and in doing so capturing the 125cc world title.

A rare paddock photograph in which both MV (left, 16) and Gilera (right, 14) are featured. The setting is Monza, September 1957.

friends from wartime days at Catterick, Peter Chapman (who later won fame as sidecar star Chris Vincent's sponsor, and as the UK's first importer of Kawasaki racing bikes). He and Jack Surtees talked things over and Chapman came up with an agricultural engineering project on which John could complete his engineering apprenticeship. Chapman was based at Guilsborough in rural Northamptonshire and was an agent for the Ferguson concern and John went to work there. The arrangement suited John, with his deep-rooted love of the countryside, very well, and he had found in Chapman an understanding partner to his studies.

After the closed season changes had been made by MV Agusta to their machinery and John was ready for another season's racing, after more testing in both Italy and England.

The 1956 MV Agusta team

As teammates for the larger classes (350cc and 500cc) John was to have Carlo Bandirola (an Italian national championship title holder) and Umberto Masetti (the 1950 and 1952 500cc World Champion with Gilera). MV were also able to call on the services of Tino Forconi and possibly Remo Venturi. For the smaller classes (125cc and 250cc) there were Carlo Ubbiali, Remo Venturi, Angelo Copota and the Swiss rider, Luigi Taveri (later to ride for Ducati, MZ and finally, as World Champion, Honda).

Early in the New Year John Surtees received a telephone call inviting him to Italy for more testing. On arrival he was booked into the Astoria Hotel in the town of Gallarate, not far from the cinema. John quite often visited the cinema as a way of improving his meagre Italian. The stay in Italy lasted 'several weeks'. During the track testing he found he much preferred the 500cc to the smaller 350cc four. The 350cc was 'too big and heavy for its power output and had a nasty temperament – sometimes very good, sometimes hopeless – which mystified the mechanics during the whole time I was associated with the factory.'

Also during this early-season stay John was able to 'sort out the riding position and get the suspension movement a little more to my liking.'

John then returned to England to resume his engineering apprenticeship duties and later his mother and father drove down to the MV factory in their van, picked up mechanic Andrea Magni (Arturo's brother) and the bikes and returned home. The 'bikes' that MV Agusta had given John for his early-season British short circuit meeting were a fully streamlined 203cc (68 x 56mm) dohc single and one

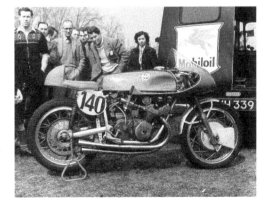

The first appearance by John as an MV rider came at Crystal Palace, south London, on Easter Monday, 2 April 1956. Here is his 500cc four-cylinder model; this view shows the frame and engine design to full advantage.

John also made winning debut on the four-cylinder 500cc MV at Crystal Palace on Easter Monday 1956. He is seen here about to cross the finishing line at the south London circuit.

of the latest 497.5cc (53 x 56.4mm) four-cylinder model. The latter machine had only a small handlebar-type fairing. Apparently no 349.3cc (47.5 x 49.3mm) four-cylinder model was ready. John's first outing was at Crystal Palace on Easter Sunday, 2 April 1956.

Strange as it may seem, before joining MV, John Surtees had never really practised bump starting any of his motorcycles – even though he had gained a reputation of being able to get off the line so quickly that it often had a demoralising effect on his oppo-

Winning the 250cc race at Crystal Palace on 2 April 1956. The machine is the dustbin-faired 203cc MV dohc single.

nents. Keen to ensure no mistakes were made for his new sponsors, 'on the paths around Crystal Palace I practiced nothing but bumping the big MV into life and getting the clutch home.' By the time he brought the machine to the line for his 1,000cc heat he felt he had 'everything taped.'

However, even the best laid plans can go awry. John's starting technique had always been to 'ride side saddle for quite a distance until I was ready to snick into second gear'. But this time he went off the line like a scalded cat, with the front wheel pawing the air – which was spectacular for the large crowd of spectators – but certainly not intended!

Apart from this minor scare, John's MV debut went off a treat with two heat wins and two final victories to his credit on the pair of MVs by the time he finally left the South London circuit. He was also placed sixth in the Invitation Handicap for the fastest 20 riders of the day. He started in scratch position and weaved a swift passage through the bulk of the field in the five laps race distance.

John Surtees's first outing at Crystal Palace that day had been aboard the fully streamlined 203cc MV single, and John recalls 'how nice the little bike seemed'. He already held the Crystal Palace 250cc lap record on his NSU, but in the heat bettered this figure by some 3mph, with a lap of 70.68mph. In the final his race speed of 70.36mph was a new record and John also improved on the morning's lap speed with a new 250cc lap record of 72.10mph.

John had requested that he be allowed to race 250cc bikes occasionally, but the factory line was that riders had already been contracted for that class and 'they didn't want me competing'. He later learned that the principal objection came from Carlo Ubbiali.

Six days after Crystal Palace, on Saturday 8 April, the Surtees MV équipe rolled up at Snetterton in Norfolk. That day his main opposition came from Norton-mounted Bob McIntyre. In the 250cc race, as *The Motor Cycle* race report says 'Surtees drew a position on the back row of the grid but at the fall of the flag he made a rocket-like getaway and was in the first three before many other competitors had settled themselves in the saddle.' Bob McIntyre finished the race runner-up to the flying 203cc MV, with Roy Mayhew (Velocette) third. The Surtees/MV combination set a new class lap record at 80.86mph. McIntyre and Surtees both won their respective heats in the 500cc event, *The Motor Cycle* again taking up the story. 'Climax of the day's racing was the 500cc final in which Surtees on the shrieking four-cylinder MV Agusta led a gallant McIntyre throughout. Again there was a new lap record, with John circulating at 88.6mph.'

John Surtees was glad of his wet test sessions at Modena, when he was confronted with one of those infamous appallingly wet days at the Northamptonshire Silverstone circuit. John describes 'a chilling, blustery wind blowing across as it only can on airfields, the track surface full of pockets and puddles of water'. The date was Saturday 14 April and the occasion the annual BMCRC championships. *The Motor Cycle* headline was most apt: 'Waterlogged Silverstone'. The report continued:

Although the unfavourable weather conditions exacted a toll of men and machines, racing was keen and interesting. John Surtees proved once again that his success as a short circuit rider does not depend on the use of the single cylinder machines. In winning the 1000cc championship on his five-hundred MV Agusta he confounded the pundits who contend that a four-cylinder machine is not a winning proposition on a wet track. At the same time he gave the lie to rumours of inferior handling of his four, at least on the smooth Silverstone circuit.

John won the first race of the day (a five-lap contest for 250cc machines) after what *The Motor Cycle* said was 'a brilliant start' on his 203cc MV single. But many observers thought that Sammy Miller (NSU), who had made a poor start and had reduced John Surtees's lead from ¼ mile on the first lap to 80 yards at the finish, would challenge and perhaps even beat the Surtees/MV combination in the main 13-lap 250cc championship race. However, the Surtees-Miller controversy was settled later in the day. At the end of the opening lap the MV led the NSU by 200 yards and that lead steadily increased throughout the remaining 12 laps. John eventually won by well over a minute; Cecil Sandford (Telfer Norton) was third.

Before the World Championship season got under way with the Isle of Man TT, John had meetings in Belgium on successive weekends: Mettet (29

Bob McIntyre

Robert Macgregor (Bob) McIntyre was born on 28 November 1928 in Scotstown, a suburb of Glasgow. His father had worked as a riveter, building ships on the shores of the River Clyde.

Bob's first job was in a large motor garage near his home and his first motorcycle a 16H Norton of 1931 vintage. After completing his national service the young McIntyre returned home and purchased an Ariel Red Hunter and it was upon this machine that he began his competitive career at a scramble event at Auchterarder, near Perth.

After competing in dirt bike events for some months and getting hooked on bikes, Bob found a job with Glasgow dealers Valenti Brothers. His job was servicing and repairing touring bikes – the firm having little connection with the sport at that time.

After watching his first road race at Kirkcaldy, Bob borrowed a friend's 350 BSA Gold Star and entered his first race at Ballado. Riding pillion to the airfield circuit on the bike, they then removed the silencer and lights. His rivals were mounted on pukka racing bikes, including KTT Velocettes and Manx Nortons, but the track was covered in loose gravel and McIntyre's scrambling experience came to the fore. The result was three wins in four races and the only reason Bob didn't win that one was because he fell off.

At that time, 1950–1, there was very little trade support for racing in Scotland. However, in 1952 Bob was asked to ride for the Troon dealers Cooper Brothers in the Clubman's TT on the Isle of Man on another Gold Star. As Bob was later to recall 'that race made me'. He finished runner-up behind winner Eric Houseley and set the fastest lap (a new class record) at 80.09mph.

That September he returned to the Island, this time to ride an AJS 7R in the Junior Manx Grand Prix. Bob not only won, but riding the same bike finished runner-up in the Senior!

From then on he mixed it with the big boys and after a spell working for AMC in Plumstead, south-east London, began a highly successful spell with tuner Joe Potts in Bellshill, Glasgow. Besides a famous 250cc Manx, Bob also rode both 350 and 500cc Manx models for the Potts stable, as did his close friend Alastair King.

By the end of 1956 the McIntyre reputation had become international. The result was that when Geoff Duke was injured at the beginning of 1957, Bob was signed to race the factory four-cylinder Gileras. He proved his worth by winning a famous double TT victory in the Jubilee races that year. He also broke the one-hour speed record (on a 350cc Gilera) at Monza later that year, after Gilera had quit GP racing.

Later Bob rode works bikes for the likes of Bianchi and Honda, but it was on the British short circuits that he continued to make his mark. And it was one fateful day at Oulton Park in August 1962 when riding his Joe Potts-tuned 499cc Norton that he crashed heavily, receiving serious injuries from which he was to die nine days later.

The *Motor Cycle* dated 23 August 1962 carried the following tribute: 'Though we mourn, we can be proud that the sport he graced and those who were privileged to enjoy his friendship are richer for his impact.' It continued 'A life of adventure was as compulsive to Bob as flying is to a bird. Challenge and conquest were food and drink to his spirit.'

April) and Floreffe (6 May). Although there was competition from the Moto Guzzi team and the BMW of Fergus Anderson, John won the 500cc race at both venues. After winning at a bitterly cold and misty Mettet from Bill Lomas (Guzzi) and Anderson, with a fastest lap of 101.62mph, largely the same riders met seven days later at Floreffe.

In comparison to a week earlier, the 8.44-mile Floreffe race was held in largely warm, sunny conditions. But sadly the meeting was to be marred by a fatal accident. Fergus Anderson, on his streamlined BMW, after setting a new lap record of 98.39mph in his pursuit of the leader, John Surtees, was killed when he crashed his BMW on molten tar in the village of Buzet, even though by this time both he and Bill Lomas (Guzzi) had given up their chase of the flying MV rider. Aged 47, Fergus Anderson had began racing in the early 1930s. Post-war he had taken delivery of the first AJS 7R built and had ridden numerous Moto Guzzi flat singles both as a privateer and works entry. His death was a major shock to the racing community. John says: 'It was a tragedy for BMW, because Fergus had shown a real ability to get the best from the Munich twin.'

The TT

Next came preparation for the TT. John recalls that although MV fielded a host of machinery in all the solo classes that year, there were none of the luxury trimmings so familiar today. 'The bikes were brought over to England by truck and van, and we actually collected two of the 500cc machines ourselves with our own van. They were all taken to London, placed on a train and we all travelled up to Liverpool, then wheeled the bikes through the streets down to the docks, on to the boat and so we arrived in the Isle of Man. Our own van took over the spares and some other equipment.' There wasn't a motor-home in sight!

After having to retire from the 1955 Senior TT (on the Norton) John admits to having 'persuaded himself that a thing like that could never happen again' – but it did! Only this time it was not in the Senior, but the Junior TT and on the smaller four-cylinder MV. For many years afterwards 'this was to leave a bitter memory'. Compared to the Norton, which could cover a lap of the 37.73-mile TT Mountain circuit to a gallon of fuel, the four-cylinder MV was much thirstier, only managing in the region of 23-25mpg.

At the start of the 264.13-mile, seven-lap Junior TT, the opposition included Bill Lomas, Duilio Agostini (not related to Giacomo), Dickie Dale and Ken Kavanagh (Moto Guzzis), Cecil Sandford (DKW), Derek Ennett, Frank Perris and G.R. Dunlop (AJS) and John Hartle, Bob McIntyre, Alan

Trow, Eddie Grant and Jack Brett (Norton). The race was run in a mixture of dry and wet conditions, depending upon which part of the circuit the rider happened to be negotiating. Only the top section of John's MV had streamlining, leaving the engine totally exposed, and the front forks were still of the leading axle telescopic type. For the first five laps Bill Lomas led the MV. But this lead had been steadily reduced from 23.4 seconds at the end of lap one, to only 6.6 seconds at the completion of lap five. Then Lomas stopped with a dead engine, leaving Surtees in the lead at the end of lap six, with Kavanagh second. Then came the last dramatic lap. John was screaming through Ramsey, then on the climb up the Mountain, at the Stonebreakers Hut signalling station, with only a quarter of a lap to go, the engine missed a beat and then cut out. Coasting to a halt, John 'looked in the tank' only to find it was empty. And although he obtained some fuel, via a milk bottle, from another machine and toured on to finish fifth, he was subsequently excluded from the official results for 'receiving outside assistance'. It was a bitter experience after so much effort.

John Surtees's build-up for the Senior TT could hardly have finished on a worse note. On the final morning of practice, putting the finishing touches to his preparation for the big event, disaster struck. When accelerating away up the steep incline from Glen Helan and round the right-hand bend at the top, as John was about to change from second to third gear an amazing thing happened: a cow leapt over a bank straight into the rapidly moving MV's path! Although the animal was bowled over, it was later reportedly 'recovered sufficiently to have breakfast in its usual pasture'. John escaped uninjured, but the same could not be said of the bike. The MV had a bent frame, scraped crankcase, damaged fairing, broken left footrest and there was an ingress of unwanted stones and dirt into the inner carburettors. But the whole incident could, of course, have been far more serious.

Senior TT success

The Motor Cycle dated 14 June 1956 began its Senior TT report with the following comments:

> *A topical query was finally settled last Friday. Until then there had been doubts as to whether John Surtees, the 22-year-old master of short circuit racing, had yet sufficient experience on the Isle of Man's 37¾ mile Mountain Course to win the Senior TT. Moreover, it remained to be shown that his four-cylinder MV Agusta had the required staying power for seven laps – 264.13 miles. Now the doubters are silent. In the most convincing manner Surtees led the*

Practice for the 1956 Senior TT. Left to right: MV chief mechanic Arturo Magni, John (seated on bike) and father Jack. Cool conditions are indicated by their attire, which in John's case included an overcoat and scarf.

race from start to finish to win in 2 hours 44 minutes 5.8 seconds, an average speed of 96.57mph. He also made the fastest lap at 97.79mph.

And this was John's 'spare' MV, not the number one machine damaged in the collision with the cow. It was a great moment for both the man and his machine, a first for both in the Isle of Man. John says, 'This success gave me a great feeling. I had notched up my first [MV] points towards the 500cc World Championship.'

When George Wilson of *The Motor Cycle* called to see John Surtees three days after his 1956 Senior TT victory for an interview, what you may ask, was he doing at his South London home? This is the answer: 'Shirt-sleeved, hair awry, surrounded by mother, father and younger brother, he was kick-starting an AJS scrambler in front of the family garage.' Though still serving

his engineering apprenticeship, Wilson discovered that John 'treats engineering as a hobby' and that the garage also housed several other bikes, including the Vincent Black Lightning-engined Norton special referred to elsewhere in this book. Even as a full works rider, his family, bikes and engineering were never very far from the surface of John Surtees's life.

After winning the 1956 Senior TT, John is flanked by his former Norton teammates John Hartle (left) and Jack Brett (right).

The Dutch TT

The next event counting towards the championship was the Dutch TT, which for the second year was being staged over the new, artificially constructed 4.79-mile circuit near the town of Assen, rather than the old 10.2-mile Van Drenthe Road course. The first year of the new venue had brought controversy, caused by a riders' strike (over the level of monies offered to privateers), which ultimately saw no fewer than 17 being suspended, including Gilera stars Geoff Duke and Reg Armstrong (although they did not take part in the strike, they supported riders who did). The effects of the suspensions were still being felt in the first few meetings of the 1956 World Championship series, and both Duke and Armstrong were not

Dutch TT at Assen in 1956. Bill Webster is signalling for John, while mother Dorothy does the time keeping at the trackside. Note the vast crowds and how close they are to the action.

Spa Francorchamps. Lap length: 8.77 miles.

given their FIM (Federation Internationale Motorcycliste) licences back until the Belgian GP in July 1956.

In the 350cc Dutch TT, after being almost the last man to leave the starting line, Bill Lomas (Guzzi) rode a fantastic race, including breaking the race and lap records, to win from Surtees, with August Hobl and Cecil Sandford (DKWs) third and fourth respectively, followed by the Guzzi trio of Kavanagh, Dale and Agostini.

Excitement abounded as engines were warmed for the 500cc event, to be held over 27 laps, 129.26 miles. Lomas had made the fastest practice lap on one of the new Guzzi V8s and Walter Zeller (BMW) and John Surtees had also improved on the Duke-Armstrong 1955 figure. But when the machines came to the line Lomas was on a single – his V8 having gone off song on the final practice circuit. From the instant the green starting light flashed until the chequered flag Surtees and the MV four were never headed. For the first three laps Zeller had attempted to keep up with John, but then the latter piled on the speed, including setting a new lap record of 83.98mph. Zeller finished runner-up, with every other rider lapped at least once!

The 8.77-mile Spa Francorchamps circuit, in the Ardennes area of eastern Belgium, was the setting for John Surtees's first double World Championship victories on Sunday 8 July 1956. It was also the first time that MV had won all four solo races at a World Championship meeting, with Carlo Ubbiali taking the 125 and 250cc races to make the quartet.

Spa Francorchamps

Of all the classic European Grand Prix circuits of the 1950s and 1960s the famous Spa Francorchamps situated in the eastern corner of Belgium, in the thickly wooded Ardennes region, was not only the fastest but one of the most spectacular in the racing calendar. Traditionally held on a Sunday in early July, it measured 8.77 miles to a lap.

From the start there was the downhill section towards the Eau Rouge curves which provided a really fast start before the long (500ft) climb to the highest part of the circuit. Before Burnenville there was a left-hand turn, then it was steadily downhill for Burnenville and the long Malmedy curve which brought one to the fast banked right-hand sweep at Stavelot, the halfway mark.

Out of Stavelot you began to climb, then negotiate several tricky corners before approaching the most arduous section of the course, La Source, a right-hand hairpin.

As the meeting invariably took place in extremely hot weather, this meant having to contend with the dangers of molten tar, and of course, the additional problems of overheated engines and clinging, sweat-laden leathers, the latter hampering a rider's movement. In such conditions, La Source was particularly dangerous and, if exactly the right line was not taken, it was exceedingly easy to crash.

The following extract from *The Motor Cycle* dated 12 July 1956 gives an insight into the pre-race tension felt of the Belgian circuit: 'The start scene was worthy of so great an occasion. Large, gaudy placards stood out in the sunlight against the background of the thickly wooded slopes and the lighter green of lush, grassy farmland. Brightly coloured national flags fluttered lazily from their masts. As zero-hour approached officials cleared technicians and well-wishers from the grid. Engines were silenced and the field formed up'.

Of the continental European circuits, John Surtees compared Spa to the Nürburgring in the way the weather could change during a lap: 'it enjoyed its own little climate zone – fine one minute, then further round it could be raining.'

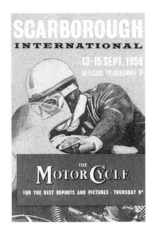

During practice for the 350cc class, five riders had shattered Bill Lomas's 1955 lap record. They were Lomas himself, his Moto Guzzi teammate Ken Kavanagh, Enrico Lorenzetti (riding an ex-works Guzzi), August Hobl (DKW) and John Surtees. When the race began, Hobl and Surtees headed the pack with Cecil Sandford and Hans Bartl (also DKW-mounted) next. The first Guzzi, with Lomas aboard, was fifth. Then Lomas went after race leader Surtees and in the process set a new class lap record at 112.22mph, but after assuming the lead the Guzzi rider was forced to retire with engine trouble (a broken valve).

A similar picture emerged in the 500cc race, run over 15 laps and 131.6 miles (against 11 laps and 96.5 miles for the 350cc event), with several riders bettering Geoff Duke's 1955 lap record in practice: Duke himself (Gilera), Zeller (BMW), Lomas (Guzzi V8) and Surtees. A vast array of exotic works machinery was entered, including not only the above but also Reg

John's mother gives him information in the pit area at one of the Continental GPs in 1956.

Armstrong, Alberto Milani and Pierre Monneret (making no fewer than five Gilera fours), Umberto Masetti (MV), Ken Kavanagh (Guzzi V8) and several more. Both Moto Guzzi V8s were destined to retire and so were the Gileras of Duke and Armstrong. Duke, having his first world championship entry since his licence was returned, led the race and set a new lap record of 117.44mph before valve trouble put him out, leaving Surtees the winner of both his races that day and also ensuring that he would be the 1956 500cc World Champion.

Solitude

For 1956, the German Grand Prix was not being held at the Nürburgring, but instead on the 7.1-mile Solitude course near Stuttgart. As John says: 'This was a vital meeting for me because I was well in the running for both the 350 and 500cc world titles.' In fact, having won the first three championship races in the 500cc category, his score stood at 24 points, and with the title race being decided on the best four performances out of six meetings

Summer 1956. Left to right: John, Count Agusta, Umberto Masetti.

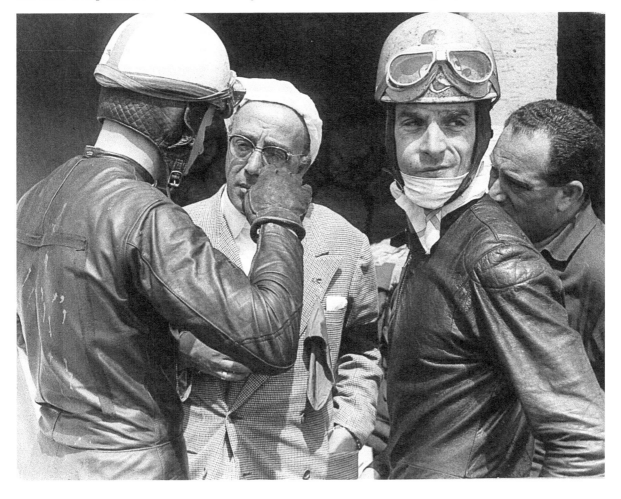

John Surtees during the ill-fated 1956 German Grand Prix at Solitude on his fully streamlined 350cc MV Agusta.

that year, only one more victory was needed to put John in an unbeatable position. His closest rival, the BMW rider Walter Zeller, had a score of 14 points. Things were less clear cut in the 350cc class. John had a score of 15. DKW's August Hobl was next with 10 and Bill Lomas, the 1955 champion, was third with 8. So a win at Solitude could also make John's position virtually unassailable.

But things didn't get off too well, for during the final practice session on Saturday morning 20 July, John crashed his 350cc MV four, twisting the frame and doing other damage. There was much frantic work by the MV mechanics overnight. John had also complained that the front end of the machine didn't feel right. What he didn't know was that the angle of the front fork had been altered – something he was not to find out about until much later. This change had been made in an attempt to improve ground clearance, and it could well have contributed to what happened in the race. John made it clear in his 1963 book *Speed*. 'That... was the only, and certainly the last, occasion on which even the slightest modification was carried out without my knowledge!' But nothing can alter what happened on Sunday 21 July 1956.

In fine, dry weather the 350cc race got away to what *The Motor Cycle* described as 'a beautiful start' and Surtees led a group of Lomas, Kavanagh and Hobl by a few yards. Then, at the end of the eighth lap, Lomas came through with a 31-second lead over Hobl – John had crashed heavily after closing right up on Lomas. This was a disaster. Not only was he out of the race but serious injuries (including a broken humerus in his right arm) meant that he was confined to hospital for several weeks and was out of racing for

the remainder of that year. John thinks that the Solitude accident was 'the worst of my motorcycle racing career'.

John's mother collected him from Stuttgart hospital, where he had had a pin inserted in his arm, and drove him back to England. He was then, as he says, 'taken off to King's College Hospital to see the team that had looked after me when I suffered the scaphoid problem [sustained during practice for the 1953 TT]'. The advice given was that he must not let the muscles waste – the doctors recommended woodwork as an ideal exercise. He later acquired a Triumph Trials Cub to further assist the 'get fit' process.

The battle for the two world titles continued without him. The German meeting had produced a victory for Bill Lomas, thus putting him in the driving (read riding!) seat in the 350cc title contest. But in the 500cc race John's most dangerous rival, Geoff Duke, had retired with mechanical trouble, as had Lomas on the Guzzi V8. And so too had Walter Zeller, who had been forced out with gearbox troubles on his BMW. The winner had been Reg Armstrong (Gilera), with John's MV teammate Umberto Masetti second and the Frenchman Pierre Monneret third on another Gilera. So with Geoff Duke now right out of the running, only one man could, theoretically at least, still take the 500cc title from John Surtees – Walter Zeller. John, still in hospital, had to wait several weeks for the result of the Ulster GP, where Zeller was unlucky once again, before he could relax in the knowledge that he was the new World Champion.

The first four-cylinder racing MV Agusta 500cc as it appeared in December 1950. Left to right: four mechanics, Count Domenico Agusta, Ing. Remor, Les Graham, Corrado Agusta, Mario Agusta, Giuseppina Agusta, Franco Bertacchini and Carlo Bandirola. Note the blade girder front forks.

By early 1951, when this photograph was taken at the non-championship Spanish GP, the front forks had been changed to tele-scopics. Other technical details of interest include dual Dell'Orto carburet-tors, Lucas racing magneto and parallelo-gram (double) torsion bar rear suspension with fric-tion damping. Like the prototype, this bike has shaft final drive.

MV Agusta 500 four-cylinder development

In 1949 Count Domenico Agusta, eager for racing success, acquired the services of Gilera designer Ing. Piero Remor and chief mechanic Arturo Magni. The new engineering duo were able to design not only a 125 dohc single, but also – far more importantly – a 500cc four-cylinder model. The latter went from drawing board to the test bench in just 15 weeks – a phenomenally short period of time.

Bore and stroke dimensions of the 1950 MV four were square at 54 x 54mm, giving a cubic capacity of 494.4cc. Running on a compression ratio of 9.5:1, the dohc four breathed through a pair of 28mm Dell'Orto carburettors (one pair of cylinders, sharing a single carb and remote float chamber). Weighing in dry at 360lb (168kg), the four-speed 1950 MV four produced 50bhp at 9,000rpm, giving a maximum speed of almost 129mph, making it faster than either the twin cylinder AJS Porcupine or single-cylinder Norton of the same era.

So, how was the bike produced so quickly? The answer was that Remor based the 'new' engine very closely on that of the 1949 Gilera. Indeed, it was

so similar that in today's litigious society, Gilera would surely have sought some sort of legal redress. Remor was clearly aware that an exact copy would not be morally acceptable, so he did introduce some features to make it different: shaft instead of chain final drive; torsion-bar suspension, both fore and aft, and perhaps most perversely gear-change levers on *both* sides of the engine! This

Carlo Bandirola's 500cc MV at the 1952 Swiss GP, much changed from the 1951 machine with new teles, frame, swinging arm, four carburettors and chain final drive.

bizarre innovation required the rider to use his heels, pushing down on the nearside for upward changes and down on the offside to change down. It was, in the author's opinion, all rather unnecessary. There is no doubt in my mind that these changes to the final drive, suspension and gear change were simply diversions from the main point – that Remor had more or less exactly reproduced the Gilera engine.

After Englishman Les Graham was signed at the end of 1950, a series of improvements began to appear. One of the first at the beginning of 1951 was the fitment of a telescopic front fork, while conventional rear suspension legs replaced the torsion bars. However, the parallelogram (double) swinging arm was retained. Additionally, reliability proved a major problem in 1951 and at the end of a disastrous season Remor quit. The design was then extensively re-engineered for 1952 by Mario Montoli and Mario Rossi, who worked alongside chief mechanic Arturo Magni.

Most notably, the engine was significantly redesigned, being given 53 x 56.4mm bore and stroke measurements (from the existing 125cc dohc single) displacing 497.5cc. Allied to other improvements, including four carburettors (first tried in mid-1951), power rose to 56bhp at 10,500rpm. Moreover, an entirely new crankcase featuring a five-speed gearbox and chain instead of shaft final drive, was a considerable improvement. There was also a new duplex frame, together with a single rear fork-type swinging arm, completing the transformation.

After a few teething troubles the results were far more encouraging. That year both telescopic and new Earles front forks were tried. Les Graham, after finishing runner-up in the 1952 Senior TT, looked a favourite on the latest MV four for the 1953 race. But, sadly, he was killed in a crash at the bottom of Bray Hill on the TT course when it is suggested a bolt jammed the front suspension.

Count Agusta was personally so shocked and saddened by the Englishman's death that the fours hardly made any appearances for the remainder of that year, but Carlo Bandirola gave the new 349.3cc (47.5 x 49.3mm) four its first victory at a non-championship race at Schotten that summer.

In the months following Graham's accident, MV gave a number of riders 'one-off' tests. These included Bill Lomas, who together with Dickie Dale was signed for 1954. The company also provided bikes for Carlo Bandirola and

Les Graham (right) seen here with Cecil Sandford (1952 125cc World Champion MV rider) inspecting the new Earles front forks which Graham used on the 500cc MV during much of 1952 and until his fatal crash in the 1953 Senior TT.

Nello Pagani; the latter now coming to the end of his riding career, was chiefly involved with the test programme (he would later assume the mantle of team manager during John Surtees's time with MV).

On the technical front the engine now yielded almost 60bhp, although the changes amounted to detail rather than major redesign. The two major areas of development centred upon the Earles front forks, which were also used featuring straight instead of curved arms and streamlining. MV tested several types of the latter, from a simple handlebar mounted device which was little more than a front number-plate holder, to a fully enclosed dustbin fairing. But as is revealed in the main text, MV for an aviation company were surprisingly slow in coming out with an effective fairing, even after John Surtees had been signed.

Results in 1954 were poor to say the least and so Count Agusta decided yet another top-class rider was needed. This turned out to be the former Norton star Ray Amm, who was tragically killed on his very first race for the company, riding the 350cc four at Imola on Easter Monday 1955.

The year 1955 was actually spent attempting to improve the four-cylinder models. Again streamlining took up a significant amount of the budget, but there was very little to show for this. The Earles front fork was eventually abandoned, particularly after John Surtees had preferred the telescopic front fork during his initial MV testing in the autumn of 1955, prior to signing to ride for MV in 1956. This fork, of MV's own manufacture, was of the leading axle type. The double-sided front brake was by now equipped with such massive air scoops that on an aeroplane these would have been referred to as air brakes! With attention to detail in areas such as compression ratios, camshaft profiles and breathing, the output of the 500cc four had been increased to between 65 and 67bhp.

Before his serious accident at Solitude in July 1956, John Surtees had amassed enough points to ensure that he would win his and MV's first 500cc World Championship. Also up to that time the bikes provided by MV had proved reliable. However, the same could not be said of the machinery in 1957, with a number of mechanical retirements caused by valves, gears and pistons. This spate of problems was not helped by overheating, caused by the centre cylinders not cooling sufficiently and problems with the piston material. There was also the matter of poorly designed streamlining. This meant that John had to sacrifice around 10 percent (up to 15mph) of maximum speed due to having to use less streamlining – typically in the 1957 Isle of Man TT. Another problem in 1957 was found to be handling. This prompted John to come up with the redesigned front fork assembly described in the main text, including a central axle. Another major change during the Surtees era was the humped frame, which again is described elsewhere.

The 500cc MV as it appeared at the beginning of 1954 and ridden by Bill Lomas and Dickie Dale. Note the revised Earles forks and the use of straight through exhaust pipes instead of megaphones.

During his five years with MV, John Surtees not only won no fewer than seven World Championships, but perfected the heavyweight four-cylinder model. It was raced thereafter by Hocking, Hailwood and Agostini with only the addition of a six instead of five-speed gearbox. However, John is firmly of the belief that MV were too conservative in their outlook and should have gone for new, lighter 500cc and 350cc fours of the type that they eventually produced in the mid-1970s, but of course they didn't and the rest is history. The slow pace of development at MV was to tip the balance when John decided to retire from motorcycle racing and try his hand in cars.

By 1955, MV were testing various types of streamlining but, as John Surtees says, 'for an aircraft company their efforts could have been much better'. The rider seen here is Carlo Bandirola.

Chapter 6

World Champion

JOHN SURTEES was the 1956 500cc World Champion, but he was not able to resume racing following his accident at the Solitude circuit in Germany until the following year, 1957. As recorded in the previous chapter, he was confined in a Stuttgart hospital for several weeks before finally being driven back to England in early September 1956.

MV Agusta did not have a stand at the Earls Court London Motor Cycle Show in November 1956, unlike rival factories such as BMW, Norton, Gilera and Moto Guzzi. So John was not 'paraded' at this event as he might have been if he had won the Blue Riband World Championship for another marque. However, he was still to be seen at lower level. For example he was recruited as a member of the panel of judges, chaired by Graham Walker, at

John Surtees and Bob McIntyre (Gilera, 78) during the eight-lap 1957 Golden Jubilee Senior TT. Even though he was to lose 10mph through not using the full fairing and the fact that they ' were not so well prepared', John still managed to finish second to Bob, averaging 97.86mph for the 302.30-mile long race.

a TT and Manx GP quiz evening organised by Bemsee and held at the Prince of Wales Tavern in Drury Lane, West London, on Tuesday 27 November. Other members of the panel included Harold Daniell, Geoff Duke, H.G. Tyrell-Smith, Jimmy Simpson, Jock West, Eric Oliver and Geoff Tanner.

Another function which John attended at around the same time was the TT Rider's Association annual luncheon at the Connaught Rooms in London during the show period. He was the guest of honour and in replying to the toast made to guests by Harold Daniell John said: 'I am sorry that British manufacturers [which meant AJS, Matchless and Norton] are to cease entering factory road racing teams, but I remain convinced that the industry could once again lead the racing world if it really put its back into the job.' After his meetings with various members of that industry prior to joining MV Agusta, he realised that this was unlikely. At the time riders and spectators still hoped for a speedy return which, as we now know, never happened.

John (left) and Bob McIntyre; both very much stars in their own right. John had recommended Bob for the MV team but the Scot chose Gilera instead. He was particularly good around the Isle of Man.

Struggling to regain form

The Solitude crash, and the only other accident of any serious consequence – when John had broken his wrist while practising for the Ultra-Lightweight TT three years earlier – were not the only mishaps he experienced during his two-wheel racing career. But all the others were, at worst, 'merely scratches and being shaken up a bit'. As a result, John had formed the 'firm belief that after a fall the very best thing to do was to get back astride a machine as soon as possible'. However, after Solitude, this was not possible. As he recalls, 'I am quite certain that it was the long time which elapsed between that July Sunday and the next time I mounted an MV, which very largely accounted for our season in 1957 being such a disaster. More time at the

Arturo Magni

In the Surtees/MV story one man looms large, besides of course, Count Domenico Agusta. That man is Arturo Magni. Magni (pronounced 'Maani') rose from a youthful spanner-man to become engineer, then projects coordinator and finally team manager of the Gallarate marque. His time with MV spanned the entire four-cylinder Grand Prix era from 1950 until the team's demise at the end of 1976.

Born in 1920 near Arcore, the home of MV's great rival Gilera, the young Arturo grew up in an Italy that was very much under the boot of the Fascist dictator, Benito Mussolini. Living in the fascist regime, however, did have one advantage, in that it positively encouraged technical achievement, particularly in the field of aviation. In his youth, Arturo was an enthusiastic aero modeller and this interest was to play a vital role in his future because it led directly to a friendship with Ferruccio Gilera, son of Giuseppe, head of the famous factory. When the aircraft works in which Arturo had worked closed its doors in 1947 he was made redundant; it was therefore perhaps natural that he should end up in the Gilera racing department. Here he soon established himself as a mechanic of rare ability. His aviation engineering proved a great asset and he was appointed head mechanic in 1948.

In this position Arturo Magni played his part in the success of the works Gilera Grand Prix squad in the 1949 500cc World Championship. Then, in a strange quirk of fate, Les Graham (who had won the 1949 500cc title on an AJS) and Magni were destined to join the same new MV team for the following season alongside Gilera's chief designer Ing. Piero Remor. Years later, Magni mentioned in conversation with the author's friend Richard Marchant how Remor had told Arturo that he was joining MV and had asked him to accompany him. Remor, Magni plus Gilera rider Arcisco Artesiani all came to join MV in the 1949–50 closed season, while Graham was signed by Count Agusta himself.

In his first couple of years with MV, Arturo continued to commute from his Arcore home to Cascina Costa, where the race shop was located within the main Agusta works. He then constructed his home (where he still lives) in Samarate, a few miles south of Gallarate.

In another life Arturo Magni might well have been a diplomat. One journalist has described him as having 'the ability to parry the most probing and often loaded questions with a polite "yes" or "no"'. Unlike many of his countrymen, he is both quiet in nature and cool under pressure. Even today, years after the death of the Count, Arturo is guarded in his accounts of the life and times of the team and its owner. There is no doubt that of all the MV riders, he has most respect for Les Graham and John Surtees.

As for Arturo Magni himself, the following extract from an article in the August 1973 issue of *Motorcyclist Illustrated* best sums up his role within the MV Agusta race setup: 'As a motorcycle manager and tactician, and above all as a company man, he must surely rate as the motorcycle racing equivalent of the legendary Alfred Neubauer of Mercedes Benz'.

factory and particularly on the track could perhaps have shown up some of the problems we encountered a little earlier'.

Conversely the arm injury did serve another purpose. During the closed season of 1956–7, John's deferment from military call-up to do his national service (which all British males were subject to from the end of World War

Two until the early 1960s) expired. The deferment had originally been granted on account of his engineering apprenticeship and not, as some readers may imagine, because of his racing. Part of the general selection process for national service with one of the British armed forces involved going before a medical board. The board turned John down as the injury to his right arm had made him 'of no further use for military purposes'. Nor were they very impressed by the 'nail' in John's humerous bone, 'nail' being the German term for the metal pin. As John later said, 'I am not going to pretend that I was really sorry about this decision'.

Towards the end of 1956 John had been asked by MV Agusta to recommend someone who could be signed up for the 350cc/500cc classes. At first he suggested John Hartle, but the latter was unable to take up the offer because at that time he was doing his national service in the British army. Bob McIntyre was another name put forward. John, together with Bill Webster, travelled to South Wales where McIntyre was competing in a race meeting at Aberdare Park on Saturday 30 September 1956. John acted as the starter for the 250cc event (which was won by the Scot) and he was under

Dutch TT 1957. Start of the 350cc event with Keith Campbell (Guzzi, 56), John Surtees (51) and Libero Liberati (Gilera, 60) pushing their bikes into life at the beginning of the 350cc event.

the impression that the arrangement between McIntyre and MV was 'virtually settled, until I read a week or so later that he [McIntyre] had signed for Gilera'. John went on to say, 'I rated Bob highly enough, particularly in the Isle of Man, to think it better to have him on an MV alongside me, rather than on a Gilera'. Finally, in early 1957 another British rider, Englishman Terry Shepherd, was signed to race the 350/500cc MVs. However, Shepherd had few outings and instead John's teammates were Italians such as former 500cc World Champion Umberto Masetti.

A poor year

John's 1957 season got off to a good start with a win at Montjuich Park, Barcelona on Sunday 7 April, but although the event was billed as the Spanish Grand Prix, it did not, in fact, count towards the World Championship. Since there were only 125cc, 500cc and sidecar events, John's sole outing in Spain came in the 500cc race on his four-cylinder MV, which he won. In fact the Italian marque had no fewer than three 'fire engines', piloted by John, Carlo Bandirola and former Norton and Guzzi works

1957 500cc German Grand Prix. Umberto Masetti (MV, 66), Dickie Dale (Guzzi, 80), John Surtees (65), Libero Liberati (Gilera, 92) and Bob Brown (Gilera, 93).

rider, Ken Kavanagh. For this event all three MVs used a small fairing, not the full streamliner which was often used on the faster circuits in 1956 and again in 1957. Although not reported at the time, John's arm was still giving him problems. For part of the race he was forced give the offending arm a rest – even his nearest challenger Carlo Bandirola didn't realise this!

In April John Surtees was upset to hear of the death of his former Norton race chief Joe Craig. He comments: 'Although I was no longer connected with Norton and Joe had ceased to manage that factory's team and gone to live on the Continent, we had continued to see a lot of each other. He attended many of the meetings and I was always grateful for the benefit of his wisdom and for the interest which he had continued to take in me. Truly, an icon of the British racing scene had passed on'.

As for races counting towards the World Championship series, it has to be said that MV had a disastrous year in 1957. The poor results were not, as people imagine, largely down to the efforts of their rivals Gilera and Moto Guzzi, but instead they were caused by a mixture of handling problems and mechanical failures. At the first round, the German Grand Prix held at the super-fast Hockenheim circuit in wet conditions on 19 May, the combined problems of high-speed instability and engine component failures reared their head. Some of the problems were associated with the use of the fully enclosed dustbin streamlining which was then in vogue. While it increased maximum speed by 10-12 percent, it also, in MV's case, had an adverse effect on the handling and on engine cooling and reliability.

Prior to the Belgium Mettet meeting (5 May) testing had been carried out at one of Agusta's associate companies, with the new streamlining in a wind tunnel. However, this was not a real trial run, as the engine was not operating. So MV engineers could not gauge the effect the dustbin shell had on cooling or engine performance. John describes the Mettet outing: 'The circuit was like a big "X" meeting in the middle. From the start we dropped down through the village, along the

EAST CURVE

4·8 MILE CIRCUIT

START AND FINISH

TOWN CURVE

Hockenheim.
Lap length: 4.8 miles.

John on the streamlined 350cc four, Germany 1957.

bottom, back up and swept round a left-hander on to a tree-lined straight. Once I got up to speed in fifth gear during practice I remember losing all steering as the thing began to take off. I just about kept it on the road, that was an experience which did not make me too enthusiastic about wind tunnel results.' The result was that the design had to go back to the drawing board, and eventually MV simply chose to copy the streamlining of Gilera and Moto Guzzi. However, overheating was to remain a problem until this form of streamlining was banned at the end of that season by the FIM.

At Hockenheim John suffered mechanical gremlins on both the 350 and 500cc MV fours. In the latter race, held at the end of the meeting and in the driest conditions of a day dogged by heavy rain, John got a flyer of a start, as *The Motor Cycle* reported. 'Using the technique he perfected in extensive short circuit racing, John Surtees led the yowling field away from the grid.' At the end of the first lap Surtees still led, with Dickie Dale (Guzzi V8), Bob McIntyre and Libero Liberati (Gileras), Umberto Masetti (MV) and Walter Zeller (BMW) making up the top six. *The Motor Cycle* described how 'the six riders were so tightly bunched that a fair-size banner might have covered them.'

Then the problems began – first McIntyre's engine went on to three cylinders, then Masetti spent some time at his pit. By almost half distance of the 27-lap, 104-mile race John was lying second behind Liberati when his rear tyre shed a section of tread and that was the end of his race. In the 350cc event earlier in the day John had been forced to retire with engine trouble.

Golden Jubilee TT

1957 was Golden Jubilee year, for it had been in 1907 that the first TT meeting had been staged in the Isle of Man. Entries totalled 279; a figure 26 higher than in 1956, even though two of the top stars, Geoff Duke and Bill Lomas, were not able to compete due to injury. Also as *The Motor Cycle* pointed out in its 'Who will be the winners?' article in the 30 May 1957 issue: 'John Surtees would by this time have unquestionably developed into another Duke if he had dodged injuries. His recent form has not been too good, but he has wisely been nursing a damaged arm, and the occasions were hardly important enough to tempt him into facing real risks.' As we know John was not one to take unnecessary risks in any case, and yes, the arm he had broken at Solitude the previous year had been giving him some problems, but also and probably more importantly, so had his machinery.

At the start of practice only one 500cc MV four had arrived. So John and Terry Shepherd (the latter having taken over Umberto Masetti's entry) had to 'share' the bike. After one lap, however, John Surtees pulled into the pits for the mechanics to inspect the rear brake linkage. Leading lap times during the early practice sessions (pm Monday 27 May) give a good example of the speeds the top riders were achieving in those days:

J. Surtees (MV Agusta)	96.22mph
J. Brett (Norton)	95.15mph
T.S. Shepherd (MV Agusta)	93.73mph
R. Anderson (Norton)	93.18mph
A.J. Trow (Norton)	92.40mph
J.J. Wood (Norton)	91.27mph

The following day brought the arrival of Bob McIntyre (Gilera) who, from a steady start, put in an amazing lap of 22 minutes 47.8 seconds, a speed of 99.3mph. Next came John in 23 minutes 10 seconds, a speed of 97.72mph. Terry Shepherd was third fastest, lapping in 23 minutes 24.4 seconds, a speed of 96.71mph. However, during the closing stages of practice Shepherd crashed heavily. *The Motor Cycle* reported: 'Coming down to the Nook toward the end of his third lap, Shepherd appeared to be travelling too fast; he applied the front brake but a wobble developed. Although he negotiated the turn at the Nook he was off line for the next left-hand bend. The machine struck the bank and careered across the roadway, throwing its rider. Having broken two fingers he was to take no further part in the proceedings.'

Held on Monday 3 June 1957, the Golden Jubilee Junior TT was staged over dry roads in warm, sunny conditions, but only after overnight fog had cleared. At the end of the first lap the top seven riders were: Bob McIntyre (Gilera), Dickie Dale (Guzzi), John Hartle (Norton), John Surtees (MV), Jack Brett (Norton), Keith Campbell (Guzzi) and Bob Brown (Gilera). The Nortons of Hartle and Brett were now fully streamlined and thus gained an additional 10mph on the fastest parts of the circuit, which put them back in the reckoning. This shows what a folly it had been to saddle the 'works' bikes in 1955 with a non-streamlined policy. But John was out of luck – he had to suffer two relatively long pit stops to change plugs. As he says he 'could reckon to be fairly fortunate to finish as high up as fourth' behind McIntyre, Campbell and Brown. John was, however, a member of the Club Award winning BMCRC team with Arthur Wheeler (Guzzi) and McIntyre (a feat the same trio of riders completed in the Senior event four days later).

The Golden Jubilee Senior TT, which took place on Friday 7 June 1957, saw history made when Bob McIntyre became the first man to lap the 37.73-mile Mountain Course at over 100mph on his way to winning the 8-lap,

301.84-mile race; McIntyre's average speed being 98.99mph. However, John came home a magnificent second – magnificent in light of the fact that his MV, unlike the bikes of his main rivals, was only clothed in a small handlebar-type fairing, rather than the fully streamlined 'dustbin' shell of McIntyre's Gilera. This was because prior to the race the MV team obtained a long-range weather report which indicated that conditions would be quite gusty; the streamlined shell was therefore removed from John's bike. At that time John's arm was not fully back to normal, but even so he says 'I chased him [McIntyre] right through the eight laps.'

The final result of the 1957 Senior TT was as follows:

1st	R. McIntyre (Gilera)	3 hours 2 minutes 57 seconds	98.99mph
2nd	J. Surtees (MV)	3 hours 5 minutes 4.2 seconds	97.86mph
3rd	R.N. Brown (Gilera)	3 hours 9 minutes 2 seconds	95.81mph
4th	R.H. Dale (Guzzi V8)	3 hours 10 minutes 52.4 seconds	94.89mph
5th	K.R. Campbell (Guzzi single)	3 hours 14 minutes 10.2 seconds	93.27mph
6th	A.J. Trow (Norton)	3 hours 15 minutes 17 seconds	92.27mph

After the Senior, *The Motor Cycle* reported: 'Injured in last year's German Grand Prix, Surtees' arm proved a bit troublesome during the first lap, but then ceased to bother him from then on. His only unwelcome excitement was a hectic slide at Glen Vine on the fifth lap as a result of oil from the chain lubricator getting on the rear tyre.' It was also observed that 'the front brake on Surtees' MV Agusta had required adjustment during the race and the rear tyre and rim were quite oily'.

A Grand Prix victory

John Surtees's first (and only) Grand Prix victory to count towards the 1957 World Championship came in Holland on Saturday 29 June at Assen. The scene was the 500cc race. Earlier in the 350cc class he had been sidelined through suspension problems; but in the 500cc event John and Bob McIntyre had streaked into the lead at the beginning of the race. Then, after seven laps of the 4.79-mile Dutch circuit, McIntyre pitted with ignition problems, but was soon back in the race only to fall while in second place with seven laps to go. John went on to win from Liberati (Gilera) and Zeller (BMW). And as *The Motor Cycle* said: 'The race provided a magnificent climax to a day's sport packed with incident and excitement. Race and lap records were broken in all solo classes.' Surtees's race-winning machine retained the small fairing used in the Isle of Man.

When the riders reached the Belgian Spa Francorchamps circuit a week after the Dutch TT, there were three riders tying on 14 points for 500cc World Championship honours: McIntyre, Liberati and John Surtees. However, as the Scot was still suffering from injuries sustained in his fall in Holland, it was left to Liberati and John to establish a definite ascendancy.

As the flag fell for the start of the 500cc Belgian GP, the field streaked downhill to Eau Rouge with Liberati ahead and John second. But by the end of the lap Keith Campbell had, as *The Motor Cycle* described, 'seared through to the forefront with the eight-cylinder Moto Guzzi and there he was to stay for more than half distance'. But as Campbell motored on to set a new lap record at 118.56mph, John Surtees had struck trouble. *The Motor Cycle* again: 'With blue smoke spurting from his exhausts he stopped at his pit for a pre-retirement consultation with the mechanics'. It was later discovered that a piston had been holed.

With Campbell also retiring Libero Liberati was eventually to cross the line as the winner, or so he thought! Then, as the result of a protest, Liberati was disqualified for changing his machine after the weigh-in (he 'borrowed' teammate Bob Brown's machine). So Norton-mounted Jack Brett found himself declared the winner. But the drama didn't end there and eventually the FIM gave the victory back to the Italian; all very confusing.

In the 350cc race at Spa Francorchamps, after lying fourth (behind Campbell, Liberati and Keith Bryan), John was an early retirement with an overheated engine (full dustbin streamlining had been refitted for the ultra-fast Spa circuit).

Next on the classic calendar came the Ulster GP over the Dundrod circuit on Saturday 10 August 1957. After the Belgian GP John had been so disappointed with the handling of his machines that he booked himself a sleeping berth next to Count Agusta on the train travelling from Brussels to Milan (he would have normally gone by car), with the express purpose of giving the Count drawings he had made of a new front fork and details of a new frame for consideration during the winter months. As John says: 'We had the new forks in time for the Ulster GP.' In fact they had been race tested at the non-championship meeting at Oulton Park on 3 August exactly a month after the Belgian round. The new forks featured central instead of leading axle location and provided much improved handling.

In the 350cc Ulster GP John hit engine trouble once more, limping into his pit at the end of lap 14 to retire. But as he admits, even though he was holding second he wouldn't have been able to catch the flying Keith Campbell's Guzzi single (Keith was to be 350cc World Champion that year).

As the Union Jack fell at the beginning of the 500cc race, John produced the type of start for which he was rightly famous and streaked away followed by the pack. At the end of the opening lap the order was: Surtees, Liberati, Brett, McIntyre, Hartle, Duke and Campbell. On the third lap John really got into his stride and knocked 3.6 seconds off Duke's lap record established the previous year, with a speed of 95.69mph. With John increasing his lead every lap it looked like he was set for his second 500cc GP victory of the year. Then mechanical failure struck again – *The Motor Cycle* reported that 'on lap 5 Surtees stopped at the hairpin, dismounted and began to push; his magneto had failed'.

At the final World Championship meeting of the year at Monza on Sunday 1 September 1957, the curtain came down, not only on that year's GP racing, but also on the true 'Golden Era' of post-war racing in which many of the major factories competed. First it had been the British AJS and Norton marques which had axed their full-blown works effort at the end of 1954, then the German DKW marque at the end of 1956 and after Monza in 1957 it was to be announced that Moto Guzzi, FB Mondial and Gilera were to quit too. But before this happened the grid was full of a variety of fully faired bikes from Gilera, BMW, Moto Guzzi and MV Agusta in the

Start of the 500cc Italian GP at Monza on 1 September 1957. Three MVs on the front row: John Surtees (2), Carlo Bandirola (60) and Umberto Masetti (36).

bigger classes, plus MV, FB Mondial, MZ, Ducati, Gilera and Moto Guzzi in the smaller categories. They provided a sight that anyone who was there would remember for the rest of their life.

In the 350cc race John Surtees was slowed by clutch problems, then at around half distance in the race he retired with valve gear problems (which had blighted the smaller four all season). The 500cc race saw John take an instant lead from Liberati. Over the next few laps, he stretched his advantage, but then his luck was out when his engine refused to reach peak revs. *The Motor Cycle* race report dated 5 September 1957 describes what happened thereafter:

> *From the sixth to the 12th laps Surtees rode like a veritable demon to offset the slowing of his engine. He got round the Italian (Liberati) on bends and swerved violently from side to side on the straights to shake him out of his slipstream. But the effort was not enough and Liberati eventually established a safe lead. Meanwhile, Duke and Milani (Gileras) battled furiously for third position, with the advantage mostly in Milani's favour. Behind them Masetti, Carlo Bandirola and Terry Shepherd, all riding MV Agustas, circled in that order until Shepherd bested Bandirola two laps from the end. What little excitement remained occurred in the final lap. Duke seized an opportunity to slip past Milani and both riders screamed by poor Surtees when his engine suddenly lost a great deal more power.*

1957 was a disaster in terms of John Surtees's World Championship hopes. Of the 12 races he had contested, he had been forced to retire in no less than eight. And in the other four he had usually suffered some form of problem; in the Isle of Man and Holland it had been handling, while in Italy the engine had been down on power. John reveals that 'by this stage I was finding it increasingly difficult to get through and speak to the Count. He was so heavily involved with his helicopter business, and I also don't think he really wanted to be reminded of the problems we were encountering. I would wait outside his office only to be told that something unexpected had cropped up and would I come back tomorrow?' Actually, as the author knows only too well from his years of dealing with the Italians, the word *domani* (tomorrow) is one of the most frequently used in the Italian language!

The MV500 six. First tested in 1957, this is the machine as it appeared in February 1958, but John Surtees had not been in favour – feeling that a better development would have been a lighter, smaller four. The six-speed gearbox later appeared on Hocking and Hailwood fours after John had quit two wheels.

However, by the end of the season, the autocratic Count was none too happy with the way things had gone. He began to take more notice of John's suggestions about improving the bikes. This led to some improvements in future years but it didn't help the 1957 results.

Non-championship events

Unlike 1956, 1957 had seen John Surtees taking part in a large number of non-championship races. As I have already mentioned, he competed at Mettet and Oulton Park, but there were many others, the results of which

Libero Liberati

Although today little remembered outside Italy, Libero Liberati is someone whom John Surtees rated highly. The 'mystery man' of 500cc World Championship winners was almost 32 years of age when he won the 1957 title and by then had been racing for 12 seasons. The reason why he has remained something of an enigma is that he mainly rode in Italy during his career. He never raced in the Isle of Man TT and raced only once in Ulster.

Besides enjoying the backing of the Gilera factory from 1950 until the company's retirement at the end of 1957, Libero was also a Gilera dealer, with a showroom in his home town of Terni, near Rome.

The son of a butcher, Libero Liberati left school at the age of 14, and began work as a mechanic. Even at this young age he was keen on motorcycling and had already obtained his first ride – on a small capacity Mas – some two years earlier. Then came the war.

When competition resumed after the conflict, Liberati, then 20, made his debut on a Moto Guzzi in a local hill climb. His roadster-based racer then gave way to a Guzzi Condor and before 1946 was out he won his first victory. Next came a Gilera San Remo. At first Libero raced privately, but after a string of excellent results he eventually received help from Gilera, who supplied him with a factory Saturno model for 1950.

At Monza in September 1951 came his debut on a four-cylinder model at the Italian Grand Prix. During 1952 Gilera entered Liberati in the home Grand Prix, plus selected other World Championship rounds including Spain and Holland. He also rode in Switzerland, where at Berne he crashed heavily, sustaining an injury which left him with a 'bent arm' riding style for the remainder of his career.

After winning the 1955 and 1956 Italian titles, Liberati scored his first Grand Prix victory on the new 350 Gilera four at Monza in September 1956; he was also runner-up behind Geoff Duke in the 500cc race. In his championship year, Libero Liberati won at Hockenheim, Dundrod and Monza – he also won at Spa Francorchamps (after initially being excluded).

Following Gilera's withdrawal from racing at the end of 1957, Liberati continued to compete in events on his own Saturno, often putting in some fantastic performances on what was by then an obsolete machine. It was also a measure of his enthusiasm for the marque that he persevered on such an outdated bike. Sadly, it was to be on his faithful Saturno that Libero Liberati was to meet his death on Monday 5 March 1962, while testing the Gilera single on public roads near his home in Terni in readiness for the coming season's racing.

are recorded in the appendix at the rear of the book. Some were ridden with machinery supplied by MV (a 203cc single and a 500cc four), but equally in many John used his own, private machines in the shape of the NSU Sportmax and 350cc/500cc Nortons.

Highlights of these outings included victories on the NSU at Oulton Park (10 June), Scarborough (13 June) and Crystal Palace (17 August). On the Nortons he achieved wins at Oulton Park (10 June, 3 August and 5 October), Thruxton (5 August), Crystal Palace (17 August),

The official opening of the West Wickham motorcycle business in February 1958. John is seen with his mother and father plus an array of bikes including an AJS Porcupine, a fully faired 500cc MV four, a works 203cc dohc MV single and in the background on the left, a BSA A7 twin.

Scarborough (14 September), Silverstone (21 September) and Brands Hatch (12 October). MV wins at non-championship events came at Montjuich Park, Barcelona (7 April), Brands Hatch (19 April), Oulton Park (3 August and 5 October), Silverstone (21 September) and Aintree (28 September). At many of these venues he set new race and lap records for good measure. And in the process he showed he had lost none of his mastery of the British short circuit scene.

Towards the end of 1957, John was asked to sign a three-year extension to his MV contract. He eventually agreed to sign once he had been promised that not only would a new frame for the 500cc be autho-rised, but also that a new, smaller 350cc would be built. Developments in the smaller classes would continue and – perhaps – there would be opportunities to race the 250cc. But the 250cc was never to materialise and as John says 'this was a matter of some sadness to me, as I would have loved to have ridden one of the full-size 250cc singles, or the later twins, particularly in the Isle of Man'.

Around the same time, John was asked by Stan Hailwood if he would 'loan' him the NSU Sportmax for his

John Surtees's motorcycle showroom, at 2 Bell Parade, West Wickham, Kent, which opened its doors in early 1958.

son Mike to ride. John admits: 'to be honest, I didn't like to see it go', but eventually he agreed to loan the bike 'just for the winter events in South Africa'. Also the spare engine was given to the Hailwood équipe. It was handed over in 'as new condition'. But neither the bike nor the engine was ever returned. John says that 'Stan Hailwood promised NSU that he would buy a load of road bikes for the King's dealership chain and that was the last I ever saw of the bike or engine.' In a similar way that's how Stan got Mike a Ducati ride – he simply became the British importer for the Bologna-made bikes!

Towards the end of 1957 John decided that he should be planning ahead, just in case he should have to give up racing. He made plans to support himself with a motorcycle business. When he came upon the type of shop premises he had envisaged as suitable, he decided there and then to buy it. The shop was at 4 Bell Parade, West Wickham, Kent. It was established under the name John Surtees Developments and opened on Saturday 16 February 1958. His brother Norman was put in charge. Special attractions at the opening were a fully faired MV four, an AJS Porcupine, a Manx Norton and the unstreamlined MV works 203cc single-cylinder racer. Agencies included Greeves, James, Matchless/AJS, Norton, NSU, Triumph and Lambretta scooters.

On Wednesday 2 January 1958, John Hartle exchanged his battledress for a civilian suit. The occasion was the ending of his period of national service. His 'working' contract with MV Agusta really began on that day. John Surtees was extremely pleased to have his old friend with him for the coming season. Even today JS rates JH highly – as a rider, teammate and as a person.

At the FIM's autumn conference in late 1957 a discussion was held at which it was agreed that from 1958 onwards the use of the streamlined 'dustbin' shell would be banned. This regulation came into force on 1 January 1958 and resulted in the new 'dolphin' type of fairing, which has been used since then. When John Surtees was interviewed after the TT in the 19 June 1958 issue of *The Motor Cycle* he said that both types were a compromise but he much preferred the dolphin.

In addition to the new type of fairing, a considerable amount of testing was carried out by MV over the closed season of 1957–8. For starters there were changes to the engine's pistons and valve springs, plus a completely new duplex frame (nicknamed 'the camel' because of the hump over the inlet camshaft). Like the Featherbed Norton this frame had duplex rails running under the power unit, but in the MV's case these were detachable for easier engine removal. This frame was designed by John and Arturo Magni. Also during the spring of 1958 MV tested the new six-cylinder 500cc; this featured a six instead of five-speed gearbox. It was only raced once, by John Hartle at the Italian GP at Monza during September 1958. With the Gilera fours and Moto Guzzi V8s now out of the picture, the need for such a bike had ceased. In any case John told the author that he was not impressed by the six, which he thought was 'a waste of time and money. Why? Well it was too big and heavy. And the limitations of its valve gear meant that it couldn't rev safely in the region it would have needed to produce maximum power. The four was safe to 10,700rpm – the six would have needed to rev to 12,000rpm.' Incidentally, after 1960 the six-speed transmission was transferred into the four-cylinder MVs, ridden by Mike Hailwood and Giacomo Agostini.

Just as 1957 had been a terrible year for John and MV in the 350cc and 500cc World Championship series, 1958 was just the opposite, with 12 races, 12 finishes and 12 victories! Of course there have been those who have pointed the finger at the fact that without rival factories, John Surtees's task was much easier than it would have been. Yes, there were no Gileras or Moto Guzzis. But many of the top stars were still around. Starting with Geoff Duke who had been signed by BMW to replace Walter Zeller who had retired; Dickie Dale was also BMW mounted. The Slazenger company had taken over the Norton factory team, in effect with the works bikes and transporters and a trio of riders: Jack Brett, Alan Trow and Michael O'Rourke. With Doug Hele now in charge of developments, Norton came out with a surprisingly large-scale development programme. There was also the formidable combination of double Jubilee TT winner and lap record holder Bob McIntyre on Joe Potts Nortons. Other notable Norton-mounted privateers in 1958 included Bob Anderson, Bob Brown, Derek Minter, Dave Chadwick, Alastair King and Keith Campbell. There were also men such as Mike Hailwood, Tom Phillis and Jim Redman who had not yet gained the recognition they hold today.

John was joined in the MV team for 1958 by his old friend and former Norton teammate John Hartle (right). The pair are seen here enjoying a cup of tea at a pre-season practice session. They enjoyed a close friendship until John Hartle's fatal accident accident at Scarborough in 1968.

So the important point about 1958 was that there was still competition and John went out and broke race and lap records and the bikes stayed together – that was why he became a double World Champion that year. The author's view is that had Gilera and Moto Guzzi been there John Surtees would still have been 500cc World Champion, probably 350cc Champion too. For proof of this you only have to go to two races – the 500cc round at Spa Francorchamps where he set a new lap record of 120.17mph (beating the previous year's Guzzi V8 record) and the 350cc German Grand Prix at the ultra-demanding Nürburgring. The Spa result shows the speed of the 1958 MV, while the Nürburgring result proves the handling improvements made over the winter and of course John's sheer riding ability.

As in previous seasons, John took in some of the early non-championship meetings to get back into the groove after the winter layoff. His arm was now much stronger than it had been a year earlier and this showed in his performances, with victories in all the races he contested. The first came on Easter Monday 7 April over a revised 3.11-mile circuit at Imola, where John secured the Shell Gold Cup in the 500cc race winning at an average speed of 84.16mph, for the 124-mile race. His fastest lap was at 86.8mph – from a standing start on the first lap – and he finished 54 seconds ahead of team-mate Remo Venturi. Australian Jack Ahearn (Norton) was third with Alan Trow (Norton) fourth.

Two weeks later on Sunday 20 April, John followed up his Imola success with another victory, this time at Montjuich Park, Barcelona. The race was held over 30 laps of the sinuous 2.36-mile Spanish circuit. *The Motor Cycle* described it thus: 'A potent five-hundred four is not the easiest of models to ride at Montjuich Park. The circuit is so tricky that the winning speeds of the 500 and 125cc races differed only by about 4mph, or six-per-cent. But Surtees swept his mount through slow and fast corners, through left-handers and right-handers, as though it was a lightweight.' MV had a factory producing motorcycles at that time in Spain, so the annual visit to Barcelona was seen as important by Count Agusta.

Junior–Senior TT double

In spite of the withdrawal from international racing of Gilera, Moto Guzzi and FB Mondial, there were still 81 entries for the Senior and 82 for the Junior TT. As for MV Agusta, they had nominated three riders for the above classes: John Hartle, Remo Venturi and John Surtees. While

John Surtees pushes out his 350cc MV Agusta on which he went on to win the 1958 Junior TT. Nello Pagani is extreme right with Bill Webster between him and John.

After winning the
1958 Senior TT one
of the MV
mechanics helps a
frozen John restore
circulation to his
hands.

in the Lightweight 125cc and 250cc races, the Italian company had entered Franco Libanori, Tarquinio Provini and Carlo Ubbiali. It is also worth recalling that both the AJS 7R and Manx Norton models had been considerably improved for 1958, including new AMC four-speed gearboxes and increases in power output figures. Geoff Duke was again a force to be reckoned with – he gained his first victory at Hockenheim in May, on his works BMW twin – so the prospects for close competition looked brighter than many pundits had thought, following the withdrawal of the manufacturers referred to above.

During the practice period for the 1958 TT series, even by Tuesday 27 May John Surtees had shown that he was in a class of his own, lapping the 37.73-mile Mountain Course in 23 minutes, 19.4 seconds – a speed of 97.06mph – from a standing start! The climax of the training sessions was when Surtees put in a lap at a shade under 100mph (99.6mph) on his Senior MV on the morning of Wednesday 28 May. On his Junior mount he was much more restrained, letting others such as McIntyre, Campbell, Duke and Dale dominate the proceedings. As for the other two MV entries, John Hartle put in a fastest lap of 98.5mph, while Remo Venturi was a non-arrival.

John Surtees totally dominated both the Junior and Senior TTs, leading on every single lap of both races. In the Junior, on 2 June, the MV World Champion completed the seven laps in 2 hours, 48 minutes, 38.4 seconds, an average speed of 93.97mph. He also set the fastest lap in 23 minutes, 43.4 seconds, at 95.42mph. Then on Friday 6 June John reeled off the seven lap Senior TT in 2 hours, 48 minutes, 39.8 seconds, averaging 98.63mph; his fastest lap in 22 minutes, 30.4 seconds represented 100.58mph, which was set on the second lap. As for teammate John Hartle, he seemed to have taken over the bad luck experienced by John Surtees the previous year, failing to finish either race. In the Junior Hartle was a first lap retirement when a piston disintegrated. Then, after lapping at 100.08mph in the Senior, his bike burnt out in Glencrutchery Road, Douglas on the fourth lap, when a fuel leak ignited!

Following his double TT victories John Surtees had joined an elite band of riders who had achieved this feat since the inception of the races in 1907: Hunt, Guthrie, Woods, Duke, Amm and McIntyre. So it seemed a good time for George Wilson to do another of his interviews for *The Motor Cycle*; this one being published in their 19 June 1958 issue. This interview is now an important piece of history, coming when John had not only become a double TT winner, but as he was to prove, the leading motorcycle racer of his era. Perhaps most interesting is how Wilson saw John as a person, commenting: 'I said a few lines back that John doesn't change much. Yet these last two years or so changed he has, for he is no longer the boy we knew. He looks older, his features are more prominent, his shoulders wider. Yet he remains as reclusive as ever, so that few people outside the Surtees ménage know him well. In spite of his long string of successes, or of the frequency with which he races, the 1958 Junior-Senior double TT winner remains chiefly a name, a face, and only to his close associates a *person*.' However, as Wilson went on to say, 'And yet, to those in the very close inner sanctum, he is all-friendly, rarely without that beaming grin, modest to a degree – so much so in fact, that he recites his success list with quite remarkable vagueness.' In many ways, in the author's opinion, John remains the same today. He has achieved his fame by his ability to carry out whatever task he sets himself to the very highest standards. He has never attempted to seek fame for fame's sake.

The Dutch TT held at Assen on Saturday 28 June 1958 saw John Surtees follow up his Junior-Senior double in the Isle of Man by winning the 350cc and 500cc classes at Assen. His average speed in the 500cc race of 83.81mph was a record. Those victories were probably the easiest of his international career. In each case he led from start to finish and was never even remotely challenged. The extent of his mastery was such that in the 350cc race he led the second man, John Hartle (MV Agusta), over the line by 1 minute, 17.5 seconds. In the 500cc event Hartle was 1 minute, 46 seconds in arrears.

It is interesting to record the leading results in these two races as they show which riders and motorcycles were John's closest rivals following the withdrawal of Gilera and Moto Guzzi from the bigger classes:

350cc Dutch TT – 20 laps – 95.75 miles
1st   J. Surtees (MV Agusta)
2nd J. Hartle (MV Agusta)
3rd K.R. Campbell (Norton)
4th D. Minter (Norton)
5th S.M.B. Hailwood (Norton)
6th L. Taveri (Norton)

500cc Dutch TT – 27 laps – 129.26 miles
1st   J. Surtees (MV Agusta)
2nd J. Hartle (MV Agusta)
3rd D. Minter (Norton)
4th E. Hiller (BMW)
5th R.H. Dale (BMW)
6th G. Hocking (Norton)

And what of Geoff Duke? After making a mediocre start, he had worked his way up to seventh, before retiring on lap 16. Geoff was having trouble adjusting to the different demands of the BMW.

120mph Belgian Grand Prix

As *The Motor Cycle* said: 'There was not a bookmaker in Spa last Sunday evening who would lay odds against John Surtees winning the world's 500cc and 350cc championships.' With what was described as: 'a faultless display', he had just swept his works MV fours to unchallenged victories in those classes of the Belgian Grand Prix on 6 July 1958, thus achieving a consecutive double in the three meetings so far staged. Now only one more victory was needed in each class at the Nürburgring, Germany, on 20 July and the titles would be his.

In the 350cc event at the meeting there were no fewer than four dohc Jawa twins, their best rider being Frantisek Stastny, who after a plug change on the first lap climbed from last place to twelfth. This combination was to become a major threat in subsequent years, although John feels that had a big star name ridden the Czech machines, they could have achieved even greater things.

The 500cc race saw John set a new lap record of 4 minutes, 22.8 seconds for the 8.76-mile circuit, at a speed of 120.25mph – the first time a rider at the Belgian GP had breached the 120mph figure. The old time, set the previous year by Guzzi V8-mounted Keith Campbell, was 4 minutes, 26 seconds; 118.56mph. This goes to show that John Surtees would almost certainly have won the 1958 500cc World Championship even if Guzzi and Gilera had still been competing.

Geoff Duke had a better meeting; after fifth place on his Norton in the 350cc, he brought his factory BMW twin home fourth in the 500cc. But the undoubted star of the non-MV riders was Keith Campbell, who was third in the 350 and a magnificent second in the 500cc, on both occasions riding Reg Dearden works development Manx Nortons. But sadly this was to be the 1957 350cc World Champion's final success, as the following weekend he crashed fatally shortly after the start at an international meeting at Cadours, near Toulouse, France, on his larger Norton.

The Motor Cycle headline summed up John's achievement: 'Surtees Makes Certain! Four Successive Double Wins Secures 350 and 500cc World Championships'. John had amassed the maximum of 32 points in each class in the minimum possible number of races. To counter those who might have argued that his task had been easy, was John's faultless ride in the appalling weather that marred the 500cc German Grand Prix. As *The Motor Cycle* went on to say, this 'was real championship stuff'.

Since the last time the Nürburgring had been used back in 1955 for World Championship motorcycles, there had been numerous long distance and Grand Prix car races which had combined to put, as one journalist said, 'a vicious polish on the surface and greatly worsened the bumps'. That meant that in dry weather the course demanded extreme caution and when the storm came there was a 'distressing' crop of spills.

The thunderstorm, which had begun during the sidecar race, reserved its full fury for the nine-lap, 127.56-mile 500cc contest. Geoff Duke had loaned sidecar star Walter Scheider his best engine; the replacement proved grossly over-jetted and Geoff retired after one slow lap. But some 20 minutes later he found some consolation in the fact that riding conditions had become incredibly bad. Rain fell, as *Motor Cycling* reported, 'with the force of hail-stones', and the track was soon awash.

At the front of the field the Surtees-Hartle MV duo was circulating at high speed, but Norton-mounted privateer Gary Hocking's performance was equally noteworthy. With no fairing to protect him, the young Rhodesian got the better of a six-way dice also involving the BMW trio of Ernst Hiller, Gerold Klinger and Dickie Dale, plus Bob Brown and Alan Trow (Norton).

Around half-distance, Hartle made the mistake of pulling down his goggles. The rain lashed his eyes mercilessly and Hocking quickly demolished Hartle's half-minute advantage to pass him – only to be repassed a lap later as Hartle gritted his teeth and pressed on. After crashes and retirements the final finishing order was:

500cc German GP – Nine laps – 127.56 miles
1st   J. Surtees (MV Agusta)
2nd J. Hartle (MV Agusta)
3rd G. Hocking (Norton)
4th E. Hiller (BMW)
5th R.H. Dale (BMW)
6th R.N. Brown (Norton)

In the dry, during the 350cc John had set a new class record of 81.83mph; in the truly awful conditions of the 500cc event he set the fastest lap of the race at 75.12mph.

Anyone who thought that it would be drier in Ulster than Germany was wrong. *The Motor Cycle* race report set the scene: 'Rainswept? That would have counted for little, but as the crowds trekked up the long, winding hill

The 1958 Ulster Grand Prix at Dundrod and John prepares for a practice session with his smaller four. To John's left is Bill Webster and further to the rear Dickie Dale (BMW, 72).

The two Johns with their 500cc four-cylinder MVs. The machine was called the 'camel' because of the hump in the top frame tubes.

from Belfast towards the circuit there was not only persistent rain but also a heavy mist shrouding the course in gloom'. However, Count Agusta was still happy, as the opening paragraph from *The Motor Cycle* dated 14 August 1958 reveals: 'Last Saturday (9 August) was a day of glory for the MV Agusta factory. In the classic Ulster Grand Prix, run over the rainswept, 7.23 mile Dundrod circuit on the heights above Belfast, John Surtees, already holding maximum points in the world 350 and 500cc championships, demonstrated the searing power of his four-cylinder mounts by bringing off yet another double win in the major races. Ten classic wins in one season must be quite a record.'

Not only this but with Carlo Ubbiali taking the 125cc race and Tarquinio Provini doing the same in the 250cc class it meant that in these categories too, the respective championship titles were going to two Italian riders and thus the MV Agusta team. This was the first time that all four solo championships had been won by a single factory. With the sureness and regularity of the Milan-Rome express train – and twice as much speed – John Surtees rounded his World Championship season off in superb style when he circled the Monza autodrome 62 times on MV fours on Sunday 14 September 1958 to win the 350 and 500cc classes of the Italian Grand Prix.

Both John Surtees and John Hartle had retained hopes that they would be allowed to race their private Nortons at the non-championship meetings during 1958. However, this was to prove a forlorn hope and the only non-championship racing John Surtees got in that year was strictly on MVs. As already explained, before the World Championship rounds got under way he had had successful outings at Imola, Barcelona and Mettet. Then, after Monza came meetings at Aintree (27 September), Mallory Park (28 September), Oulton Park (4 October) and Brands Hatch (12 October).

The highlight of these British short circuit appearances came at Aintree when he broke Geoff Duke's Gilera lap record of 83.85mph, with a speed of 86.36mph; nearly 3mph faster! *The Motor Cycle*

After winning the double World Championship in 1958, John took in a number of British short-circuit events including victory on his 350MV and a record lap at Aintree, near Liverpool, on 27 September.

A practice photograph of John Hartle (4) leading John Surtees (2) on their 350cc four-cylinder MV Agustas at Monza in September 1958.

John and his mother on the MV pit wall at the 1958 Italian Grand Prix at Monza.

John with the garlands of victory after winning the 500cc race at the Italian GP in Monza, 1958.

Aintree race report ended by saying: 'If ever a rider had a successful season, this young Londoner has had one in 1958. But let there be no doubt about his deserving it; for in the saddle he is true genius.'

John had hoped to be wintering in South Africa. But when he appeared at the Earls Court Show on Press Day, Friday 15 November 1958, in company with Nello Pagani the MV Agusta team manager, he told journalists that unfortunately he would not after all be going to make the trip. MV would give him permission to race at only two meetings, and as he said: 'South Africa is a long way to go for that.'

MV developments

On Wednesday 12 February 1959, John left London by air for Milan to discuss his racing programme for the coming season. At the time the 1958 double World Champion said he: 'hoped to see new 250 and 350cc models'. A week later he returned with a nasty bout of flu caused by 'waiting at airports for fog to lift'. But he was able to report that progress with the new MV 350cc was 'splendid', and that he hoped to do some testing with it at

Monza in three weeks time. John commented that the machine was a scaled-down version of the model used the previous year. The 500cc was unchanged.

When he left London again bound for Italy in early March to 'carry out tests with the 350cc at Monza', John also revealed that he would be taking in the French Grand Prix course at Clermont-Ferrand, which had recently been completed. The purpose of the visit was to make a reconnaissance on behalf of the factory so he could make suggestions for gearing the MV lightweights. He was also travelling to Munich; he was about to add the BMW agency to his dealership in West Wickham and was keen to arrange for a factory course for his mechanics. While in Italy he also travelled to Rome and the Vatican where, together with Carlo Ubbiali and Tarquinio Provini, he was presented to Pope John XXIII.

Much as John attempted to push them, MV Agusta's main thrust during this period was on the development and testing of their lightweight 125 and 250cc machinery. For example, not only did they build a new 250cc twin-

The Sportsman of the Year presentation ceremony towards the end of 1958. John is pictured with Lord Selsdon, chairman of the *News of the World* newspaper (centre) and Formula 1 car driver Mike Hawthorn (left). It was Mike who first suggested John should try four wheels. Sadly Mike was killed in a road accident in his Jaguar on the Guildford bypass in January 1959.

cylinder model, but they also tested experimental 125cc and 250cc twins featuring desmodromic valve operation. The problem for John was that MV saw the competition coming in the smaller classes, notably Ducati and MZ. It is important to remember that this was before Honda made their bow in Europe the following June at the Isle of Man TT.

In addition at that time there was considerable uncertainty about whether the 500cc class would continue to allow factory specials such as the MV. This was because at the FIM's spring conference in 1958 a decision had been made to exclude the 500cc bikes from the World Championships in 1960. For 1959 the FIM had planned that a season of Formula 1 events should be staged, alongside the existing Grand Prix races. Quite frankly this was an ill-conceived idea. The concept was probably that by only allowing production models (such as the Manx Norton or Matchless G50 singles), it would encourage other manufacturers to take part. But the FIM simply didn't organise the series properly. The result was poor entries at the few venues that ran F1 races and much confusion. For example, a little-known fact is that Honda originally entered a trio of CB92 125cc street bikes in the Isle of Man F1 TT, which was only for 350cc or 500cc bikes! Only much later were the Japanese company's entries changed to pukka race machines, which scooped the team prize in the 1959 125cc Ultra Lightweight TT. This partly explains why Count Agusta saw fit to concentrate his resources on the smaller classes at that time.

At Imola on Easter Sunday, 12 April 1959, John Surtees repeated his success of the previous year, by winning the 500cc Shell Gold Cup on the four-cylinder MV. The race was sadly marred by the fatal accident of the Australian Harry Hinton Junior who crashed his Norton two-thirds of the way through the 30-lap race when lying second. *The Motor Cycle* reported: 'John Surtees' superiority on his MV Agusta four was so emphatic that he was able to stop his machine and tell officials of a serious crash by Harry Hinton and still beat teammate John Hartle by 1 minute 23 seconds.'

Only six days later John took part in his only British short circuit meeting of the year, the BMCRC Silverstone Saturday, held on 18 April. He described the setting at the bleak Northamptonshire circuit at the start of the day as 'icy-cold, wet and windy'. This didn't stop him winning the 350cc race, with a new class lap record of 93.87mph. But things didn't go according to plan in the 500cc race. After making one of his lightning starts he crashed out on the first lap. John says: 'The rain started to come down again for the 500 event and I suppose I must have had one of those lapses; I don't quite know. Perhaps it was some oil on the track but after getting away comfortably, going into Club Corner on the first lap I lost it

John with his parents at a cold, wet Silverstone, Saturday 18 April 1959.

completely. It was something of a rarity for me to fall off at that stage of my career, but it was quite a big accident which was to have further repercussions relative to my getting permission from MV to race in non-championship events.'

'Surtees Back in the Groove' was *The Motor Cycle* headline in the 21 May 1959 issue. It came in response to John following the pattern he had set the previous year of scoring double victories. He led both 350 and 500cc classes on Sunday 17 May, in spite of the fact that the five-mile Circuit de Montague, south-west of Clermont-Ferrand in central France, was so twisty and undulating that the performance advantage of the four-cylinder MV could never really be exploited. In the 350cc race teammate John Hartle could only manage third, with the two MVs split by hard riding Gary Hocking (Norton). In the 500cc contest Hartle was replaced by Remo Venturi. The the result was:

1st   J. Surtees (MV Agusta)
2nd   R. Venturi (MV Agusta)
3rd   G. Hocking (Norton)
4th   R.H. Dale (BMW)
5th   T. Shepherd (Norton)
6th   E.G. Driver (Norton)

Surtees set the fastest laps in both races; the 350cc at 74.54mph, the 500cc 75.60mph.

Back to the Island

Then it was back to the Isle of Man. Only one MV was out at the start of official practice for the 1959 TT series on Saturday 23 May and this was John Hartle, who lapped in 24 minutes 25.4 seconds, a speed of 92.72mph. The talking point at the following Monday's breakfast tables was the lap that John Surtees had put in earlier that morning: 22 minutes 29.2 seconds, 100.67mph. But even that didn't tell the full story, as John put in three of his four laps at under 23 minutes each, the last of them in 22 minutes, 34.2 seconds (also over 100mph) from a standing start and with a coasting finish! The condi-

Negotiating Waterworks Corner during the 1959 Isle of Man Junior TT. His victory in both the Junior and Senior races that year was the second successive TT double, thus equalling the achievement of Norton rider Stanley Woods almost a quarter of a century earlier.

Teammate John Hartle during practice for the 1959 Junior TT on the smaller MV four-cylinder model.

tions had been ideal for high speeds; the day dawning cloudless and bright, with virtually no wind. Then the riders concentrated on the Junior MVs. During the early morning session on Tuesday 26 May, John Surtees went round at 94.43mph; John Hartle at 93.54mph.

The whole practice period and all the races except the Senior were held under perfect weather conditions. As expected, Surtees brought his four-cylinder MV home to a comfortable victory in Monday 1 June's Junior TT. As *Motor Cycling* reported: 'He rode his usual well-judged race and, although never unduly pressed, established a new race record of 95.38mph.' John Hartle on the other MV was runner-up, averaging 93.65mph and Alastair King (Norton) third, with a speed of 93.56mph. The top six leader-board was completed by Geoff Duke, Bob Anderson and Dave Chadwick (all Norton mounted).

Appalling weather on Friday 5 June 1958 saw the Senior TT put back 24 hours until Saturday 6 June. In so many ways the race was one of John's greatest performances, culminating in a magnificent victory. Postponed it may have been, but for six of the seven laps the race was lashed by storm-force wind and furiously heavy rain. On the first lap, the only one in totally dry conditions, from a standing start, John set a new course lap record of 101.18mph – bettering by 0.06mph the previous figure set by Gilera-mounted Bob McIntyre in 1957.

John's second victory of the week gave him the honour of the double-double (Junior and Senior victories in each of two successive years) which

John flanked by teammate John Hartle (1), MV runner-up, and Alastair King (Norton), after winning the 1959 Junior TT. MV team manager Nello Pagani is pictured between his two riders.

only one other rider, Stanley Woods, had achieved in 52 years of TT history. Woods had won both races in 1932 and 1933; he too had been successful on one make of machine, in the Irishman's case, Norton. Only once before had it been necessary to hold over the Senior TT until the following day; that had been back in 1935. John Surtees led the race from start to finish. His team-mate John Hartle was second before he crashed out on lap 3. By now the conditions were at their very worst and one rider, Alan Trow, was 'blown off the road' at Alpine Cottage, near Ballaugh. At the end of lap three Surtees had refuelled in 31 seconds with the knowledge that his nearest challenger, Alastair King (Norton) was some 2¼ minutes astern. By now retirements were coming thick and fast as the combination of high winds and rain began to take its toll. Everyone expected the race distance to be shortened but it never was. At the end of the race John Surtees, like many others, had to be lifted off his bike, his hands frozen and his body chilled to the bone.

Only 22 of the 58 starters finished. John's average speed for the seven laps, which he completed in 3 hours 13.4 seconds, was 87.94mph. The final result was:

1st J. Surtees (MV Agusta)
2nd A. King (Norton)
3rd R.N. Brown (Norton)
4th D.T. Powell (Matchless)
5th R. McIntyre (Norton)
6th E.G. Driver (Norton)

At the evening's presentation at the Villa Marina, Douglas, John said he 'felt that everyone who finished in the Senior this year deserved a silver replica'. Later, at a small private ceremony, John received a most unusual trophy from Japan – a Samurai warrior's helmet, a superb affair of golden horns and pink silk chinstraps, known as a *kabuto*. It was a traditional Japanese symbol of bravery, and was the first of a series of awards which were to be made annually by *The Motor Cyclist* magazine of Japan.

Continental European GPs

A mere eight days later John was taking part in the German Grand Prix at Hockenheim on Sunday 14 June. As he says: 'Thankfully, the meeting at Hockenheim took place in somewhat better weather and I had good races in the 350 and 500cc events, winning them both.' It was then on to the Dutch TT, where on Saturday 27 June he not only clinched the 500cc world title, winning from Bob Brown (Norton), Venturi (MV) and Dale (works

John Hartle was not only a great friend and teammate of John Surtees (at both Norton and MV Agusta), but he was also someone that John rated highly as a rider, likening Hartle's style to that of Geoff Duke. John Hartle was also responsible for probably saving John Surtees's life when the latter got into difficulties swimming in a Swedish lake during 1955.

John Hartle

Hailing from Chapel-en-le-Frith in the English Peak District, John Hartle was born in 1933. He was destined to become a teammate of John Surtees both at Norton and MV Agusta. He was, as John says, 'a true friend'.

For a couple of years after leaving school, Hartle took a job in a local garage where as he once said he was 'required to delve into the internals of cars and lorries'. His interest, however, lay more with two wheels than four, and with a certain degree of what he described as 'hero worship' Hartle visited various trials and scrambles in which local star Eric Bowers was competing.

The lure of motorcycle sport proved too strong to resist and so in 1950, then aged 17, he joined Bowers's Chapel-en-le-Frith dealership. By this time Bowers had retired from active competition, but was sponsoring a couple of road racers, including Eric Houseley; Hartle was recruited as a 'weekend race mechanic'. When Houseley subsequently won the 1952 Junior Clubman's TT on a BSA Gold Star, the young Hartle was there to look after the spanners and pitboard.

The following year, Hartle made his own race debut at Brough on a BSA single – alongside the likes of Houseley, Peter Davey and Ken Kavanagh (the latter on a factory Norton). In September 1953 John Hartle took part in the Manx Grand Prix on an AJS 7R in the Junior and a Manx Norton in the Senior. But after refuelling the 7R in around tenth position, he braked too hard at Quarter Bridge and ended up inspecting the tarmac at close quarters. However, he remounted to finish 21st. In the Senior race he brought the Norton home in 15th place and, as a result of two very respectable finishes, collected the Newcomer's Award.

Even better was to come the following year, when not only did Eric Bowers provide two new bikes, an AJS and a Norton, but after finishing third on the 7R in the 1954 Manx Grand Prix, he led the Senior race in awful weather until running out of fuel on the last lap, a major disappointment. He had also finished third behind Geoff Duke and Bob Keeler in the Hutchinson 100 at Silverstone.

These performances led to him being invited to join the Norton team alongside Jack Brett and John Surtees for 1955. A friendship started between the two John's that lasted until Hartle's fatal accident at Scarborough during September 1968. Hartle rode for Norton in 1955 and 1956, and in 1957 he had the use of a fully streamlined Norton machine.

There is no doubt that John Surtees was instrumental in getting his friend John Hartle as co-rider in the MV Agusta team for the 1958 season, a position which was retained for 1959. He rode for the Italian factory in the 1960 TT and

Hartle at Union Mills during the 1957 Junior TT. His flowing riding stance made him especially good at circuits such as the Isle of Man and Ulster Grand Prix.

John Hartle with his 350cc MV at the assembly area behind the grandstand at the 1958 Isle of Man TT. In the Junior a piston disintegrated at the Bungalow on the first lap, while in the Senior his machine caught fire and burnt out. This unfortunately was typical of the appalling bad luck this talented rider suffered while a member of the MV team.

was subsequently sacked, which John Surtees thought 'unjust'. There is no doubt that luck seemed to pass Hartle by during his MV days – he had more than his fair share of crashes, breakdowns and even a fire.

After MV John Hartle went back to racing as a privateer on his own Norton machinery. He was recalled as a works rider to the Scuderia Duke team riding four-cylinder Gileras in 1963. But this team disbanded at the end of that year and John returned to the ranks of the privateers. Even though by now John Surtees had quit bikes for cars, the two remained in touch. John Hartle tested John Surtees's desmo Ducati JSD twin during 1962-3. By the mid-1960s he had switched from Norton to Aermacchi, riding for importer Syd Lawton. In 1967 he set up a racing spares business, but he was fatally injured while racing at Scarborough the following year, aged 34.

Preparing for the start of the 1959 500cc German Grand Prix at Hockenheim with his teammate John Hartle (2). Other machinery in the picture includes a BMW Rennsport (5) and a Manx Norton (14).

BMW), but also set a new lap record. There was no 350cc round at Assen that year.

The Belgian Grand Prix at Spa Francorchamps on Sunday 5 July saw John again in winning form on his 500cc MV – again setting a new lap record, this time with a speed of 120.39mph. And again there was no 350cc Grand Prix event; as in Holland, this was due to Formula 1 races being staged. It was not until the Swedish GP at Kristianstad on 26 July that John Surtees made certain of the 350cc World Championship.

This left two rounds of both the 350cc and 500cc classes to be contested, in Ulster and Italy, even though John had already retained both titles. For once the hilltops above Belfast, the home of the 7.42-mile Dundrod circuit, were bathed in bright, warm sunshine for Saturday 8 August 1959 and the Ulster

John Surtees studies one of the MV fours he rode to a double victory in the 350cc/500cc races at the Ulster Grand Prix in 1959. Unchallenged, he averaged 91.32mph on the smaller bike and 95.28mph on the 500cc model.

Grand Prix. In the 350cc race, although John Surtees won, averaging 91.32mph for the 20-lap, 148.32-mile race, it was his MV teammate John Hartle who broke the class lap with a speed of 93.35mph. However, Hartle clouted the bank with his foot at Jordan's Cross, breaking a small bone and forcing him out. This meant that Hartle was a non-starter in the 500cc race, in which John Surtees not only won but also broke the lap record at 96.73mph.

Monza and a Spanish Farewell

As was usual MV practice for the home round at Monza, Italian riders were also put out on four-cylinder models. In this case Remo Venturi and Ernesto Brambilla were chosen. In the opening miles of the 350cc Italian Grand Prix on Sunday 6 September 1959, it was Brambilla who was second behind the flying Surtees. But then on lap two the Italian crashed at Vendano and Venturi took over the runner-up berth. Riding a rapid Jawa twin, Frantisek Stastny stuck to Venturi's wheel tracks for 11 laps before a broken rear wheel spindle sidelined the Czech entry. Surtees and Venturi ensured another MV one-two in the 500cc race later that day. In this race John set a new two-wheel lap record for the 3.57-mile Monza circuit at 119.2mph. The previous record had been set by Gilera's Libero Liberati at 118mph in the year when he became 500cc World Champion, 1957.

John Surtees receiving the main trophy of the day for winning the 500cc race on his four-cylinder MV from General Franco's wife, at Parque Del Retiro, Madrid, on 11 October 1959.

Instead of allowing John to take in the end of season British short circuit meetings on either his own private Nortons or works MVs, Count Agusta limited the Englishman to one final event in 1959 – a meeting in Spain at the Madrid circuit on Sunday 11 October. Staged in the honour of General Franco, it was held in the city's central park. Arriving early to inspect the course, John was not impressed: 'It was a typical park-style circuit. Polished by continuous traffic, it was largely made up of wet tar in the really hot weather.' John realised that it was potentially extremely slippery and there was one particular long left-hand curve which seemed even more treacherous than the rest. John noticed a grandstand was being constructed on the outside of this section of the course – just where a motorcycle could expect to go off the road if anything went wrong. When John enquired he was informed that this was a special stand for General Franco, his staff and his guests! After John had explained the potential danger, the organisers moved the grandstand slightly out of harm's way further round the corner.

When the race took place John, who was only entered in the 500cc event, found that the crowd had a nasty habit of coming on to the circuit en masse to get a better view. This dangerous practice continued to the end of each race. Luckily no one was hurt and a very relieved John Surtees won from teammate Carlo Bandirola, thus bringing the 1959 season to a close.

Crossing swords with the Count

During 1959 John had used his enthusiasm and engi-

THE 1959 CLASSICS

ITALIAN GRAND PRIX

SEPTEMBER 6, 1959

350 c.c.	500 c.c.
1st J. Surtees (M.V. Agusta)	1st J. Surtees (M.V. Agusta)
2nd R. Venturi (M.V. Agusta)	2nd R. Venturi (M.V. Agusta)
3rd R. Brown (Norton)	3rd G. Duke (Norton)
	Record lap J. Surtees 119.2 m.p.h.

125 c.c.	250 c.c.
1st E. Degner (M.Z.)	1st C. Ubbiali (M.V. Agusta)
2nd C. Ubbiali (M.V. Agusta)	2nd E. Degner (M.Z.)
3rd L. Taveri (Ducati)	Subject to official confirmation

won on **AVON** to-day's leading tyres

At the Italian GP at Monza on Sunday 6 September 1959 John scored yet another 350cc/500cc double for MV. Second place in both races went to teammate Remo Venturi, seen here at bottom left in the picture. John also raised the circuit lap record to 119.2mph.

neering skills to construct a couple of lightweight British singles. The 350cc was powered by an AJS 7R engine (described in detail in Chapter 8), while the 500cc featured a Manx Norton power unit and used a Weslake cylinder head; an MV front wheel was also fitted. However, due to Count Agusta's tough line that year, it was not possible for John to ride either bike at any meetings.

John was not happy with this situation and at the end of that year he had a long, but largely unproductive meeting with the Count in Italy. John recalls that the Count seemed unmoved by his senior rider's arguments, saying 'No, you will do World Championship events only', which on reflection John feels 'was partly due to the Italian press'. The result was that ultimately John Surtees would quit two wheels for four. It was also to mean that as there was now no chance of his racing the lightweight AJS and Norton specials, these were sold off. The AJS went to Rex Butcher, who rode it for a while before selling it on to Tom Arter, in whose care it found much fame as the Arter AJS, ridden notably by Peter Williams. The Norton was sold to Stan Hailwood for use by his son Mike.

In the summer of 1959 six million viewers of the popular BBC television feature *Sportsview* watched 'Let's go motorcycling with World Champion John Surtees'. John is seen here in action on a BSA Gold Star Clubman's machine at Oulton Park during filming of the programme.

The closed season of 1959–60 was one of award ceremonies and receiving trophies for John Surtees. He was also involved, when time allowed, with his motorcycle dealership at West Wickham. At the shop an interesting exhibition of AJS and Matchless products took place in mid-November 1959. There were two AJS Porcupine racers, a separate Porcupine engine on a plinth, sectioned Matchless twin and single-cylinder engines, including a sectioned gearbox and one of the very old models usually seen in the 'Pioneer Run' (the Vintage Motorcycle Club annual outing for Pioneer bikes) – a 1913 AJS.

On Thursday 3 December John was presented with the Sportsman of the Year award at the Sports Writers' Association annual ceremony at the Waldorf Hotel, London. This was the first time a motorcyclist had gained the award, the previous highest placing being Geoff Duke in fourth. Among John's rivals were many of the most famous sporting names of that era. Runner-up was Donald Campbell, the world's water-speed record holder, and third was Ronnie Dawson of Ireland, who captained the successful British Lions Rugby team which toured Australia, New Zealand and Canada. In the other positions were Arthur Rowe, British and European shot-put record holder, fourth; Stirling Moss, fifth; and Louis Martin, World Champion weightlifter, sixth.

Besides winning no fewer than three awards in Britain during 1959, John Surtees was also voted the Italian Sportsman of the Year, a fantastic achievement and proof of his great popularity at that time.

John pictured in December 1959 with the BBC Sportsman of the Year Award, his parents and younger sister Dorothy.

Then in mid-December John followed the Sports Writers' Award by winning the national Sportsman of the Year ballot organised by the *Daily Express* newspaper. In this ballot John led Stirling Moss, Brian Hewson (runner), Bobby Charlton and Dave Mackay (footballers) and Brian Phelps (diver). A week later John Surtees topped the votes in BBC Television's Sportsview Personality of the Year ballot, thus becoming holder of the three major British popularity titles. Before millions of viewers the double 1959 World Champion received the prestigious trophy from Sir John Hunt, leader of the Hillary-Tensing expedition which had conquered Everest in 1953.

One more year

As he entered 1960, John Surtees 'had more or less decided that I would continue racing motorcycles for one more season.' After that he would prob-

In 1960 John got his season under way with a couple of non-championship meetings in Italy. The second of these was at Imola on 25 April. He is seen here lapping a Norton rider on his way to victory in the 500cc race.

ably retire to concentrate on running the motorcycle business bearing his name, or he would put his engineering training to good use. However, as is recorded in Chapter 7, the germ of an idea had been sown at a Sportsman of the Year gathering towards the end of 1958 when he had shared a table with Mike Hawthorn and Tony Vandervell, among others. From this chance meeting was to come another career – motor racing.

However, before the start of the 1960 season, it was

Mike Hailwood

S.M.B. (Stanley Michael Bailey) Hailwood was born on 2 April 1940, the son of a self-made millionaire motorcycle dealer. His father Stan had competed pre-war on two, three and four wheels, before going on to build up the largest grouping of dealerships seen up to that time in Great Britain.

Mike Hailwood began his racing career aboard a 125cc MV Agusta under the watchful eye of his father and Bill Webster, a close friend of factory boss Count Domenico Agusta. This was at the Oulton Park circuit near Chester just after his 17th birthday. At the end of the 1957 season Stan packed his son off to South Africa, equipped with the ex-John Surtees 250cc NSU Sportmax and a 350cc Manx.

South Africa proved an excellent training ground and Mike came back not only with several wins, but also experience enough to score an incredible trio of British Championships (125, 250 and 350cc).

In 1959 Mike secured his first Grand Prix win on a 125cc Ducati (his father had become the firm's British importer). He also won all four British Championships – a feat he repeated the following year and one which no man before or since has equalled.

For 1961 Mike rode 125 and 250cc works Hondas, plus a 350cc 7R AJS and a 500cc Manx Norton. He gained his first world title, the 250cc, on the four-cylinder Honda, took the 125 and 250cc TTs and the 500cc on his Norton. On the latter machine he averaged over 100mph for the six-lap, 226-mile race. He then signed for MV Agusta and won the 500cc world title four years in a row (1962–1965). Mike rejoined Honda in 1966 and won both the 250 and 350cc classes on the new six-cylinder models, equalling this feat the following year before switching his attention to four wheels.

For more than a decade he largely stayed away from bikes (except for a couple of outings on BSA and Yamaha machines) before making an historic comeback TT victory on a Ducati V-twin in 1978. The following year, 1979, he rode a Suzuki to a final TT victory. Then he retired once more – becoming a partner in the

Hailwood & Gould bike business (with fellow World Champion Rod Gould) in Birmingham.

Mike died tragically in a road accident while driving his Rover car home after collecting a fish and chip supper in the spring of 1981.

Mike Hailwood largely followed in John Surtees's footsteps. He began young, progressed to dominate British short circuit events before becoming a works rider, became a motorcycle multi-World Champion, then drove cars including Team Surtees models. This photograph was taken at the beginning of his motorcycle career in the late 1950s.

Mike cranking over the 500cc MV Agusta at Mallory Park's Race of the Year, 26 September 1965. This is the final version of the heavyweight model developed by John Surtees during his time with the Italian company. The only major difference was a six instead of five-speed gearbox.

John Surtees in typically smooth style on his way to victory in the 500cc French GP at Clermont-Ferrand on 22 May 1960, the first round of the World Championship series.

motorcycles which really commanded John's attention and effort. As we have seen, Count Agusta's attitude drove a wedge between John Surtees and his motorcycle racing aspirations and enthusiasm for the sport. Except for a couple of early season Italian outings on the MVs before the World Championship rounds began at Cesenatico, a narrow street circuit, on 18 April and Imola a week later on 25 April, John's first racing in 1960 came on four wheels, not two, with outings at Goodwood (19 March), Oulton Park (2 April), Aintree (30 April) and Silverstone (14 May).

From then on during that year the name John Surtees in a programme could equally have meant bikes or cars. But in this chapter we are concerned with his final year of racing MV motorcycles. Compared to the 100 percent record of finishes and victories in the two previous years at this level, 1960 was not quite as good, even though once again he was to complete the year as double 350cc and 500cc World Champion.

The first of the 1960 World Championship rounds came at the French GP at Clermont-Ferrand; here John displayed his mastery of this difficult circuit by setting new lap records for both the 350cc and 500cc classes, at 75.49mph and 76.77mph respectively. But he didn't win both races, only the larger capacity event. In the 350cc class victory went to MV's new signing Gary Hocking on a 284.8cc (56.9 x 56mm) version of the 250cc twin-cylinder MV. John rode his usual four-cylinder model, which two-thirds of the way through the race went

Clermont-Ferrand.
Lap length: 5 miles.

Clermont-Ferrand in central France was a particularly sinuous circuit and not the easiest for the 500cc MV, but this made no difference to John – he still won the 500cc race and set a new lap record.

on to three cylinders. As *The Motor Cycle* reported, 'Finishing his 12th lap Surtees swung calmly to his pit with the MV engine firing on three. Furiously he and his team mechanic began to whip out the plugs. Luck ran badly for Surtees for the offending plug was the last to be removed.' Eventually he rejoined the race in fifth position, but even though he rode like a demon to get within striking distance of Hocking and Stastny (Jawa), the race ended a lap or two too early.

The 350cc MV had been improved for 1960, but it still struck problems. Before the French Grand Prix the engine had received a new cylinder head. However, glitches with the gear-change (caused by the movement of the peg which located the selector spring) brought selection problems in the Isle of Man, which followed the French round. In consequence during the TT the smaller four suffered when the exhaust valve seats retreated into the head and the valves no longer closed. This meant a loss of about 1,500rpm in top (fifth) gear. So in the Junior race John was forced to keep the engine buzzing at peak revs by staying in fourth gear. As he said when interviewed after the race: 'With a sick engine I knew I could not hope to hold John Hartle, but I don't believe in retiring unless I am forced to and so I kept pegging away for second place.' So, after setting a new Junior TT lap record on the Wednesday 15 June 1960, on his second lap in 22 minutes, 49.4 seconds (99.2mph), John was forced to accept the runner-up berth to teammate Hartle.

If he had wanted to go out in style, in what was destined to be his final TT race, Friday 17 June 1960 could not have been better. He set a new race

Doing carburation tests up on the Mountain during practice week of the 1960 Isle of Man TT series.

John leaps Ballaugh Bridge during the 1960 Junior TT. After setting a new class lap record of 99.2mph he was slowed by first and third gears jumping out of engagement due to selector troubles and the valve seat inserts in the new cylinder head also gave him trouble. Although the engine lost its edge, he still finished second behind teammate John Hartle.

average speed of 102.44mph and a fantastic record fastest lap (on lap 2) in 21 minutes, 45 seconds, a speed of 104.08mph. Even those folk rarely given to colourful expressions muttered words such as fabulous, fantastic and incredible.

The Motor Cycle race report dated 23 June 1960 was equally enthusi-astic: 'Friday's Senior was a spell-binder. The out-and-out speed, the sheer virtuosity of the champion, froze the imagination. Never before had a race demanded such unbroken concentration from every man, woman and child around the course. Yet Surtees, the golden boy, rode with his characteristic smoothness and finished relaxed and unruffled, his quiet smile suggesting he felt contentment more strongly than elation'.

John Hartle's MV contract as Surtees's teammate had not been renewed at the end of 1959, but MV asked Hartle to ride for them again at the 1960 TT. Hartle won the Junior for them, but was then dropped again. As a result he rode his private Nortons at Assen for the Dutch TT on Saturday 25 June. The weather, as was usually the case at Assen, was perfect. John Surtees recalls that 'my 350cc was going as well as I had ever known it to perform' and he beat his new teammate Gary Hocking with a record race average of 83.53mph. In doing so John regained the lead in the 350cc title stakes – he had scored a win, a second (TT) and a third (France). Then in the 500cc race, after setting the fastest lap, John struck problems. A blocked carbu-rettor jet caused his engine to misfire. He made one, two, three and finally four pit stops in an attempt to solve the problem and then took a tumble when attempting to make up lost ground. This left Remo Venturi to win on another four-cylinder MV.

At the Belgian Grand Prix at Spa Francorchamps on Sunday 3 July, there was no 350cc race. But this time the 500cc four ran perfectly and John won at a record average 120.53mph and also set a new lap record of 122.67mph; Venturi was second.

Then came what is probably a unique event in post-war motor sport. John participated in a world championship race on the 500cc MV (which he won) and in a car race with a Porsche Formula 2 (in which he retired) on the same day. This historic occasion took place in Germany at the Solitude circuit near Stuttgart on Sunday 24 July 1960. Unfortunately, this meeting was marred by a fatal accident to the Australian Bob Brown, who crashed while practising on a works four-cylinder Honda 250cc. So it was with sadness that John Surtees left Stuttgart, even though his win had ensured he had retained his 500cc world title.

Clinching the Championship

John always enjoyed taking part in the Ulster GP, but the meeting staged on Saturday 6 August 1960 saw John experience unexpected problems. In the 350cc race the 'problem' was the spirited riding of AJS-mounted Alan Shepherd, who put up a tremendous fight with Surtees for the lead. The gallant struggle ended on the seventh lap when the 7R's timing chain snapped. At the end of the race MV lodged a protest, complaining that the

During the 350cc Ulster GP John was pushed hard by AJS 7R rider Alan Shepherd (30), but Shepherd's gallant attempt was ended when his timing chain broke.

John's younger brother Norman also took part in motorcycle sport. At first this was off-road (trials and scrambling) but he later switched to tarmac. Norman is seen here on an AJS 7R at Brands Hatch in March 1961. John says Norman was not committed enough in his approach to the sport.

British single-cylinder engine was oversize. Yet when it was measured it was found to be exactly 349.209cc. John recalls: 'I was deeply disappointed that MV chose to challenge the size of the AJS engine. I had been telling them time and time again, and had shown them timing sheets to indicate that I had actually lapped faster than the MV with my own AJS special.' When Shepherd dropped out John won the race and thus took the 350cc title, making him double World Champion for the third year running.

In the 500cc Ulster GP John had to replace a broken gear lever and then fought back from 42nd place in the remaining 13 laps to finish runner-up behind old friend John Hartle (Norton). In the process he set a new lap record of 99.32mph.

Swansong

A loose megaphone and subsequent engine trouble on his 350cc four robbed John Surtees of an Italian Grand Prix double at Monza on Sunday 11 September 1960. He completed the afternoon in style with a win in the 500cc race, but even this didn't go according to plan. He fell after hitting oil at Vedano Curve, but like a true champion he got back aboard and still won.

Retirement

'Will He Quit?' asked the headline in *The Motor Cycle* on 15 September. But at that moment no retirement decision had been taken by John Surtees, even though it was thought that his father, for so long his trusted advisor, had told John he should switch from bikes to cars. When interviewed in the week following Monza, John had told journalists:

I think it is fair to say that in the five years I've been with MVs the three-fifty four has been my biggest disappointment. The machine is

so unpredictable. Reviewing the results of my rides on it during the past two or three years, it seems that progress has been totally absent. I tried the lighter version as well during practicing at Monza, but though it accelerated better I decided not to race it. It's low build gave rise to serious grounding on the bends and that kills a rider's confidence stone dead.

1960 Ulster GP. Although John Hartle (right) was back on his private Norton, he and John Surtees remained the best of friends as the photograph shows.

John also revealed that the MV factory had tried to do too much: 'Heaven knows we've had mechanical trouble enough this year.' He went on to say: 'Competing in all four solo classes, it is quite enough to aim at getting two machines to the grid in tip-top fettle for each race; anything more jeopardizes our chances.'

In the autumn of 1960 there were several reasons why John's retirement from motorcycling looked likely. First, after taking part in only a few events, he had shown real potential in car racing. Second, Count Agusta had done his best to upset John by pouring cold water over the World Champion's attempt to ride his own motorcycles, after John had spent a lot of the

Rhodesian Gary Hocking joined the MV team after some excellent GP results in 1959 aboard Norton and MZ machinery. His first race on a four came in the 1960 Dutch TT where he finished second behind John Surtees. After John quit bikes at the end of that year Hocking went on to become double MV World Champion in 1961.

previous winter building lightweight AJS and Norton machinery. Third, the Count had made tactical mistakes by refusing to allow John to race his own motorcycles, and by failing to exclude car racing from his number one rider's contract.

After Monza John departed to North America to see through a car racing commitment. Then everything went quiet until early December when he finally announced that he was 'for definite retiring from motorcycle racing'. The reasons he gave were as follows:

1. MV's insistence that machines would only be available for the Grand Prix, and that John should not ride his private bikes on the home circuits. This was not to John's liking as he 'loved his racing'.
2. Initially, it was agreed that MVs would be available for lesser meetings and entries were made. But often machines were not forthcoming and spectators were let down at a lot of tracks. This upset John in a big way. John also feels 'it would have been nice to have had the opportunity to ride a 250cc (MV)'.
3. A general lack of planning. Believing himself free of commitments for MV, John made arrangements to go to the United States Grand Prix to race a Lotus-Climax car. Four days before he was due to leave a telegram arrived from Italy to say MVs were competing at Syracuse and that he was wanted to ride.
4. The straw which broke the camel's back. John telephoned Italy to query the Syracuse decision, but though there was no international opposition in the Syracuse race, Agusta insisted that he ride. John went to America. Since then he had tried to contact the Count but without success. That being so, he felt that a decision to retire had to be made. As he said in *The Motor Cycle* dated 15 December 1960: 'That being so, I felt that a decision to retire could no longer be delayed. There has been no split, no harsh words – no words in fact'.

So John took up a new challenge and ultimately repeated what he had achieved on two wheels by winning the World Championship in the blue riband of the sport, Formula 1. John Surtees carved his special place in history. But for Count Domenico Agusta's autocratic rule this might never have happened. Even so it is important to note that John's relationship was still good with the Agusta family. He was the only ex-rider ever to be given a four-cylinder racing machine, though it took many years to arrive. The promise was first made in 1960 and the Count also offered to build a Grand Prix car 'if I would resign'. But John quit. The bike (a 350cc) was eventually sent by Corrado Agusta in 1980.

Chapter 7

Quitting two wheels for four

ALTHOUGH it might not be obvious today, high-speed motorcycling was in years gone by the breeding ground for many of the greatest names in the four-wheel world, certainly in the first half of the 20th century. Tazio Nuvolari, probably the greatest Grand Prix driver of all time, began his career on two wheels. So did his compatriot, Achille Varzi, a pre-war Champion of Europe in the car world and post-war member of the invincible Alfa Romeo works' team. The same went for Bernd Rosemeyer, who as the star of the Auto Union GP squad up to his death in 1938, not only kept the upper hand over a 600bhp/1-ton car, but actually and incredibly made it look easy. There were other notable names too: Ernst Henne, for many years the fastest man on earth on two wheels; Georg Meier, the first foreign winner of the Senior TT on a foreign bike (and also the fastest TT winner of the inter-war years); and Sir Malcolm Campbell, the greatest of all record breakers on both land and water.

But since World War Two and the advent of World Championship racing, only one man has become champion on both two and four wheels – John Surtees.

Raymond Mays, that great racing driver of the inter-war period and forever connected with the ERA and BRM marques, called the connection between getting the best from both bikes and cars 'adhesion sense'. As explained earlier in this book, John Surtees had the talent to get the best out of whatever car (or motorcycle) he had at the time, and he had an immense sympathy for his machinery. But most important of all, and the real reason for his greatness on both two and four wheels, was the combined skill of braking and getting on the power again – in other words the changeover from deceleration to acceleration. He also had the ability to learn circuits quickly. With these great gifts he was always a leading competitor. They also meant that he had the minimum of crashes and mechanical failures during his long career.

Interestingly, when the first mention of racing cars came up – at the 1958 Sportsman of the Year awards evening when John found himself in the company of the Formula 1 World Champion Mike Hawthorn, Vanwall boss Tony Vandervell and Aston Martin team manager Reg Parnell – he simply replied 'No, no, no… that's not for me. I'm a motorcyclist.' However, this response didn't stop both Tony Vandervell and Reg Parnell leaving open invitations to try their respective cars – Vanwall and Aston Martin.

John had purchased his first car, a Jowett Jupiter, back in the days of his Vincent apprenticeship at Stevenage. Later came a Porsche 356 Super 'a fabulous little machine', an Aston Martin DB2/4 and then a BMW 507 (which he still owns to the present day, saying: 'I'm still very fond of it and it holds many special memories'). So John was not new to cars, just new to racing them. However, after that Sportsman of the Year evening at the end of 1958, he honestly never thought about the idea of switching camps. Instead he got on with what he knew best, racing motorcycles, which in his case were the Italian MV Agustas.

Then one day in October 1959 he received a phone call from Reg Parnell asking if he would like to come down to Goodwood and have a run in the Aston Martin DBR1 which Stirling Moss had used to win the Nürburgring 1,000 kilometres event. John, together with his MV teammate John Hartle: 'hopped into my BMW507 and went off to Goodwood, a circuit which I had never seen before, one morning a few weeks later.' And after successfully completing some 30 laps and 'Almost before I had climbed out of the car, Reg Parnell was at my elbow saying "Right, we would like you to sign a contract to drive next year". But my reaction was still as it had been at the awards evening.'

Even so more tests were arranged and John continued to fend off Reg Parnell's attentions. When Tony Vandervell got to hear of these sessions, he asked John to make another trip to Goodwood, this time to try the Vanwall F1. John remembers it as 'a big car' and he was 'very impressed with the whole Vanwall organisation'. The design of the Vanwall had a strong motorcycle connection. The cars were powered by what was, in effect, four single-cylinder Norton motorcycle engines that had been combined into one unit. This arrangement had been conceived by Leo Kusmicki, the Norton works engineer, while Tony Vandervell was a Norton director.

During a meeting in late 1959 John told Count Domenico Agusta 'that, since he didn't seem to want me to race other bikes outside the World Championship series, I would start driving cars.' This is the point where John's four-wheel racing career really started. After much thought, on 19 January 1960, he went to visit John Cooper at his Surbiton, Surrey factory and 'ordered a Formula 2 Cooper-Climax for £2,437'. Then came the task of obtaining an RAC competitions licence – his motorcycle one being of no use for this new form of motorsport. At this stage Ken Tyrrell became involved – he offered John a drive in a Formula Junior Cooper-Austin. Ken had been at the Cooper works when John had made his visit because of his interest in the budding car racer.

John's debut in Tyrrell's car came at Goodwood on 19 March 1960, when he took runner-up spot behind Jim Clark (works Lotus-Ford) in the Formula Junior event. Through successes in the Ken Tyrrell car and John's own F2 Cooper-Climax, came the offer of a Formula 1 drive from Lotus team boss, Colin Chapman, even though the Lotus team's number one driver Innes Ireland was said to be 'none too keen' because he was somewhat fearful of the new driver's potential.

John's first outing in the F1 car came at Silverstone on 14 March 1960, where John was 'sidelined from this race by a leaking oil filter'. Then on 29 May came the really big one, John's F1 World Championship Grand Prix debut drive, at no less a venue than Monaco. This, John reveals, was 'quite an experience because although I had taken part in the occasional bike race on street circuits, I had never encountered anything like the challenge of the Mediterranean principality.' Gearbox gremlins and some engine problems during practice meant a poor grid position and a retirement in the race after 19 laps due to final drive failure.

It is important to point out that this car racing was going on side-by-side with John's contractual outings in the World Motor Cycle Championships on 350 and 500cc MV Agustas. For example, immediately after Monaco John went back to the Isle of Man for two weeks of practice and racing in the TT.

The next outing for the Lotus F1 team came at the British GP at Silverstone on 16 July and, although qualifying only eleventh (due to a persistent misfire, caused by chafed plug leads), John finished what can only be described as a brilliant second to Jack Brabham's Cooper-Climax. This was only John's second World Championship event, and in the process he beat his teammate Innes Ireland.

On 14 August it seemed that John might go one better, when he qualified in pole position for the Portuguese Grand Prix at the Oporto road circuit. He built up a lead of almost half a minute, in a field which included Innes Ireland, Jim Clark and Stirling Moss in identical cars, and it looked as though he was on course for a victory that would have been a sensational one for someone so new to F1. However, it was not to be. A slight leak from the Lotus's petrol tank had allowed fuel on to the soles of John's shoes.

During 1960 John Surtees began his four-wheel racing career driving Lotus, Cooper and Porsche cars, together with his World Championship motorcycle duties with MV Agusta. The following year, 1961, he concentrated on the Cooper T53-Climax 4 shown here.

When he braked the front wheels locked up and the resulting incident split open the water radiator. The chance of victory and glory passed by.

The combined car and motorcycle racing season continued, with John winning both the 350 and 500cc bike world titles for MV. John admits now that he did not realise the 'mood of aggravation between the Count and myself over his decision not to let me ride my own bikes'. At the end of the year, after another meeting with the Count, John decided to retire from motorcycle racing after a decade of achievement. The story of the behind-the-scenes events is covered in Chapter 6.

In 1961 John competed solely on four wheels and, except for an outing at Silverstone on 6 May where John at last drove a Vanwall, the season was taken up with the Cooper T53-Climax 4. He decided not to drive for Lotus, even though they had offered him number one position in the team, because of 'political problems' with Innes Ireland. Apart from a win at Goodwood in the Glover Trophy on 3 April and fifth places in the Belgian and German Formula 1 Grand Prix, 1961 was destined to be a major disappointment. As John candidly admits: 'I made the wrong decision'.

Then came 1962 and a switch to the Lola Mk4-Climax. The first part of the season featured a host of retirements. Then came some good mid-season Formula 1 results, including runner-up in both the British and German Grand Prix. Unfortunately more mechanical failures followed, including valve and piston problems in Grand Prix events. More successful were the outings in a Ferrari 250GTO in sports car events, including second place with Mike Parkes in the Paris 1,000-kilometre race on 21 October.

Ferrari

During the course of the 1962 season John had received an approach from Ferrari, via Keith Ballisat of the Shell Oil Company. John had declined an invitation to visit Maranello the previous year. At the time John felt the idea of meeting Enzo Ferrari solo was: 'a bit too daunting'. When he eventually did go to meet Mr Ferrari he found 'a sort of old world atmosphere which immediately reminded me of Count Agusta's office in Gallarate'. A few months later came a second meeting with Enzo Ferrari 'in a different location and with a different atmosphere'. John began to feel that he might be 'part of the team'.

John's 1963 Ferrari season actually got under way in March, not in a Formula 1 car, but instead at the American Sebring 12-Hours, which he won with co-driver Lodovico Scarfiotti in a 250P. This victory came after their original car had been 'taken over' by fellow driver Willy Mairesse. This was the first time John experienced the politics behind the racing at Ferrari, in particular the problems created by team manager Eugenio Dragoni.

Driving a Ferrari 156 (a 1.5-litre V6) in the 1963 Formula 1 series, John showed his potential, including a victory in the German GP at the Nürburgring, second in the British GP (Silverstone), third in the Dutch GP (Zandvoort) and fourth in Monaco. However, a series of retirements – in Belgium (injection feed pipe), France (fuel pump), Italy (piston), United States (valve spring), Mexico (excluded) and South Africa (con-rod) – ruined his championship prospects.

1964 was the year when John achieved one of his greatest ambitions – to add a motor racing World Championship to the seven he had won on two wheels. Yet he now admits that 'in some ways it was a year which I wanted to forget.' In fact, it was a time of tremendous frustration and as John says, 'a year in which many things went wrong which had no right to go wrong and, more significantly, could have been avoided.' John felt that 'once again, too much was being attempted [by Ferrari] for the resources available. There was simply not the manpower – or, I now realise, money – available to run an intensive F1 and sports prototype programme, without one or the other suffering from lack of attention.' And, if all this was not enough, there was also the continuing irritation of 'Ferrari politics', which, in the author's opinion, probably made the trouble John had encountered at MV Agusta pale into insignificance. Finally, there was the saga of the V8 engine. John still feels that Ferrari 'should have gone straight from the V6 to the flat 12'. However, the decision had been made and he had to do the best he could with the V8. As history records, John's early season F1 record of one finish (second in Holland) and three retirements from the first four rounds of the

After finishing fourth in both the 1962 and 1963 Formula 1 World Championships, in 1964 John made history by becoming F1 Champion. He is seen here in that year's Ferrari 158 car, having become the only man to have won the world title on both two and four wheels.

1964 F1 World Championship shows that the new car was far from championship material.

Third place in the home round at Brands Hatch in mid-July was encouraging. But at the Nürburgring on 2 August 1964 John's championship aspirations really came alive. He set pole position and went on to an impressive race victory. A slight set-back occurred in Austria later in August when he retired when leading with suspension breakage. Then came another victory, this time at Monza on 6 September, followed by the runner-up spot in the two remaining races – in the US and Mexican GPs in October. The Mexican result gave him the Formula 1 World Crown, and he became the first and only man in history to win the ultimate championship titles, on both two and four wheels.

Thereafter John's career with Ferrari went largely downhill. However, there were some successes too, because unlike Count Agusta, Enzo Ferrari did not object to John 'racing in the classes we don't make cars for'. It may come as something of a shock to many readers to discover that John 'wasn't earning much money with Ferrari', and this was another reason for him to drive other people's cars. In 1965 he excelled in the Lola T60-Cosworth and Lola T70-Chevrolet. The Lolas were campaigned on both sides of the Atlantic and John won at Oulton Park, Mosport Park, Brands Hatch and Ste Jovite. There were no wins in F1 for John Surtees in 1965, the best result being a third in the British round. Then on Friday 25 September that year, while practicing at Mosport Park in the Lola T70-Chevrolet, as John says: 'a twist of fate brought me face to face with the most serious accident it had ever been my misfortune to encounter.' This came while John was trying out Jackie Stewart's Lola T70. He says: 'I remember climbing into the car, but recall nothing more until about four days later'. The crash was caused by losing a front wheel, due to an upright failure. He had suffered spinal injuries, a broken pelvis and a ruptured kidney.

The results of this accident were to be far reaching, even though his condition was a lot better than had first been feared when the accident occurred. John was able to leave London's St Thomas's hospital early in 1966, but the effects of the accident were to be with him for many years to come.

After a convalescent holiday with his wife Pat (whom he had married in 1962), John returned to Ferrari in Italy for discussions. As he says, 'The Italians may have their strange ways, but the honest and sincere manner in which I was greeted on my return to Maranello gave me a great boost.'

The accident did bring about a slight change in John's feelings about the dangers of racing. After the crash he began to worry more about mechan-

ical failure, which had not bothered him when he was racing bikes. Like most racers, John had always felt that a serious accident was unlikely to happen to him, although he did take the dangers seriously enough to try to reduce the risks to a minimum – through careful machine preparation and a thorough knowledge of the capabilities of both the bike/car and himself.

1966 was the year when the new 3-litre F1 regulations came into force. Ferrari's new 312 F1 car was powered by a V12 engine. Although everyone at the company said it would 'go', it didn't. For example, when testing John was 2½ seconds slower around the Modena circuit than in the 2.4-litre V6-engined 1965 car which had been prepared to take to the Tasman series in Australia and New Zealand.

The first part of the season saw not only problems with the car, but also within Ferrari. John puts it like this: 'In any normal company, I feel I could have sorted everything out on a man-to-man basis, but Ferrari, with all its intrigue, was not a normal company and the only way to resolve the problem in such a situation was to make a clean break of it, no matter how much it hurt in the short term.' Again team manager Dragoni hadn't helped the situation and in fact, as John says, 'he had been busy for some time trying to undermine my position'. The result was 'the divorce of Ferrari and myself' which, as John puts it, 'brought to an end a very special period in my life'. He did, however, have the satisfaction of winning in his last Ferrari F1 race, with the 312, at the Belgian GP on 12 June 1966.

Immediately after leaving Ferrari, John received an approach from Roy Salvadori on behalf of the Cooper-Maserati team, Salvadori having been a teammate in the Bowmaker Lola days. In the seven remaining rounds of the 1966 F1 title hunt, John suffered retirements in four races, but he won the final race (the Mexican GP), was second in the German GP and third in the US GP; discounting the DNFs, this was impressive stuff. Once John's Ferrari win in the Belgian GP is included, the final 1966 Surtees F1 scorecard reads: two wins, one second, one third and five retirements. He was second in the World Championship. In addition John won that year's Can-Am sports car series in North America driving a Lola.

Honda

Then came John's next big move, to Honda. During the final round of the 1966 F1 season, at the Mexican GP, John had 'first made the acquaintance of Honda's Yoshio Nakamura'. Honda had first appeared on the F1 scene in mid-1964 at the German GP with a car driven by Ronnie Bucknum. Then in 1965 they mounted a full-blown effort and were rewarded when their driver Richie Ginther won the Mexican GP, the last event held under the 1.5-

litre regulations. Things didn't go well with the new 3-litre V12-engined car the following year. Quite simply, although the engine put out 320bhp, the car weighed in at a mammoth 600kg. Nakamura felt that the company was about to pull the plug on its F1 effort, but might be dissuaded if John would agree to join them and 'run the car on their behalf'.

John joined Honda in 1967. The car shown here is the RA301 introduced for the 1968 season and it is seen in that year's Belgian Grand Prix. The car was designed by ex-Cooper engineer Derrick White and Honda's Soicho Sano, and had a slightly revised V12 engine.

There is little doubt that John's decision to join Honda was heavily influenced by what the Japanese company had achieved in motorcycle racing. He also imagined he would be free of the Ferrari style political infighting. Unfortunately, he was to be proved wrong on both counts. First, Honda was very much in the infancy of its car involvement and in addition, the car team had financial pressures on them that the motorcycle division had not experienced in its drive towards the top. For example, there were no facilities (or budget) to rebuild engines at the Surtees headquarters in Slough, England, so these had to be air-freighted back to Japan for their scheduled overhauls. But John is full of praise for key Honda personnel: 'They are engineers running an engineering company, rather than accountants.' He goes on to say 'I used to fume when Honda seemed to turn over staff so quickly on the F1 project, but from their viewpoint, in terms of getting the necessary experience into the company, they did themselves an immense amount of good.' With the benefit of hindsight it is clear that Honda were actually *learning* the technology of the car world, whereas in the bike world they had *created* it.

As a consequence John's ability to win races for Honda was compromised from the start. Even so in his first race for the Japanese company, the South African GP at Kyalami, he took his RA273 V12 to third place (though the car finished with a serious misfire). Then came a trio of mechanical retirements in Monaco, Holland and Belgium, which effectively ruined any chances he might have had. The new RA300 debuted at Monza in September 1967 and John outsprinted Jack Brabham's Brabham-Repco to the finish line to score what was to turn out to be his only Honda F1 victory.

As far as John was concerned he 'personally had no doubt that we had been promised some new developments for the start of the 1968 season'. Unfortunately the major development was an oil/air-cooled V8 (the car being coded RA302), which proved a major failure because of serious overheating problems. Even worse was the fact that the V8 signalled the end of development for a lightweight and compact V12 – which was really what John wanted. The whole sad episode effectively killed off the entire Honda F1 programme. As John recalls 'All in all, I was very disheartened. I'd spent two more years of my career putting together something which I looked on rather in the way I'd regarded Ferrari: the team with which I would stay for the rest of my career. Now it was over and I had to look elsewhere.'

From Honda, John went to BRM. Based in Bourne, Lincolnshire, BRM (British Racing Motors) had been created in the immediate post-war period to further British racing prestige. But by the time John joined the team 'morale was pretty low'. Although the BRM V12 engine produced considerable power, out on the circuit John found this power disappearing as a race progressed and this, coupled with a number of gearbox problems, restricted results during the 1969 season. And again there were political reasons why things did not go well. So John decided that he 'wasn't going to get involved in anybody else's Formula 1 projects and, since the Surtees TS5 was going pretty well in F5000, we decided to take the plunge for 1970 and build our own Grand Prix car.'

Team Surtees was largely born out of a partnership with Eric Bradley and Lola Racing, whereby Team Surtees had a contract to test, develop and race Lola products. It began in 1965 with the T70s and later went on to include the F2 T100 car, which ran in 1967, using Cosworth FVA and BMW-Apfelbeck radial-valve engines. But as John reveals: 'I got involved in race car manufacture totally by mistake'. Film star James Garner, who was keen to establish a Formula 5000 team, asked Team Surtees to help him. The original idea was that Garner would operate a race team and market the cars in the US, Len Terry of Leda Cars would build the cars and Team Surtees would act as agents and look after the test programme.

Then it transpired that Leda Cars simply wasn't sufficiently capable of carrying out their part of the agreement to a high enough standard – for example, various brackets and components failed. So John ended up taking over the basic Leda design and subsequently developing it into the Surtees TS5 (Team Surtees 5000). Initially, it was intended to build a batch of 12 TS5s, but in the event around 25 were made and they were, as John says, 'pretty successful'. One of the Lola drivers competing against Team Surtees was eight-times World Motorcycle Champion, Mike Hailwood. After Mike suffered a catalogue of problems, John spoke to him saying 'Come on Mike, let's get together. We'll understand you', and eventually Hailwood was persuaded to join the Surtees squad to drive the new TS8 F5000 car for 1971.

Of course, Mike and his father Stan were no strangers to John Surtees – they had known each other for many years. In addition, Mike had followed in John's wheeltracks at MV Agusta. Both Mike and John were great competitors, but in terms of personality they were vastly different. For example, whereas John was described as being 'as cold as ice' before a race, Mike was someone who, as John recalls, was 'a bag of nerves before the start'. John feels that Mike's reputation as a 'man-about-town' largely stemmed from the fact that 'had he lain in bed, he would have sweated himself to pieces'.

John found that working with Mike 'brought a certain simplicity and honesty' – qualities that, it has to be said, were often lacking within the car fraternity, where personalities and politics often ruled. This side of the motor racing world was something John found difficult to come to terms with during his four-wheel career, as both driver and constructor.

John describes Mike in the following terms: 'Very honest, so you could work with him, but you needed to understand Mike and the vehicle and put them *together* to get the best result'. Also Mike had 'the ability to carry through what he had started'. One has only to study photographs of Mike and John together to realise that they were at ease in each other's company. If truth be known, their collaboration was probably one of John's best moments in the car world.

The first Surtees F1 car, the TS7-Cosworth, had made its debut in the British Grand Prix at Brands Hatch on 18 July 1970, retiring due to oil pressure problems. It wasn't until the new TS9 arrived for the 1971 season that real progress was made in Formula 1. 1971 was also the first year of Mike Hailwood's Team Surtees racing campaign, so not only was John driving in Formula 1, he was also overlooking Mike's activities.

Hailwood's 1972 European Formula 2 winning season was also John's final year of driving. As he says: 'I gradually wound down my own competitive driving because the pressure of trying to run the company as well meant

At the Saltzburgring in 1972, the 'dream team' of John Surtees and Mike Hailwood (right), both driving for Team Surtees. John's final race was at Oulton Park on 16 September in a Surtees TS10-Hart car.

Hailwood (1) leading the Shell F2 race at Imola on 23 July 1972.

Mike Hailwood in the Surtees TS14-Cosworth during the Formula 1 Italian GP at Imola, 10 September 1972. Although John and Mike were different in terms of personality, John says 'we got on very well and he brought a certain simplicity and honesty to the team'. They could also share their two-wheel experiences, which other members of the car racing fraternity could not.

that I could no longer be so dedicated to the business behind the wheel.' In retrospect, John's final driving season was more about testing his products than actually racing them, which included the new TS14, the prototype of the 1973 Formula 1 car. Nonetheless, the season included wins in Formula 2 with the Surtees TS10-Hart car at Mount Fuji, Japan and Imola, Italy. These victories came 24 years after he had clambered aboard his father's sidecar for his first competitive outing in the Trent Park speed trials at Cockfosters, North London. However, luck wasn't always with Team Surtees – for example, there was Jody Scheckter's crash at Woodcote on the first lap of the 1973 British Grand Prix at Silverstone, which wrecked all the Surtees cars and gave John a massive headache. Another problem during the mid and late 1970s was John's health, which became more and more of a concern as the decade progressed. It was also increasingly difficult to raise enough money from sponsors for each season.

In fact it was a failed sponsorship deal which was to cause the demise of Team Surtees. The deal concerned was with the Danish company Bang and Olufsen, and on the strength of it a new factory was built. But when the sponsorship was not forthcoming, the team was placed under such severe financial pressure that it eventually floundered. John recalls that 'Partly as a consequence, perhaps, of all the stress, my health problems came to a head in 1978 – the result being a 12-week stay in hospital.'

The end came for Team Surtees when the organi-

John and Mike Hailwood with the Brooke Bond Oxo publicity girls, in 1972. Sponsorship, or lack of it, was to be the downfall of the Team Surtees constructors team.

A smiling John Surtees shakes hands with Duckham's Competition Manager Ron Carnell (left) to conclude another sponsorship deal for Team Surtees.

The Team Surtees factory in Edenbridge, Kent. Its owner is seen inspecting the front end of a TS14 car, bottom left of picture. Note the use of a Ford V8 engine.

sation's 'position' in F1 was sold to Frank Williams. As John says: 'With the funds realised from that, we basically managed to save Team Surtees. The company eventually paid every single creditor by 1984, six years after we last raced in a Grand Prix.' And so came to an end the motorsport career of one of its greatest figures. However, this, as future pages reveal, was far from the end for John Surtees himself and, recharged, he emerged into the world of classic cars and classic motorcycles with an unbridled enthusiasm which continues to the present day.

Honda

Soichiro Honda was born on 17 November 1906, the eldest son of the village blacksmith in Komyo, long since swallowed up by the urban sprawl of modern-day Hamamatsu. From these humble beginnings was to emerge a man who would, like John Surtees, achieve huge success with both two and four-wheel vehicles.

Honda's first motorcycle was produced in the aftermath of World War Two, thanks to a cache of 500 ex-Japanese War Department stationary petrol engines, which had been used by the military authorities to power small generators. Soon he was overwhelmed with orders and the 500 engines rapidly ran out, so to meet demand, Soichiro Honda set out to design and build his own engine. From then on expansion was rapid, even though in 1953 he was almost forced out of business by cash flow problems. By the end of the 1950s Honda had become the world's largest motorcycle manufacturer – a position the company has retained to the present day.

In 1959 Honda sent a team of riders to compete in the Isle of Man TT, winning the team prize in the process. By 1961 their machines were good enough to win the 125 and 250cc World Championships. Honda usually dominated the smaller motorcycle classes in Grand Prix events until they retired at the end of 1967.

Honda's ventures into the four-wheel world – their first production car, the S500, was launched in 1962 – received considerable publicity in the west, thanks to their participation in the Formula 1 World Championship series. Their first racing car, which debuted in the 1964 German Grand Prix, featured a 1.5-litre, V12 engine producing 215bhp. There is also no doubt that their choice of American drivers Ronnie Bucknum and Richie Ginther was influenced by commercial considerations. Ginther gave Honda its F1 victory in the 1965 Mexican Grand Prix, the last event for the 1.5-litre formula, which was succeeded by a 3-litre formula for 1966.

1967 saw John Surtees join the Japanese company as its number one driver. At first he drove the RA273. This was followed towards the end of the season by the new RA300, with which John scored a brilliant debut victory at Monza in September that year. For 1968 the RA300 was replaced by the troublesome RA301. A poor record of car reliability saw John Surtees quit Honda at the end of that season. John was expecting great things from Honda following their huge success with the Grand Prix motorcycles. Unfortunately, it was not until many years later that Honda really produced the goods on four wheels, both with its range of series production cars and its Formula 1 power units.

F1 driver John Watson, John Surtees and the Duke of Edinburgh at Silverstone, in 1975.

Chapter 8

Reborn

AFTER he had retired from active competition in 1972, John Surtees MBE (awarded in November 1961) had put his full effort into making a success of Team Surtees. However, as he now recalls: 'that period taught me a great deal about the frustrations of going racing and not being able to follow the path you believe in because of commercial considerations'.

Team Surtees did produce some very competitive cars, but in the final analysis it was never able to reach its full potential – for purely financial reasons. The end came after John was able to take stock of himself when forced to have a period in hospital to put right the after-effects of the serious crash he had suffered years earlier at Mosport Park in Canada during September 1965. The effects of this accident, together with the stress of running Team Surtees, conspired to wear him down during 1977 and 1978. There is no doubt that this period was the lowest point of John Surtees's motorsport career. He once confessed: 'The team had taken virtually everything I had ever earned in motor sport but, more importantly, I hadn't been able to do it as I believed it should have been done.'

After all the pain and heartache of problems surrounding the demise of Team Surtees and a lengthy stay in hospital in 1978, John Surtees (seen here with Giacomo Agostini) was to find that two wheels was the key to a rebirth of his fortunes as the 1980s dawned. His first ride came on a four-cylinder MV Agusta in the newly introduced Isle of Man TT parade lap in 1979.

Mike Hailwood and Ducati factory mechanic Oscar Folesani at Silverstone getting ready to test the brand new 250 Desmo twin in early April 1960. The machine had just arrived in Britain from the Italian factory.

The JSD Project

The JSD (John Surtees Ducati) saga came about following John's disposal of the remaining motorcycle stock from his West Wickham dealership in 1961 to the Kings of Oxford organisation, headed by Stan Hailwood. Part of the payment was made up by various bikes and spares which Stan Hailwood had commissioned Ducati to build for his son Mike.

These motorcycles, of 249.7cc (55.25 x 52mm) and 349cc (64 x 54mm), were desmodromic dohc parallel twins. The first machine to arrive in England, in late March 1960, had been a 250cc which was taken to Silverstone for testing almost immediately. Even though Mike Hailwood was to make a victorious debut on this bike at Silverstone on Saturday 9 April, and in the process take the prestigious Mellano Trophy for a second year, the design was not without its problems.

The work of Ducati's chief designer, Ing. Fabio Taglioni, the 250 Desmo twin put out 37bhp at the rear wheel (equivalent to 43.3bhp at the crankshaft), at 11,600rpm; both it and its 350cc brother featured a six-speed transmission. At the time of its introduction the 250cc Ducati was the most powerful quarter-litre four-stroke racer around. But, unfortunately, it had a trio of major drawbacks.

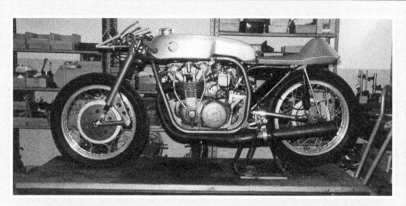

The JSD (John Surtees Ducati) was constructed in the closed season of 1961/2 with a Reynolds frame and leading link front fork. There were both 250cc and 350cc versions.

First, the design needed at least a year's development on the race circuit with the full support of the factory; second, it was at least 50lb overweight; and third, to quote Mike, 'It was the fastest five-bar gate in the world.' The best results gained by Mike on the 250 Desmo twin in the World Championship had been fourth places in Belgium and Ulster. Reflecting on the Ulster result in *The Motor Cycle* at the time, John Surtees commented: 'Mike Hailwood's Ducati twin was a bit disappointing. As with the MZs I think it is wrong to hang a Manx Norton front fork to a lightweight frame; it doesn't help the power-to-weight ratio even if it is a good stop-gap where handling is concerned. The Ducati has stacks of power but the machine as a whole is too bulky; it needs paring down to make better use of the power.'

The Desmo twin-cylinder engine, like other Ducati power units, carried its oil in a sump below the crankcase, which in John's view 'creates a somewhat tall engine'. The multi-World Champion set out to cure this by enlisting the help of Reynolds Tubes (with whom he had worked closely on the lightweight AJS project). John suggested 'a detachable lower-run frame tube on one side' (as on his MV four). But Ken Sprayston of Reynolds came up with a design which was similar to a Norton Featherbed frame, but with one vital difference. There was no bottom offside frame tube. Instead the right loop was bent across the frame in front of the crankcase and was welded to the nearside (left) tube. A similar procedure was followed at the rear, with the right tube bent across to meet the left tube behind the gearbox. Main frame material was 1¼in diameter 18 gauge tube, plus a rear sub frame in ¾in diameter and 17 gauge material.

Steering was by a Reynolds leading link fork of the type pioneered by Geoff Duke during the late 1950s for his privately entered Nortons. John Surtees purchased a total of three frames, although he had, in fact, received a total of four machines (two 250s and two 350s). He carried out much of the testing himself during late 1961 and early 1962 at Brands Hatch and Silverstone.

Brother Norman raced the 250 version throughout 1962 at venues all over the UK, including Brands Hatch and Cadwell Park; Fred Neville also raced an original-framed 250cc in the summer of 1961, before his death in the Manx GP that September.

For 1963 John had hoped his former Norton and MV teammate John Hartle would race both the 250 and 350 JSDs that year. Tests did take place, but the plan fell through when Hartle signed to race the Scuderia Duke Gilera fours.

By now John's four-wheel career was gathering pace and although other riders were linked with the JSDs, eventually he ran out of time and the whole project ground to a halt. The machines were sold off over a number of years, the final deal being done with a German enthusiast during the early 1980s.

John riding one of the last of the 500cc four-cylinder MVs from the mid-1970s in the 1982 Isle of Man TT parade lap...

(Inset) ...a similar machine with the fairing removed. This was very much the lightweight four-cylinder machine that John had envisaged at the end of the 1950s.

John Surtees riding his 998cc Vincent V-twin at the Old Timers meeting at the Saltzburgring in 1981. The other machine in the picture is a 500cc BMW flat twin being piloted by the late Walter Zeller.

But every cloud has a silver lining; in John Surtees's case there were two. First, if he hadn't gone into St Thomas's Hospital he would never have met Jane, who was a sister on the ward during his stay there. He married Jane in 1986 (his first marriage having ended in the 1970s). Together they produced a new 'team': Edwina (born 9 November 1987), Leonora (born 25 May 1989) and Henry John (born 18 February 1991). Today the two girls are very much involved with horses, while Henry John has already followed

Surtees lightweight AJS

As is revealed in the main text, John Surtees would probably have continued to race motorcycles rather than switch to cars had Count Agusta allowed him to race his own privately owned machines in 1959 and 1960. These machines would have been Norton (500) and AJS (350). The latter machine was a bike which went on to achieve great things in the hands of others, thanks to the Count effectively banning its use by John.

The Surtees 7R Special was first tested by John himself at Silverstone after its completion in late 1959. The idea for this particular machine came from John's involvement with a standard 7R during 1958 and early 1959. When I asked John why he had chosen the 7R engine in preference to the Manx Norton with which he is usually associated, he gave several reasons. Firstly the 7R engine was lighter than the Manx. Secondly, Jack Williams was then in charge of the 7R's development at AMC and had been a good friend of John's father while at Vincent. And finally, unlike the Norton, the AJS had an enclosed valve gear and so it 'kept the oil in'.

John's 7R Special was in many ways a masterpiece of design work; a project on which he could use his considerable engineering skills to the full. The frame was designed by John himself along with Mr Frick of Birmingham-based Reynolds Tubes and manufactured by Ken Sprayston of Reynolds. The 7R engine was modified by fitting lighter flywheels from the works 3-valve engine, twin spark ignition, a longer inlet tract with the carburettor (both Amal GP and an Italian Dell'Orto SS1 were tried) rigidly mounted, and a modified Dell'Orto remote float chamber. The gearbox, a modified Manx Norton assembly, employed an elektron shell and a one-off close ratio, stronger gear cluster.

It was the cycle components which attracted the most attention, giving the machine a much lower and compact feel than the standard AMC product. The engine was mounted 1⅛in lower than the standard 7R. A trio of tubes, 1¼in diameter and of 18 gauge, formed a rigid, lightweight structure. Norton Featherbed fashion, the twin front down tubes were connected to the top of the steering head, but instead of sweeping downward and backward in straight lines they were bent approximately halfway down so that the lower sections were almost vertical. This, said John at the time, 'gives better support for the steering head and allows the engine to be mounted further forward'.

The pair of tubes passed beneath the power unit, then swept upward behind the gearbox. The twin top frame rails were joined to the base of the steering head, splayed outward around the front down tubes, then continuing rearward to join the upper extremities of the main loops. Gusset plates at the joints were employed to form upper anchorage points for the reversed (to save unsprung weight) Girling rear shock absorbers. The upper and lower tubes were both cross-braced by a pair of short tubes.

John ensured enhanced rigidity by using a third pair of tubes. These extended from halfway along the upper tubes to the region of the swinging arm pivot pin. Oil for lubricating the primary chain was held in the nearside frame tube. What appeared to be a small gusset plate was welded into the joint on each side; in fact the 'plate' was hollow and fabricated from 16 gauge sheet steel. The pivot pin for the swinging arm passed through the above mentioned gussets, which also formed the footrest mountings.

A long, low, slimline aluminium petrol tank held 3½ gallons and was held in place by an aerolastic which passed over an ear at each end of the tank, clamping it down on to the rubber-covered frame top rails. Considerable thought had been given to the triangular-shaped oil tank which, again of aluminium construction, was set lower in the frame than on the standard 7R.

Weighing in at 265lb (some 25lb lighter than the production 7R), the Surtees Special had spring poundages 15 percent lower than the standard 7R front and rear suspension systems. A Manx Norton Roadholder front fork had been shortened by ¾in and the sliders switched to accept an Italian Oldani front brake; there was a Manx Norton hub at the rear. The forks also featured modified dampers and employed lightweight SAE 5-rate oil.

A second frame type was also constructed; in this design the top tubes ran to the top of the steering head, which was dropped, thus allowing the use of shorter front forks. It is worth mentioning that a pair of Reynolds leading link forks were available, but these were never tested on the Surtees 7R.

After John had retired from motorcycle racing he sold the 7R Special to fellow rider Rex Butcher in 1962, the latter then sold the machine on to dealer/entrant Tom Arter at the end of 1963. Riders such as Mike Duff, Peter Williams and finally Dave Hughes enjoyed considerable success with the machine. A 500cc Matchless G50-engined version was also built, which gained even more glory for the design. During the late 1990s John built a replica of the machine for the American Barber Collection.

in his father's footsteps by racing karts. Second, when John came out of hospital in late 1978 and began on the path to recovery, his original love of motorcycles was revived. He dragged out all the assorted motorcycle components he had kept in his garage at home and this included enough bits to enable construction of a Vincent Grey Flash to commence. John was also able to visit the scene of so many of his motorcycle triumphs, the Isle of Man, for the Millennium TT in June 1979. He undertook a demonstration

The start at the Saltzburgring, with a collection of classic bikes. The front row includes two Moto Guzzi singles, John's ex-Meier BMW twin (49), the Velocette Roarer and a 1930s 500cc NSU single.

A famous foursome at Spoleto, Italy, during the early 1990s. Left to right: Mario Lega (1977 250cc World Champion-Mobidelli), John (with his 1973 500cc Benelli four), Tarquinio Provini (ex-FB Mondial, MV, Morini and Benelli works star) and Remo Venturi (seated on a 1957-type 500cc Gilera four).

Circuit Paul Ricard Le Castellet, French Grand Prix, 1986 Historic Race, with John riding a 499cc Manx Norton.

around the famous Mountain Course on an MV Agusta, which the Italian factory kindly provided. This sparked a passion for collecting the machines with which he had been associated during his 11-year motorcycle racing career.

There is absolutely no doubt in talking to John Surtees of his deep and genuine enthusiasm for the motorcycle world. John is very much of the old school in how he sees things. For example, he says 'I always remember Dad, many of his friends and indeed myself, competing simply for the pleasure of taking part in a sport we loved.'

This love of the sport has seen John Surtees turn the clock back and not only restore many of the bikes he formerly rode in his heyday, but also ride them – in a style which many riders years younger would find it hard to

John trying Andrew Stroud's Britton V-twin during the mid-1990s. Since his return to the motorcycle fold, John Surtees has given enthusiasts the world over great pleasure with his displays of skilful riding on a huge variety of bikes.

match in terms of speed and style. He has also ridden many motorcycles
which were only memories before, including the pre-war supercharged
BMW flat twin, the Moto Guzzi horizontal single and V8 models from the
1950s, the Benelli four, Mike Hailwood's 1967 Honda 500 four and Phil
Read's 1973 MV Agusta 500 four. He has also been able to take to the wheel
of some of the finest racing cars ever produced, including the Mercedes-Benz
W125, W154, W196 and 300SLR, pre-war Auto Unions and a Maserati
250F. In addition John became the only former MV rider to be given one of
the factory's GP bikes, when totally out of the blue a 350cc four arrived by
air from Italy during 1981.

Georg Meier (centre) with
John Surtees and the
historic 1939 BMW super-
charged twin.

Chapter 9

The Restorer

WHEN JOHN SURTEES'S renewed love affair with motorcycles took place after his illness and subsequent winding up of the Team Surtees business during the tail-end of the 1970s, it was originally very much a way of coping with all the problems which beset the great man during this period in his life. However, the rebuilding of the machinery, as opposed to actually riding it, was also something which John had found particularly enjoyable since his very earliest days. Therefore both the riding and restoration acted as therapy.

His early boyhood 'tinkering' had progressed to that of a proficient engineer, thanks in no small part to John's five-year long engineering apprenticeship during the first half of the 1950s; first with the Vincent motorcycle factory and finally with Peter Chapman's Northamptonshire-based agricultural engineering business and the Ferguson company. John's great attention to detail and his determination to 'do things properly' has ensured that all his motorcycle restorations carried out over the last quarter of a century have been to the very highest standards of both engineering, and wherever possible, originality.

Vincent

John Surtees's first restoration projects concerned the Vincent marque. In many ways this was a fitting outcome, given his involvement with the former Stevenage-based company at the beginning of his career. Not only had John first found fame riding the Vincent Grey Flash, including winning his first ever race at Aberdare Park in the summer of 1950, but he had also served the first four years of his five-year apprenticeship with the company. He had also been responsible for the construction of a 998cc Vincent V-twin engined Norton special, with which he had planned to take on the might of Geoff Duke and the Gilera four-cylinder, prior to his joining the Norton factory as a works-supported rider for the 1955 season; but events conspired to ensure that this particular bike was never raced. At some stage in the future he hopes to complete and show off this machine to the public (see photograph on p.41).

John Surtees with his first restoration project, a Vincent Grey Flash seen here at Brands Hatch in 1981. He admits 'loving to tinker with anything mechanical'.

Although John had sold his original Grey Flash to finance his first new Featherbed 500cc Manx Norton in mid-1952, he had retained most of the components of the spare machine which Vincent had provided him with as a back-up during his two years of riding the 499cc single. By the end of the 1970s these components were 'lying around in various bits, some of which were virtually buried in my garden'. As not everything was there, this particular machine was not entirely rebuilt in its original guise. Instead the main priority at that time was to create a motorcycle which could be used in the burgeoning historic racing events which were, as the 1980s dawned, springing up all over Europe.

Another motorcycle close to John Surtees's heart had always been the Vincent V-twin. Although he had only raced an example on one occasion (his father's machine without the sidecar in spring 1951), he had been closely involved in helping his dad at the family's South London Vincent dealership, and obviously working at the Vincent factory itself during his apprenticeship from 1951 until 1954. John is still of the opinion that compared to the mainstream British motorcycle industry of the immediate post-war period such as BSA, Norton and Triumph, Vincent was far ahead in terms of outlook and design and would have been better able 'to cope with the demands of the 1960s'. But as it was, following Philip Vincent's unfortunate accident while testing one of his products in 1949, the company went into decline. But, with the correct build quality, the Vincent V-twin can be a formidable machine. John's performances on the Black Lightning,

Another early project was this 1973 Benelli 500cc four-cylinder, seen here at the Donington Park Classic Fest, Sunday 27 July 1986.

John with his 1939 ex-Georg Meier BMW super-charged twin...

witnessed by those fortunate enough to see the maestro in action at historic events, particularly during the early 1980s, demonstrated a great combination of riding skill and sheer naked (the machine was unstreamlined) power. A particular day to remember was the John Surtees 'weekend' at Brands Hatch in 1981.

Benelli four

John's Benelli four is actually a 1972/73 500cc model, as raced occasionally by the likes of Jarno Saarinen and Walter Villa during the period when the Pesaro factory was under the ownership of the Argentinian business tycoon Alejandro De Tomaso. John's bike is one of the last in a distinguished line of development that began shortly before World War Two. The first four-cylinder Benelli, a supercharged liquid-cooled 250cc, debuted in 1940, but Italy's entry into World War Two in June that year sealed this promising design's fate. The next model, this time normally aspirated and air-cooled, but still a 250cc, arrived in 1960, but wasn't raced until 1962. A 322cc version arrived in 1965, followed a few months later by a 343cc model. The Italian Grand Prix at Monza in September 1968 saw the new 494.6cc (54 x 54mm) five-hundred make its bow. In 1969 the Australian Kel Carruthers won the 250cc World Championship on the latest version of the smaller four. This was Benelli's second title, the first having come back in 1951, albeit with a dohc single.

John's 500cc sports a six-speed gearbox and triple disc brakes, while the engine puts out around 75bhp, giving it a maximum speed approaching 140mph. The seven-times World Motorcycle Champion chose to ride the Benelli in the 'Parade of Past Masters' event at Classic Fest, Donington Park on 31 July 1986. John has also ridden the Italian bike at numerous other events, including the Ulster Grand Prix.

Georg Meier's 1939 TT BMW

The supercharging technology which BMW employed on their Kompressor 500 works road racers which debuted in 1935, was based on the same firm's record breakers with which Ernst Henne captured world speed records from 1929 onwards. Both the record breaker and road racer were fitted with a Zoller blower built on to the front of the crankcase assembly and coupled to the rearward facing inlets by long pipes under the cylinders. The displacement was 492.6cc (66 x 72mm) and the dohc horizontally opposed twin put out over 80bhp at 8,000rpm, offering a maximum speed (in racing guise) of around 140mph, subject to circuit conditions.

By 1937, the Kompressor racer had become competitive on the European stage and not only did Karl Gall become German champion, but Englishman Jock West won the Ulster Grand Prix on one of the fleet BMW twins. In 1938 Georg Meier became European Champion (the forerunner of the World Championship series). But it was Meier's 1939 Isle of Man Senior TT victory which really made the news. Not only was this event the premier race at that time anywhere in the world, but it was the first time a foreign rider on a foreign machine had won it.

Several of the works' machines survived the war which followed, either to race on German soil again or end their days as war booty. BMW subsequently modified some of the bikes for use in the German Championships in 1950. Only one machine remained to original specifications. That machine is reputedly Georg Meier's TT winner, which was taken from its place of storage in Germany by a Frenchman when the Allies entered Germany. This machine is the one John Surtees has used extensively around the world, sporting number 49 (Meier's 1939 TT number). The machine has now returned home where it will form part of the BMW Museum in Munich.

...and the motorcycle itself.

The Norton F-Type

The Norton F (Flat) Type was the machine which could have put the Bracebridge Street, Birmingham company back on the top in Grand Prix racing. Instead, it was to become as *The Daily Telegraph* called it in their 14 March 1998 issue: 'The Secret Norton'. Luckily it has been saved for future generations thanks to John Surtees's enthusiasm and commitment. A full working restoration was carried out during the mid-1990s.

The F-Type was the machine which would have carried Norton's hopes had they continued with factory-built works specials after the end of 1954. However, AMC's acquisition of Norton in February 1953 meant that the F-Type was never to be used in anger. Joe Craig, Norton's team manager and development engineer, was responsible for getting former Vincent designer Ernie

1952 499cc works Norton with 16in rear wheel.

John with the F-Type in the paddock at Mallory Park's Post TT meeting, June 2001.

Ray Amm's 1954 Junior TT Norton.

Walsh to create the radical new Norton single during late 1953 and into 1954. The horizontal cylinder layout was inspired by the success which had been achieved by the Italian Moto Guzzi factory and its designer Ing. Giulio Carcano.

The work was carried out in secret – certainly the normal Norton employee knew nothing of the 'F' project. Finally, in October 1954, Norton race mechanic Charlie Edwards, together with works rider Ray Amm, took the newly completed prototype to the MIRA (Motor Industry Research Association) test track near Nuneaton for testing. These tests went well enough for the team to return home to Birmingham excited at the F Type's prospects.

Unfortunately there was to be no future for the design, as shortly afterwards, following the death of Charlie Collier (the last remaining family member of AMC's founding Matchless marque), Norton's new owners were now in the hands of accountants rather than motorcycle men. AMC's supremo, Donald Heather, promptly axed the works racing programme of the entire company, which not only meant AJS, but also Norton. As a result Amm left to sign for MV Agusta, while Edwards took the F-Type and as John Surtees says 'hid it behind a bunch of suspension boxes in a store room. His anger was heightened by the fact that its demise was not directly a Norton decision'.

A mock-up of the bike was assembled for an article by journalist John Griffiths in 1960, but otherwise the F-Type remained largely a forgotten

Historic Racing

Along with the massive upsurge of interest in vintage and classic street bikes has come a parallel growth in the sporting side of older bikes, most notably in racing. Today, classic and vintage racing is an integral part of the road racing scene on a worldwide basis.

In the past, when a racing bike became uncompetitive it was simply pensioned off, but since the end of the 1970s this trend has been reversed and many thousands of previously unwanted racing machines have been put back into service. At first it was simply a case of original bikes being re-raced, often by their original riders, but with the subsequent rises in values towards the end of the 1980s many bikes started to change hands for super-inflated prices. Often they had become too valuable to risk on the track. This has led to the building of replicas of the originals. The process started with Seeley G50s and Manx Nortons, but has grown to include many exotic works bikes including four-cylinder Gileras and MV Agustas.

One of the first organisations for old racing machinery was the VMCC (Vintage Motor Cycle Club) which began running meetings during the 1960s. Next came the CRMC (Classic Racing Motorcycle Club) in 1979. Another organisation, the IHRO (International Historic Racing Organisation) began in the mid-1980s. This is essentially a group of enthusiasts who aim to recreate the atmosphere of the Continental Circus of Grand Prix racing spanning the early 1950s until the late 1970s, with selected international events throughout Europe during the summer months. In addition there are a host of other clubs and organisations which run historic events.

John Surtees has played an important role in the growth of the classic movement, not only through his restoration of many important motorcycles and his outstanding displays of skilful riding, but also through the special meetings he has helped to organise, including events at Brands Hatch and Goodwood.

John Surtees's pet restoration was, without doubt, the F-Type Norton single, which because Norton quit racing works specials at the end of 1954, was never raced in anger. With help from former Norton race engineer/mechanic Charlie Edwards, the F-Type finally came to life in January 1998.

secret. In the late 1970s John Surtees became involved. John, who had recently closed his car racing team and regained his enthusiasm for motorcycles, and Nortons in particular, made a visit to Sid Mularney's dealership in Leighton Buzzard, Bedfordshire, where, as he says, 'my eyes fell immediately upon the F – or at least its remains'. He was keen to see the bike rebuilt:

...my mind was made up, especially as I had always felt cheated that I had never been able to ride it. I desperately wanted to see it together and try it out and Mularney promised he would try to rebuild it. Sadly, he died before this was possible. But I kept in touch with his son Michael and during one of my regular calls, on 14 November 1992, he agreed to sell me what remained of the original.

John then contacted Charlie Edwards and 'pumped him for every piece of knowledge from our Norton days'. Gradually John uncovered the original

Mallory Park Post TT, June 2002. Even though it rained cats and dogs, John was as keen as mustard to show fans his superbly restored Norton F-Type; machine 69 is an Aermacchi 350cc.

specification and with that knowledge 'was able to search the country and follow up every lead for parts. Some I found at auto-jumbles, others I discovered among parts I had purchased with a standard works Norton.'

Slowly, the F-Type was reborn, being finally completed in January 1998. Since then it has made appearances at several historic racing events, with John in the saddle. It takes pride of place among other former works Nortons he has lovingly restored. Charlie Edwards has played, as John says, 'a vital role with advice on the F-Type and other Nortons during the restoration process'.

The REG twin

A future restoration project for the John Surtees stable is an example of Bob Geeson's home-spun double overhead camshaft REG parallel twin 250cc, which is described in detail in Chapter 3. A complete engine and gearbox assembly was discovered in Australia by John and has been shipped back to the UK. The idea is to rebuild the machine using the frame and suspension which John and Bob had intended to use back in the 1950s but never did.

Since its constructor is now dead, the restoration of the REG is likely to prove a challenging task. However, knowing John Surtees's ability to painstakingly undertake a detailed 'rebirth', it will, I'm sure, eventually join the other restored motorcycles in his growing collection of machines that played a part in the his racing career.

The collection and restoration of the motorcycles with which John Surtees has in one way or another been associated over the years has become a very important part of his life; something of a passion in fact. Some bikes, such as the supercharged pre-war BMW twin and the post-war Benelli four, are bikes he had previously admired from afar. Others – the Vincent singles and V-twins, the various Nortons (excluding the F); the MV Agusta four and the REG twin – are motorcycles with which he was closely involved during his 11-year motorcycle racing career. The restoration process has allowed the engineer in John Surtees to come to the fore. This skill is on a par with the undoubted riding talents he displays in historic racing circles.

Chapter 10

A place in history

JOHN SURTEES is truly a living legend. Someone who already has a special place in motorcycle (and motoring) history, as the first and only man to have won premier World Championship titles on both two and four wheels.

John Surtees is someone who has taken fame without showing it. He is a modest man, whose ability is proven by what he has achieved, not by some great publicity machine which has hyped up lesser achievements to look good.

The facts are simple. John Surtees began his road racing career in spring 1950, when just 16. He won his first race later that year. By August the following year he was good enough to be the runner-up behind World Champion Geoff Duke at a big international Thruxton event in two 500cc races. In 1952 he took part in his first World Championship race: the 500cc Ulster Grand Prix, finishing sixth. Only a practice accident prevented John joining the factory Norton team in 1953. In 1954 he dominated British short-circuit racing, before extending his wings in 1955 to include his first Continental race and first World Championship victory.

After signing for the Italian MV Agusta team at the end of 1955 John became 500cc World Champion in 1956. Although 1957 was, by his standard, a poor year, he proceeded to not only become the first man to win the 350/500cc world titles three years running, but also to take consecutive Junior/Senior TT victories in 1958 and 1959.

In 1960 John Surtees combined two and four wheels – winning his final two bike titles while also taking part in 17 car races. In one of these he took part in bike and car races on the same day at Solitude in Germany. He was also runner-up in only his second Formula 1 car race, the British Grand Prix at Silverstone, and he put

John (left) and his great friend, the late Jim (Bill) Oliver outside Puttenham Manor, August 1996. The latter had accompanied the former to his first road-race meeting with the Triumph Tiger 70 at Brands Hatch back in April 1950, and was fellow racer Michael O'Rourke's uncle.

Cutting the cake on his 63rd birthday, 11 February 1997. The smile shows the man behind the name, someone who enjoys the company of his friends and family.

his works Lotus on pole position in just his third F1 drive in Portugal. If all that was not enough he went on to win the 1964 Formula 1 World Championship driving a Ferrari. Besides Porsche, Lotus and Ferrari, John also drove Cooper, Honda, Vanwall, Lola, Matra, BRM, McLaren, Chaparral and his own Surtees cars before retiring from competitive driving in 1972.

The driving side of his four-wheel career came naturally to him, but other aspects of the motor-racing scene he found difficult to cope with. He admits now that 'I didn't know my fellow competitors.' Having grown up in the bike world, John didn't have this trouble on two wheels. Recently in *MCN Sport* magazine he revealed that 'my biggest problem was handling all the people involved. Team managers, hangers-on, members of the trade – they were all strangers. People would say "Do this, do that", and in some ways I lost my way.'

This frankness is something which I as an author have discovered while writing *John Surtees: Motorcycle Maestro*. John gives a straight answer to any question, in a very open way. When he has made a mistake he owns up to it, with no excuses. For example, John openly admits that he made an error when he attempted to build his own cars and continue to drive them. He sums it up in the following way:

That was a mistake. We bought a Formula 5000 project for the actor James Garner, but he disposed of the sponsor's money and left me holding the baby. I put my own team together, we sorted the car, and came second in the 1969 American F5000 championship. When we built a F1 car, we had such a limited budget that I was the driver, mechanic, engineer, sponsorship finder, the lot. It was too much, but we did get our cars to where we were probably the third or fourth best team on the grid.

This statement really puts John Surtees, the man, in context. He *can* and *has* done virtually everything in motorsport. He has raced both bikes and cars at the very highest levels, has acted as an engineer and mechanic, has dealt with sponsors, and has even organised events. No one else has combined all these tasks so successfully. However, John gave a revealing reply when he was asked recently by *MCN Sport* whether anyone would be able to repeat his achievement in winning the ultimate double – the motor-cycle Grand Prix championship and F1 car title. John said: 'I don't see any reason why not, with youngsters starting as young as they do today. If you have an ability to coordinate yourself, and if you apply yourself and show the right attitude, there's no reason why you shouldn't get success.'

The author is not the only commentator who considers John Surtees to have been the greatest racing motorcyclist of all time. Back in 1966, *Motor Cycle News* published a short series of articles entitled 'The Greatest by the Greatest'. Bill Lomas, himself a TT winner and World Champion, placed John Surtees as his number 1. Here is a small extract from that piece:

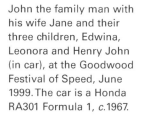

John the family man with his wife Jane and their three children, Edwina, Leonora and Henry John (in car), at the Goodwood Festival of Speed, June 1999. The car is a Honda RA301 Formula 1, *c.*1967.

Besides riding motorcycles at historic events, John Surtees also maintains a presence in the four-wheel world including, as shown here, with Mercedes-Benz. John remains very much a living legend and appears at motorcycle and motoring events all over the world – long may this continue.

It is in braking and turning on the power again that the great rider shows his superiority over the merely good riders. In other words, the changeover from deceleration to acceleration. This was where John Surtees was supreme, where he left everyone else standing. There are a great many riders and ex-riders – myself included – who will testify to John's almost uncanny ability to brake just at the right point for the machine he was riding... and do it EVERY time. He would adjust this braking point with all the slightest changes in conditions, so that he went into the corner completely in control and in exactly the right position... The ability to ride in the wet is probably of equal importance. John could do this so beautifully, seeming to know by instinct just how much earlier to start applying his brakes, how much slower to go round each and every corner, and how much more careful he had to be with the twistgrip.

To the author's mind one word describes John Surtees' motorcycle racing talent – *maestro*. He was a master craftsman, someone who went about his racing in a truly professional manner. To him the riding was not the only important aspect of racing – he attended equally to his mental approach and his tactics and to the meticulous preparation of his machine. This single-minded attitude was critical to his success. Second best in anything was never an option.

Postscript
by John Surtees

AS I write this piece, the sad news has just come over the radio that Barry Sheene has died of cancer. It signals the end of an era, as in my opinion Barry was the last British motorcyclist to be a true household name. He revelled in the explosion of television coverage and media attention and the sponsorship that it brought in all sports. His enthusiasm and personality ensured that motorcycle sport maintained its fair share of media coverage.

However, I have seen change in recent times with what would appear to be a dumbing-down of motorcycle sport. There is no doubt that there is still an enormous amount of enthusiasm for the sport among the young and not so young, and that motorcycle racing is one of the most thrilling and exciting activities to watch. But it has become more and more isolated from the mainstream British sporting scene. When I go to the BBC Sports Personality of the Year presentation and sit there I see practically no reference to British motorcycle sport. It receives little press attention other than in specialised publications. I think that this is the result, partly, of self-destruction. We are fortunate in this country to have a superb selection of race circuits. But we haven't produced a World Champion who could perform and communicate at the highest levels since Barry. The British scene would appear to have developed many champions of this or that – but some seem to rest on their laurels and carry on doing what they know they can do. Others have the talent and ambition but don't have the support. It is a familiar story. I think that the ACU governing body, if it were a bit more far-sighted, would pay attention to ensuring that the structure of our racing here on the mainland allows the real talent to come through. It would give those riders a chance on the world scene. Other nations have done this with both two and four-wheel competitors.

I know my mention of Barry Sheene being the last champion will get some jumping up and saying 'Fogarty'. But with all due respect Super Bike can only be looked upon as a stepping stone for any really ambitious and totally confident rider. It is a second-grade championship that is preparation for going into what really counts, Grand Prix. No one will ever know how good Fogarty was because he never pitted his skills against the top people in Grand Prix racing, although he had a number of opportunities to do so. However, I was pleased to see, after watching the final of the Super Bike championship at Imola in 2002, that that the main contestants said 'right, that's done, away we go' and took up the challenge of Grand Prix. That is the way it should be done and I applaud them for it.

There is some hope for motorcycle sport though, because the BBC is showing a greater interest. I have been pressuring them for years to try and think more about motorcycling. With greater coverage it is to be hoped that more support will be forthcoming to back up British talent. It might even induce the manufacturers to start thinking about the benefits of putting a British rider on the world scene in Moto GP. For too long they have concentrated on the Isle of Man, which is now a purely local affair since it no longer counts for any form of World Championship. The Isle of Man has a very special place in motorcycling history. It can still play its part within the motorcycle world, but it should not divert the main interests of manufacturers from the most important thing – achieving success on the world stage at Grand Prix level. What we really need here in Britain is a young star like Valentino Rossi to pique interest. Perhaps the initiative of the BBC, and some change of thinking by the main manufacturers who market in this country, will help to bring that about.

Another of the uncertainties facing the sport in this country is what will happen to the circuits at Brands Hatch, Snetterton, Oulton Park and Cadwell Park. All of these belong to a single company, which has now stated that it wants out. I can only hope that the circuits end up in the hands of those who want to continue their development as part of the racing scene. All the circuits certainly played a vital part in my evolution as a rider and I applied the skills I learnt there to both the circuits of Europe and the TT course. The numerous circuits we have available in this Britain are the envy of the world.

My career on first two and then four wheels took me through from being Formula 1 World Champion to a race car constructor. In the aftermath of trying to come to terms with the end of some dreams and the closing of my team, a call came through asking me if I would attend the 1979 Millennium TT celebrations in the Isle of Man and do a lap of the circuit. A call to Count Corrado Agusta brought forth the ready offer of a bike, but it wasn't a bike like I had ridden before, it was one from the Phil Read/Agostini period, a small compact four-cylinder. I hadn't ridden a bike for something like 18 years, and certainly not a race bike. So that one standing start lap where they told me that I had gone round at something like 98 miles an hour was a surprise to say the least. But then the circuit had been unrecognisable to me on certain sectors. Widened, corners straightened out and some not there. Also, the all-important focal points that showed you just where to be on the road that were etched on my mind from years before had often gone. The bike, though, responded beautifully and as the lap went on I began once again to feel part of a two-wheeled machine, rekindling the emotions that were to take me back to my first love.

On my return from the Island I looked in the shed and dragged out all the pieces of Vincents, Nortons and MV Agustas that had lain there for years. I went searching for other machines I had been associated with. Projects like the F Norton took countless hours to put together. I was supposed to have ridden it in 1955 for the works Norton team but the AMC takeover stopped all that and it was never seen until I rebuilt it a few years ago. Only an artist's impression to the wrong specification existed. Luckily, that long-term stalwart of the works Norton team, Charlie Edwards, was able to help me get it right.

On my travels around the world I have been heartened to see the enthusiasm that exists for my time in motorcycling, now commonly referred to as the classic period. Events at Brands Hatch, Mallory Park and Goodwood have had a wonderful effect, uniting enthusiasts old and new. They have been able to enjoy the sight and sound of one to six-cylinder bikes.

I therefore despair when I see the so-called world governing body apparently creating a World Championship for classic machines. How many more World Championships do we need to create? They devalue what has gone on before and the real World Champions of today. The genuine race machines from the classic period have served their time, shown their abilities and are in the history books. Why should we create a race in their name for machines that are largely designed and built today? The most original part on the machine is probably the transfer on the tank. To me it makes no sense to call a bunch of specials 'classics' and create a World Championship for them. What the authorities should do is give support to those people who are preserving our heritage by keeping original machines to original specifications and running them.

Throughout my life involved with two, three and four-wheeled motorsport I have considered myself very fortunate to have been paid for doing what I love. Perhaps I was a little too early to get the sort of rewards that a Schumacher or Rossi gets today. But their satisfaction and pleasure when they get things right can't be any more than I enjoyed. I suppose I have always been a bit of a dreamer as well. In my car racing career I would have done well to have paused for a moment and brushed aside my enthusiasm for a new project, and instead concentrated on ensuring that I put my bottom into the best and most competitive car, something that I often failed to do.

In recent years I have had a chance to sit on and in bikes and cars of other champions from different eras and for a moment bring my life closer to theirs. I have felt the same sensations as them, whether it be Georg Meier with a BMW Kompressor, Geoff Duke on a 1952 works Norton, Ray Amm on that proboscis 500 Norton and F, Mike Hailwood and the Honda 500cc four-cylinder or the 500cc MV Agustas of Read and Agostini. I have driven Fangio's 300cc SLR from 1955 round the Mille Miglia circuit. I have driven Gonzalez' first-ever Grand Prix Ferrari winner round Monza and in the 600hp W125 1937 Mercedes-Benz I sat in Caracciola's seat. I drove the V12 W154 of Lang and a host of others on circuits around the world.

They say a cat has nine lives. If I could pick nine moments from motorsport history to live, they would be these: 1937 – the chance to compete with one of those W125s with the likes of Caracciola, von Brauchitsch, Nuvolari and Rosemeyer; 1939 – jump on a BMW Kompressor with Georg Meier; 1950 – the birth of the Featherbed Norton and the new star Geoff Duke; 1954/55 – the revival of the three-pointed star domination of the race circuits and Moss and Fangio at Mercedes-Benz with the Silver Arrows; 1958 – join Moss in the Vanwall team sitting behind what was basically four works Norton engines; 1966 – back to two wheels, joining Hailwood for the challenge of the 500cc Honda four-cylinder; 1974 – riding the last model of the MV Agusta four-cylinder with Phil Read; 1986 – in the turbo-charged Formula 1s join Piquet and Mansell in the Williams Formula 1 team to get back a little of the investment I made in the Honda company; last but not least – what better place to be than in Italy with the Ferrari team of 2002.

But back to reality. The world of motor sport, whether it be two or four wheels, is a unique one. This is because, whatever the sporting pages may say, motorsport is the only sport that benefits the country economically as well as providing entertainment and boosting morale. An enormous business has developed around the sport. The technology now involved in Formula 1, which will become more and more important in motorcycling now that we have the GP Moto class with four-strokes, is largely based in this country. I live in hope that the media will realise that we do live in a motoring age. Motorsport is important for our world prestige, national pride and our motorsport industry. It is therefore sad to see that of all the millions of pounds spent from the lottery fund by organisations like Sport England, motorcycling, karting and car racing receive not a penny piece (except in Scotland, where some support has been forthcoming). It seems to me incredible that our sport, which means so much to so many people, should have been bypassed in such a fashion. Apart from the fact that it is important to have national heroes who are successful on the world stage, I believe that many of the problems that exist with motivating youngsters and pointing them in a direction which will give them something to live for could be resolved if a little more attention was paid to what motorsport and motorsport engineering have to offer.

These days I am not spending as much time as I would like on my long-standing projects – finishing off some of the machines in my works Norton collection, including the desmodromic. The reason for this is that another generation of Surtees is involved in motorsport: my son Henry, with karting. So at weekends that I am turning the clock right back and experiencing the same sort of mental stress, together with pleasure when things go right, that my father and mother must have gone through when they were helping me. But at the events we attend I also see both boys and girls working with pieces of machinery from the ages of eight upwards. They do not always behave quite as you would like them to, but just the same they are giving of their all and enjoying themselves and getting involved, while showing an astounding degree of skill. When I see this I think back and realise how fortunate I was to have been born to parents who loved motorsport.

John Surtees, March 2003

Appendices
John Surtees Motorcycle Road Racing Results

1951

Position	Class	Machine	Circuit	Date
2	1000cc	Vincent Black Shadow	Thruxton	26 March
3	1000cc	Vincent Grey Flash	Boreham	30 April
1	500cc	Vincent Grey Flash	Brands Hatch	3 June
1	1000cc	Vincent Grey Flash	Brands Hatch	3 June
1	Handicap	Vincent Grey Flash	Brands Hatch	3 June
6	350	Norton Plunger Manx	Boreham	21 July
5	500cc	Vincent Grey Flash	Boreham	21 July
6	1000cc	Vincent Grey Flash	Boreham	21 July
2	500cc	Vincent Grey Flash	Thruxton	6 August
2	1000cc	Vincent Grey Flash	Thruxton	6 August
2	350cc	Norton Plunger Manx	Boreham	1 September
2	500cc	Vincent Grey Flash	Boreham	1 September
1	500cc	Vincent Grey Flash	Brands Hatch	16 September
3	1000cc	Vincent Grey Flash	Thruxton	29 September
1	500cc	Vincent Grey Flash	Brands Hatch	30 September
5	Handicap	Vincent Grey Flash	Silverstone	7 October

1952

Position	Class	Machine	Circuit	Date
1	1000cc Championship	Vincent Grey Flash	Brands Hatch	12 April
2	1000cc	Vincent Grey Flash	Brands Hatch	12 April
3	500cc	Vincent Grey Flash	Thruxton	14 April
Unplaced	500cc	Vincent Grey Flash	Silverstone	19 April
1	500cc Scratch	Vincent Grey Flash	Brands Hatch	20 April
1	500cc Invitation	Vincent Grey Flash	Brands Hatch	20 April
Retired	500cc	Vincent Grey Flash	Boreham	27 April
1	1000cc Scratch	Vincent Grey Flash	Brands Hatch	25 May
1	1000cc Invitation	Vincent Grey Flash	Brands Hatch	25 May
2	350cc	Norton Plunger Manx	Brands Hatch	29 June
Retired (crash)	1000cc	Vincent Grey Flash	Brands Hatch	29 June
4	Handicap	Vincent Grey Flash	Cadwell Park	6 July
4	350cc	Norton Plunger Manx	Ibsley	12 July
1	1000cc	Vincent Grey Flash	Brands Hatch	13 July
1	Handicap	Vincent Grey Flash	Brands Hatch	13 July
6	500cc Ulster GP	Featherbed Manx Norton	Clady	16 August (first World Championship race)
5	500cc	Featherbed Manx Norton	Boreham	23 August
1	1000cc	Vincent Grey Flash	Brands Hatch	24 August
1	500cc	Vincent Grey Flash	Aberdare Park	30 August (RL)
1	500cc	Featherbed Manx Norton	Castle Combe	6 September
4	500cc	Featherbed Manx Norton	Scarborough	20 September
1	350cc	Works AJS 7R	Thruxton	4 October
1	500cc	Featherbed Norton	Thruxton	4 October
2	350cc	Featherbed Norton	Brands Hatch	5 October
1	1000cc	Featherbed Norton	Brands Hatch	5 October
1	Handicap	Featherbed Norton	Brands Hatch	5 October
1	500cc Scratch	Featherbed Norton	Blandford	11 October
1	500cc Invitation	Featherbed Norton	Blandford	11 October

1953

Position	Class	Machine	Circuit	Date
1	350cc	Manx Norton	Brands Hatch	3 April
Retired (crash)	500cc	Manx Norton	Brands Hatch	3 April
3	350cc	Manx Norton	Thruxton	6 April
1	500cc	Manx Norton	Thruxton	6 April
2	350cc	Manx Norton	Silverstone	18 April
2	500cc	Manx Norton	Silverstone	18 April
1	350cc	Manx Norton	Brands Hatch	19 April
1	1000cc Scratch	Manx Norton	Brands Hatch	19 April
1	1000cc Invitation	Manx Norton	Brands Hatch	19 April
1	350cc	Manx Norton	Snetterton	2 May (RL)
1	500cc	Manx Norton	Snetterton	2 May (RL)
1	1000cc	Manx Norton	Snetterton	2 May
1	350cc	Manx Norton	Aberdare Park	23 May (RL)
1	500cc	Manx Norton	Aberdare Park	23 May (RL)
1	1000cc	Manx Norton	Aberdare Park	23 May (RL)
1	350cc	Manx Norton	Brands Hatch	24 May (RL)
1	1000cc Scratch	Manx Norton	Brands Hatch	24 May (RL)
1	1000cc Invitation	Manx Norton	Brands Hatch	24 May (RL)
Did not start	350cc Junior TT	Works Norton	Isle of Man	8 June
Did not start	125cc Ultra Lightweight TT	EMC*	Isle of Man	11 June
Did not start	500cc Senior TT	Works Norton	Isle of Man	12 June
1	350cc	Manx Norton	Ibsley	11 July (RL)
1	350cc	Manx Norton	Castle Combe	18 July (RL)
1	500cc	Manx Norton	Castle Combe	18 July
1	350cc	Manx Norton	Brands Hatch	19 July
1	1000cc	Manx Norton	Brands Hatch	19 July
Retired (startline collision)	1000cc Invitation	Manx Norton	Brands Hatch	19 July
3	250cc	REG	Blandford	3 August
Retired (engine trouble)	350cc	Manx Norton	Blandford	3 August
2	500cc	Manx Norton	Blandford	3 August
Did not start	(practice crash)	Did not race	Crystal Palace	22 August
1	500cc	Manx Norton	Aberdare Park	29 August
1	500cc	Manx Norton	Snetterton	5 September (RL)
3	350cc	Works AJS 7R	Scarborough	19 September
Retired (crash)	500cc	Manx Norton	Scarborough	19 September
6	350cc	Manx Norton	Silverstone	26 September
5	500cc	Manx Norton	Silverstone	26 September
1	250cc	REG	Brands Hatch	27 September
2	350cc	Manx Norton	Brands Hatch	27 September
1	500cc	Manx Norton	Brands Hatch	27 September

*Practice crash due to forks breaking

1954

Position	Class	Machine	Circuit	Date
3	350cc	Manx Norton	Silverstone	10 April
1	1000cc	Manx Norton	Silverstone	10 April
1	250cc	REG	Brands Hatch	16 April
1	350cc	Manx Norton	Brands Hatch	16 April
1	1000cc	Manx Norton	Brands Hatch	16 April
1	250cc	REG	Crystal Palace	19 April (RL)
1	350cc	Manx Norton	Crystal Palace	19 April (RL)
1	1000cc	Manx Norton	Crystal Palace	19 April (RL)
1	250cc	REG	Brands Hatch	25 April
1	350cc	Manx Norton	Brands Hatch	25 April
1	1000cc Scratch	Manx Norton	Brands Hatch	25 April

Position	Class	Machine	Circuit	Date
1	1000cc Invitation	Manx Norton	Brands Hatch	25 April
1	350cc	Manx Norton	Aberdare Park	8 May
1	500cc	Manx Norton	Aberdare Park	8 May
1	1000cc	Manx Norton	Aberdare Park	8 May
1	250cc	REG	Brands Hatch	9 May
1	350cc	REG	Brands Hatch	9 May
1	1000cc Scratch	REG	Brands Hatch	9 May
1	1000cc Invitation	REG	Brands Hatch	9 May
1	350cc	Manx Norton	Oulton Park	15 May
1	1000cc	Manx Norton	Oulton Park	15 May
11	350cc Junior TT	Manx Norton	Isle of Man	14 June
15	500cc Senior TT	Manx Norton	Isle of Man	18 June
Retired (engine trouble)	350cc Ulster GP	Manx Norton	Dundrod	26 June
5	500cc Ulster GP	Manx Norton	Dundrod	26 June
1	250cc	REG	Cadwell Park	4 July
1	350cc	Manx Norton	Cadwell Park	4 July
1	500cc	Manx Norton	Cadwell Park	4 July
1	250cc	REG	Crystal Palace	17 July
1	350cc	Manx Norton	Crystal Palace	17 July
Retired (water in carburettor)	500cc	Manx Norton	Crystal Palace	17 July
1	250cc	REG	Brands Hatch	18 July
1	350cc	Manx Norton	Brands Hatch	18 July
1	1000cc	Manx Norton	Brands Hatch	18 July
1	250cc	REG	Castle Combe	24 July
1	350cc	Manx Norton	Castle Combe	24 July
1	500cc	Manx Norton	Castle Combe	24 July
1	350cc	Manx Norton	Snetterton	1 August (RL)
1	500cc	Manx Norton	Snetterton	1 August (RL)
2	350cc	Manx Norton	Thruxton	2 August
1	500cc	Manx Norton	Thruxton	2 August (RL)
1	350cc	Manx Norton	Silverstone	7 August
Retired (engine trouble)	500cc	Manx Norton	Silverstone	7 August
2	250cc	Telfer Norton	Ibsley	21 August
1	350cc	Manx Norton	Ibsley	21 August (RL)
1	500cc	Manx Norton	Ibsley	21 August (RL)
1	350cc	Manx Norton	Brands Hatch	22 August
1	1000cc	Manx Norton	Brands Hatch	22 August
1	250cc	Telfer Norton	Aberdare Park	28 August
1	350cc	Manx Norton	Aberdare Park	28 August (RL)
1	500cc	Manx Norton	Aberdare Park	28 August (RL)
1	1000cc	Manx Norton	Aberdare Park	28 August (RL)
1	250cc	Telfer Norton	Brands Hatch	12 September
1	350cc	Manx Norton	Brands Hatch	12 September
1	1000cc	Manx Norton	Brands Hatch	12 September
1	350cc	Works Norton	Scarborough	18 September
2	500cc	Manx Norton	Scarborough	18 September
1	350cc	Manx Norton	Cadwell Park	19 September
1	500cc Scratch	Manx Norton	Cadwell Park	19 September
1	500cc Invitation	Manx Norton	Cadwell Park	19 September
3	350cc	Manx Norton	Aintree	25 September
2	1000cc	Works Norton	Aintree	25 September
1	350cc	Manx Norton	Cadwell Park	10 October
1	500cc	Manx Norton	Cadwell Park	10 October
1	350cc	Manx Norton	Brands Hatch	17 October
1	1000cc	Manx Norton	Brands Hatch	17 October (RL)

1955

Position	Class	Machine	Circuit	Date
1	350cc	Manx Norton	Brough	3 April
2 (crash, remounted)	1000cc	Manx Norton	Brough	3 April
1	250cc	NSU	Brands Hatch	8 April
1	350cc	Manx Norton	Brands Hatch	8 April (RL)
1	1000cc	Manx Norton	Brands Hatch	8 April (RL)
1	250cc	NSU	Snetterton	10 April
1	350cc	Manx Norton	Snetterton	10 April
1	500cc	Manx Norton	Snetterton	10 April (RL)
1	250cc	NSU	Crystal Palace	11 April (equalled lap record)
1	350cc	Manx Norton	Crystal Palace	11 April (RL)
1	1000cc Scratch	Manx Norton	Crystal Palace	11 April
1	1000cc Invitation	Manx Norton	Crystal Palace	11 April (RL)
1	250cc (5-lap)	NSU	Silverstone	23 April (RL)
1	250cc (10-lap)	NSU	Silverstone	23 April (RL)
1	350cc	Manx Norton	Silverstone	23 April
1	500cc	Manx Norton	Silverstone	23 April
1	250cc	NSU	Brands Hatch	24 April
1	350cc	Manx Norton	Brands Hatch	24 April
1	1000cc	Manx Norton	Brands Hatch	24 April
2	350cc	Works Norton	Mettet	1 May (first Continental European race)
2	500cc	Works Norton	Mettet	1 May
1	250cc	NSU	Oulton Park	7 May
1	350cc	Manx Norton	Oulton Park	7 May (RL)
1	1000cc	Manx Norton	Oulton Park	7 May (RL)
1	250cc	NSU	Aberdare Park	14 May
1	350cc	Manx Norton	Aberdare Park	14 May
1	500cc	Manx Norton	Aberdare Park	14 May
1	1000cc	Manx Norton	Aberdare Park	14 May
1	250cc	NSU	Brands Hatch	15 May
1	350cc	Manx Norton	Brands Hatch	15 May (RL)
1	1000cc	Manx Norton	Brands Hatch	15 May (RL)
4	350cc Junior TT	Works Norton	Isle of Man	6 June
29 (ran out of fuel, pushed home)	500cc Senior TT	Works Norton	Isle of Man	10 June
1	250cc	NSU	Crystal Palace	18 June (RL)
1	350cc	Manx Norton	Crystal Palace	18 June
1	500cc	Manx Norton	Crystal Palace	18 June
Retired (crash)	German GP	NSU	Nürburgring	26 June
3	German GP	Manx Norton	Nürburgring	26 June
Retired (misfire)	German GP	Works BMW	Nürburgring	26 June
1	350cc	Manx Norton	Scarborough	1 July
1	500cc	Manx Norton	Scarborough	2 July
1	250cc	NSU	Castle Combe	9 July
1	350cc	Manx Norton	Castle Combe	9 July
1	500cc	Manx Norton	Castle Combe	9 July
2	350cc Swedish GP	Works Norton	Hedemora	23 July (non-championship)
2	500cc Swedish GP	Works Norton	Hedemora	23 July (non-championship)
1	250cc	NSU	Thruxton	1 August (RL)
2	350cc	Norton	Thruxton	1 August
1	500cc	Norton	Thruxton	1 August
1	250cc	NSU	Snetterton	2 August
1	350cc	Manx Norton	Snetterton	2 August
1	500cc	Manx Norton	Snetterton	2 August
3	350cc Ulster GP	Works Norton	Dundrod	11 August (First World Championship victory)
1	500cc Ulster GP	Works Norton	Dundrod	13 August (First World Championship victory)
1	250cc	NSU	Ibsley	20 August (RL)
1	350cc	Norton	Ibsley	20 August (RL)

Position	Class	Machine	Circuit	Date
1	500cc	Norton	Ibsley	20 August (RL)
1	250cc	NSU	Brands Hatch	21 August
1	350cc	Manx Norton	Brands Hatch	21 August
1	500cc	Manx Norton	Brands Hatch	21 August
1	250cc	NSU	Aberdare Park	27 August
1	350cc	Manx Norton	Aberdare Park	27 August
1	500cc	Manx Norton	Aberdare Park	27 August
1	1000cc	Manx Norton	Aberdare Park	27 August
Retired (seized piston)	250cc Italian GP	NSU	Monza	4 September
1	250cc	NSU	Snetterton	10 September
Retired (crash)	350cc	Manx Norton	Snetterton	10 September
1	500cc	Manx Norton	Snetterton	10 September (RL)
1	250cc	NSU	Cadwell Park	11 September
1	500cc	Manx Norton	Cadwell Park	11 September
1	350cc	Works Norton	Scarborough	16 September (RL)
2	500cc	Works Norton	Scarborough	17 September
1	250cc	Manx Norton	Brands Hatch	18 September (RL)
1	1000cc	Manx Norton	Brands Hatch	18 September
1	350cc	Works Norton	Aintree	24 September (RL)
2	500cc	Works Norton	Aintree	24 September
1	350cc Open Handicap	Works Norton	Aintree	24 September
1	250cc	NSU	Brough	25 September (RL)
1	350cc	Manx Norton	Brough	25 September (RL)
1	1000cc	Manx Norton	Brough	25 September
1	250cc	NSU	Silverstone	1 October
1	350cc	Manx Norton	Silverstone	1 October (RL)
1	500cc	Manx Norton	Silverstone	1 October (beat Duke-Gilera)
1	350cc	Manx Norton	Brands Hatch	2 October
1	1000cc Scratch	Manx Norton	Brands Hatch	2 October (beat Duke-Gilera)
1	1000cc Invitation	Manx Norton	Brands Hatch	2 October (beat Duke-Gilera)

1956

Position	Class	Machine	Circuit	Date
1	250cc	MV Agusta 203cc	Crystal Palace	2 April (first race on MV)
1	500cc	MV Agusta four	Crystal Palace	2 April
1	250cc	MV Agusta 203cc	Snetterton	8 April
1	500cc	MV Agusta four	Snetterton	8 April (RL)
1	250cc	MV Agusta 203cc	Silverstone	14 April
1	250cc Invitation	MV Agusta 203cc	Silverstone	14 April
1	1000cc	MV Agusta four	Silverstone	14 April
1	500cc	MV Agusta four	Mettet	29 April
1	500cc	MV Agusta four	Floreffe	6 May
Disqualified (ran out of fuel on last lap when leading)	350cc Junior TT	MV Agusta four	Isle of Man	4 June
1	500cc Senior TT	MV Agusta four	Isle of Man	8 June (first TT victory)
2	350cc Dutch TT	MV Agusta four	Assen	30 June (RL)
1	500cc Dutch TT	MV Agusta four	Assen	30 June
1	350cc Belgian GP	MV Agusta four	Spa Francorchamps	8 July
1	500cc Belgian GP	MV Agusta four	Spa Francorchamps	8 July
Retired (crash, broke right arm)	350cc German GP	MV Agusta four	Solitude	21 July

1956 500cc World Champion

1957

Position	Class	Machine	Circuit	Date
1	500cc	MV Agusta	Barcelona	7 April
1	250cc	MV Agusta	Brands Hatch	19 April
2	1000cc Scratch	MV Agusta	Brands Hatch	19 April

1957 continued

Position	Class	Machine	Circuit	Date
2	1000cc Invitation	MV Agusta	Brands Hatch	19 April
Retired (crash)	250cc	MV Agusta	Oulton Park	22 April
Retired (gearbox)	500cc	MV Agusta	Oulton Park	22 April
2	350cc	MV Agusta	Mettet	5 May
Retired (handling problems)	500cc	MV Agusta	Mettet	5 May
Retired (engine failure)	350cc German GP	MV Agusta	Hockenheim	19 May
Retired (engine failure)	500cc German GP	MV Agusta	Hockenheim	19 May
4	350cc Junior TT	MV Agusta four	Isle of Man	3 June
2	500cc Senior TT	MV Agusta four	Isle of Man	7 June
1	250cc	NSU	Oulton Park	10 June
1	350cc	Manx Norton	Oulton Park	10 June
2	500cc	Manx Norton	Oulton Park	10 June
1	250cc	NSU	Scarborough	15 June
Retired (crash)	500cc	Manx Norton	Scarborough	15 June
Retired (suspension)	350cc Dutch TT	MV Agusta four	Assen	29 June
1	500cc Dutch TT	MV Agusta four	Assen	29 June
Retired (overheating)	350cc Belgian GP	MV Agusta four	Spa Francorchamps	7 July
Retired (holed piston)	500cc Belgian GP	MV Agusta four	Spa Francorchamps	7 July
2	250cc	NSU	Oulton Park	3 August
1	350cc	Manx Norton	Oulton Park	3 August
1	500cc	MV Agusta four	Oulton Park	3 August (RL)
1	350cc	Manx Norton	Thruxton	5 August
1	500cc	MV Agusta four	Thruxton	5 August
Retired (engine problems)	350cc Ulster GP	MV Agusta four	Dundrod	10 August
Retired (engine problems)	500cc Ulster GP	MV Agusta four	Dundrod	10 August
1	250cc	NSU	Crystal Palace	17 August (RL)
1	350cc	Manx Norton	Crystal Palace	17 August (RL)
1	500cc	Manx Norton	Crystal Palace	17 August (RL)
Retired (engine problems)	350cc Italian GP	MV Agusta four	Monza	1 September
4	500cc Italian GP	MV Agusta four	Monza	1 September
Retired (engine problems)	350cc	Manx Norton	Scarborough	14 September
1	500cc	Manx Norton	Scarborough	14 September
1	250cc	MV Agusta	Silverstone	21 September (RL)
1	350cc	Manx Norton	Silverstone	21 September (RL)
1	500cc	MV Agusta	Silverstone	21 September
1	250cc	MV Agusta single	Aintree	28 September
2 (later disqualified as riders only allowed 2 races)	350cc	Manx Norton	Aintree	28 September
1	500cc	MV Agusta four	Aintree	28 September
1	350cc	Manx Norton four	Oulton Park	5 October (RL)
1	500cc	MV Agusta four	Oulton Park	5 October (RL)
2	350cc	Manx Norton	Brands Hatch	12 October
1	1000cc Scratch	Manx Norton	Brands Hatch	12 October
1	1000cc Invitation	Manx Norton	Brands Hatch	12 October

1958

Position	Class	Machine	Circuit	Date	
1	500cc	MV Agusta four	Imola	7 April	
1	500cc	MV Agusta four	Barcelona	20 April	
1	350cc	MV Agusta four	Mettet	4 May	
1	500cc	MV Agusta four	Mettet	4 May	
1	350cc Junior TT	MV Agusta four	Isle of Man	2 June	
1	500cc Senior TT	MV Agusta four	Isle of Man		6 June
1	350cc Dutch TT	MV Agusta four	Assen		28 June
1	500cc Dutch TT	MV Agusta four	Assen	28 June	
1	350cc Belgian GP	MV Agusta four	Spa Francorchamps	6 July (RL)	
1	500cc Belgian GP	MV Agusta four	Spa Francorchamps	6 July (RL)	

1958 contintued

Position	Class	Machine	Circuit	Date
1	350cc German GP	MV Agusta four	Nürburgring	20 July
1	500cc German GP	MV Agusta four	Nürburgring	20 July
1	350cc Ulster GP	MV Agusta four	Dundrod	9 August
1	500cc Ulster GP	MV Agusta four	Dundrod	9 August
1	350cc Italian GP	MV Agusta four	Monza	14 September
1	500cc Italian GP	MV Agusta four	Monza	14 September
1	350cc	MV Agusta four	Aintree	27 September (RL)
1	500cc	MV Agusta four	Aintree	27 September
1	Open Handicap	MV Agusta four	Aintree	27 September
1	350cc	MV Agusta four	Oulton Park	4 October
1	500cc	MV Agusta four	Oulton Park	4 October
1	350cc	MV Agusta four	Brands Hatch	12 October
8 (plug trouble)	1000cc Scratch	MV Agusta four	Brands Hatch	12 October
2	1000cc Invitation	MV Agusta four	Brands Hatch	12 October

1958: 350 and 500cc World Champion

1959

Position	Class	Machine	Circuit	Date
1	500cc	MV Agusta four	Imola	12 April
1	350cc	MV Agusta four	Silverstone	18 April
Retired (crash)	500cc	MV Agusta four	Silverstone	18 April
1	350cc French GP	MV Agusta four	Clermont-Ferrand	17 May
1	500cc French GP	MV Agusta four	Clermont-Ferrand	17 May
1	350cc Junior TT	MV Agusta four	Isle of Man	1 June
1	500cc Senior TT	MV Agusta four	Isle of Man	6 June
1	350cc German GP	MV Agusta four	Hockenheim	14 June
1	500cc German GP	MV Agusta four	Hockenheim	14 June
1	500cc Dutch TT	MV Agusta four	Assen	27 June (RL)
1	500cc Belgian GP	MV Agusta four	Spa Francorchamps	5 July (RL)
1	350cc Swedish GP	MV Agusta four	Kristianstad	26 July
1	350cc Ulster GP	MV Agusta four	Dundrod	8 August
1	500cc Ulster GP	MV Agusta four	Dundrod	8 August (RL)
1	350cc Italian GP	MV Agusta four	Monza	6 September
1	500cc Italian GP	MV Agusta four	Monza	6 September (RL)
1	500cc	MV Agusta four	Madrid	11 October (RL)

1959: 350 and 500cc World Champion

1960

Position	Class	Machine	Circuit	Date
1	500cc	MV Agusta four	Cesenatico	18 April
1	500cc	MV Agusta four	Imola	25 April
3 (plug trouble)	350cc French GP	MV Agusta four	Clermont-Ferrand	22 May (RL)
1	500cc French GP	MV Agusta four	Clermont-Ferrand	22 May
2 (gearbox problems)	350cc Junior TT	MV Agusta four	Isle of Man	15 June (RL)
1	500cc Senior TT	MV Agusta four	Isle of Man	17 June (RL)
1	350cc Dutch TT	MV Agusta four	Assen	25 June (RL)
Retired (crash)	500cc Dutch TT	MV Agusta four	Assen	25 June (RL)
1	500cc Belgian GP	MV Agusta four	Spa Francorchamps	3 July (RL)
1	500cc German GP	MV Agusta four	Solitude	24 July
1	350cc Ulster GP	MV Agusta four	Dundrod	6 August
2 (broken gear pedal)	500cc Ulster GP	MV Agusta four	Dundrod	6 August (RL)
Retired (loose exhaust pipe)	350cc Italian GP	MV Agusta four	Monza	11 September
1	500cc Italian GP	MV Agusta four	Monza	11 September

1960: 350 and 500cc World Champion

Index

ND - #0356 - 270225 - C0 - 260/195/15 - PB - 9781780912158 - Gloss Lamination